Contested Utopia

University of Nebraska Press   Lincoln

Contested Utopia

JEWISH DREAMS and ISRAELI REALITIES

Marc J. Rosenstein

The Jewish Publication Society   Philadelphia

Grateful acknowledgment for use of the following: Asaf Yedidya, *"Chadash Mi-lo Yashan: Ha-utopia Hagenuza shel Zeev Yaavetz"* [New from the Not Old: Zev Yavetz's Unpublished Utopia]. *Cathedra* 148 (June 2013): 110–48. By permission of Yad Ben Zvi. Meir Or, *"Rosh Hashana Bakfar"* [Rosh Hashanah in the Village] *Batira* 2 (1950): 13. By permission of Reuven Or, Kibbutz Tirat Zvi. Mark Zborowski and Elizabeth Herzog, *Life Is with People* (New York: Schocken, 1969), 216–32. Siegfried Lehman, *Ra'ayon Vehagshamah* [Idea and Realization], edited by Abraham Yakel. (Tel Aviv: Tarbut Vechinuch, 1962), 113–15. By permission of Ada Lehman-Schair. Jabotinsky, Vladimir. "Tristan da Runha." In *A Pocket Edition of Several Stories Mostly Reactionary*, 141–202. Paris: n.p., 1925. By permission of the Jabotinsky Institute. Theodor Herzl, *Old New Land*, trans. Lotta Levensohn (Princeton: Wiener, 1997), 29–251. By permission of the publisher.

Manufactured in the United States of America. ∞

Library of Congress Cataloging-in-Publication Data
Names: Rosenstein, Marc, 1946– author.
Title: Contested utopia: Jewish dreams and
Israeli realities / Marc J. Rosenstein.
Description: Lincoln: University of Nebraska Press;
Philadelphia: The Jewish Publication Society, 2021. |
Includes bibliographical references and index.
Identifiers: LCCN 2020031223
ISBN 9780827614727 (paperback)
ISBN 9780827618633 (epub)
ISBN 9780827618640 (mobi)
ISBN 9780827618657 (pdf)
Subjects: LCSH: Zionism and Judaism. | Utopias—Religious aspects—Judaism | Zionism—History. | Israel—History.
Classification: LCC DS149 .R6278 2021 | DDC 320.54095694—dc23
LC record available at https://lccn.loc.gov/2020031223

Set in MeropePonca by Mikala R. Kolander.

To my children

Joshua, Ilana, and Lev

Rabbi Tarfon said:

It is not for you to complete the work, but
neither are you free to desist from it.

— *Mishnah Avot* 2:16

Contents

**PART 3. The Modern State of Israel:
Reality Meets Utopia**

Maps

Preface

Envisioning a Jewish State

If you had a magic wand and could create the ideal Jewish state, with no outside constraints, what would it look like? How would it be governed? Where would its borders lie? What would be the status of religion? Of minorities? Of immigrants? What policies would it enact in social welfare? Environment? Education? What would be uniquely Jewish about it?

In the course of my career as a tour educator, facilitator, and lecturer on Israel, I have stood in front of hundreds of groups—diaspora Jews and Israelis, youth, students, teachers, clergy, ordinary tourists—and posed that challenge. While the response is often an awkward silence, sometimes suggestions are ventured: "Jewish state" means a state

with a Jewish majority

where Jewish culture is dominant

governed by Jewish law

where Jews, as a nation, have political sovereignty and military power

whose behavior conforms to Jewish values

where Jews are "more equal" than others

as envisioned in biblical prophecy

where the Jews can live normally

where Judaism is the established religion

where life has a Jewish flavor

existing within biblical borders

Alas, suggestions such as these raise more questions than they answer. For example: Who counts as a Jew in judging a Jewish majority? Who is authorized to determine Jewish law? Where are Israel's biblical borders? What are Jewish values and who determines them? What is normal?

Moreover, while some of these definitions dovetail, others seem to conflict with each other. For example, can a normal state base its policies and borders on biblical revelation? Or can a modern sovereign state be ruled by a legal system based on life in a nonsovereign, minority community?

These and other uncertainties and inconsistencies bedevil any attempt to reach a clear, consistent consensus on what the ideal Jewish state should look like. It seems everyone has an opinion about what is wonderful—and what is distressing—about Israel as it is, but we rarely pull back from advocacy and criticism to reflect on what we really mean when we say "Jewish state." On the one hand, this lack of a clear vision has enabled a broad-based common effort to build and sustain the State of Israel, despite deep ideological divisions. On the other hand, those divisions have made it impossible to resolve fundamental questions such as borders, relations with neighbors, minorities' status, the public role of religion, and immigration policy.

I believe that with the passing of time, the costs of not having a shared guiding vision have come to outweigh the benefits of consensual vagueness. Indeed, it is not far-fetched to suggest that the increasingly strident polarization of public discourse might actually pose a threat to Israel's survival.

Several years ago it occurred to me that it was unfair to challenge others to envision a Jewish state if I couldn't do so myself, so I undertook to try. As I explored the sources, I discovered that over the course of its history, the Jewish people has articulated several different visions of the ideal Jewish state. Some of these were consonant with each other; some were dissonant. As I examined these images more closely, I kept finding myself returning to the idea of utopia. From Abraham to the present, it seems that the Jewish people has never stopped imagining a more perfect place than the present location, a more perfect existence than our present experience. These images have always been based on promises, dreams, values, memories—and current realities. In providing inspiration and sustenance, they have become central pillars of individual and collective Jewish identity.

In the past two centuries, forces of secularism and nationalism have placed these images in a new context, blurring the boundaries formerly taken for granted: boundaries between inspiration and aspiration, between guiding principles and concrete action plans, between utopian dreams and facts on the ground.

Living in Israel, it is hard to navigate in such an environment, to know what we Israelis really want, what we really mean to implement, now that the power is, or seems to be, in our hands. And yet, that navigation—by which I mean clarifying, and then living with, the delicate balance between desire and hope, between utopian image and practical action—is, I believe, the crucial challenge of our times. For example:

- How should a modern Jewish state relate to the Jewish religion, its rituals, and its moral imperatives? (Already in biblical times, the relationship among state, morality, and ritual—among kings, prophets, and priests—was often fraught and contentious.)
- How should we read God's biblical promise of sovereignty from Sinai to the Euphrates—a promise the Jewish people longingly read and reread over three millennia—over against our—and the world's—longing for peace, fairness, and stability?
- How do we reconcile the biblically rooted ideal of a homogeneous Jewish polity with the obligation to see all humanity as created in God's image? As a start: How should we respond, in our world, today, to the biblical utopian image of a land "cleansed" of Canaanites?

In other words: What do we, Israelis and diaspora Jews, too, *really desire*—and how should we live in the meantime, with the unsettling awareness that we may never achieve it? This is the honest, open, painful conversation I believe we must have, now.

This book, begun as my personal quest to articulate a vision of a Jewish state that would be convincing, at least to me, in addressing the value conflicts inherent in such a project, led me on a fascinating journey of discovery. As I visited the far-flung islands of utopia scattered through the sea of Jewish history and thought, I gained new perspectives on Judaism—and Jewish survival—in general, and on Zionism in particular. *Contested Utopia: Jewish Dreams and Israeli Realities* is the explorer's journal in which I have recorded my observations. As such, it is focused on the specific topic of how utopian images affected Jewish and especially Zionist thought across the centuries. Thus, the book is neither a comprehensive study of utopian thought nor a general survey of Zionist thought. It does, however, offer a unique perspective, examining how the interface of the two—utopia and Zionism—influences public discourse in and about Israel today. But it goes beyond historical analysis, for it offers my own vision of a Jewish state, grounded in that analysis.

As a historian I have done my best to present divergent utopian ideals and their champions objectively, including and analyzing extensive text passages from each utopia. However, there is no getting around the fact that my own beliefs and experiences affect my commentary, especially regarding the ways in which these utopian visions collide in modern Israel. I grew up in the liberal American-Jewish milieu; attracted to what I learned about Israel, I spent several extended sojourns studying and working in the country, before deciding in 1990, at the age of forty-four, to immigrate with my family to a small community in the Galilee. So while I have experienced both Israel and the Diaspora from both outside and inside, that experience remains inevitably idiosyncratic. This book makes no claim to be an exhaustive, systematic history of the development of the state and its policies.

Again, I see this volume as an entryway for both Israelis and diaspora Jews into a more transparent dialogue, one illuminated rather than occluded by our individual utopian dreams. I end the book with an opening foray: my own vision of utopian Israel. While I would be pleased if many people were convinced that my vision is worth working toward, I also hope that readers, having benefited from the exploration of Jewish utopian thinking in the first eleven chapters, will be inspired to articulate their own alternative utopias. Then we could have an orderly—well, at least knowledgeable—discussion on the implications, merits, and deficiencies of each vision. A utopian conversation.

Acknowledgments

This book has been cooking for a long time.

In 1982, given the opportunity to write a doctorate at the Hebrew University in the Jerusalem Fellows program for diaspora Jewish educators, I consulted with Prof. Jacob Katz, retired by then from active teaching. I told him that as a liberal Jewish educator in the Diaspora, I constantly found myself frustrated by my task of socializing young Jews into a nonexistent society (for example, being assigned to teach children rituals, like Sabbath observance or daily prayer, that no adult in their home or community actually modeled). I wondered if he could suggest other moments in Jewish history illustrating the same dilemma. He suggested the attempt of pre-1948 Zionist educators to create a "New Jew." And he suggested Dr. Emanuel Etkes as advisor. There ensued an enriching and exciting three years, during which I learned a great deal about Zionism, Israeli history and culture, and the daunting challenge of education for social and cultural change.

My fascination with the challenge of translating ideal models into real social institutions stayed with me throughout my years as a Jewish teacher, both in American Jewish day schools and in informal education frameworks in the Galilee. From 2000 to 2017 Rabbi Jan Katzew offered me the opportunity to reflect, in writing, about this challenge in my weekly "Galilee Diary" on the Union for Reform Judaism "Ten Minutes of Torah" website.

Then, in 2014, another fellowship gave me time to study the matter in depth. My month as a Coolidge Fellow at Auburn Theological Seminary in New York yielded a first attempt at a theoretical exposition, "Toward a Vision of a Democratic Jewish State," published in the Spring 2016

CCAR Journal. I thank Charles Henderson at Auburn and Rabbi Paul Golomb at the *CCAR Journal*.

There ensued a long epistolary dialogue with Rabbi Barry Schwartz, director of The Jewish Publication Society (JPS), as I struggled to find a framework to say what by then I felt I needed to say, in a convincing and grounded way. In the midst of this, the idea of utopia arose as a unifying concept.

And here we are, but not without several false starts and major revisions. A number of friends and colleagues generously agreed to read drafts of all or part of the book; their concerns and suggestions have been invaluable, and I am grateful to them all for their corrections, insights, and encouragement: Rabbi Zvi Berger, Dr. Joel Duman, Professor Lisa Grant, Rabbi Avi Kadish, Professor Michael Marmur, Rabbi Sigalit Ur, Noam Zion, and members of the Shorashim Book Club.

I am also grateful to Reuven Or, archivist at Kibbutz Tirat Zvi, for sending me the original of his father's essay on Rosh Hashanah in the kibbutz, and Shuki Shukrun and Dr. Avishai Berland, of the Ben Shemen archives, for helping me locate the original of Siegfried Lehmann's essay on the New Jew.

And special thanks are due to:

Rabbi Barry Schwartz at JPS for his encouragement and guidance in refining the concept of the book.

Joy Weinberg, the JPS managing editor, for relentlessly and thoughtfully pushing and leading me to make the book coherent, clear, and readable.

The University of Nebraska Press for the advice and support of their professional staff.

Cartographer Erin Greb for the maps.

The librarians at Hebrew Union College, Jerusalem, for their cheerful help.

Friends and neighbors at Shorashim, who attended study sessions and endured dinner-table conversations on utopia.

My wife, Tami, without whose example I would surely have given up on utopia a long time ago.

Introduction

The Jewish State as Utopia

In 2011, the popular Israeli author Eshkol Nevo wrote in his novel *Neuland*:

> This Tel Aviv of yours, nu, how would you be able to suffer it if you weren't imagining another, more beautiful city all the time? And this state of ours, what? Jews on top of Jews, all living in one place, but in their heads they have another place from which they came here, and another place to which they want to flee tomorrow. And it is very fortunate that this is what they have in their heads . . . because only thus, in the thoughts and imaginings of wanderings, is it possible to give up on real wanderings. To stay.[1]

In 1902, five years after he founded the Zionist movement by convening the First Zionist Congress, Theodore Herzl published a futuristic novel, *Altneuland* (*Old New Land*), describing his vision of life in an imaginary Jewish state twenty years hence. *Altneuland* was in the tradition of a popular literary genre invented by Sir Thomas More in 1516: utopian fiction. Since the publication of More's *Utopia*, hundreds of authors have used the literary vehicle of a visit to an imaginary society in a far-off land or a future time to express criticism of the status quo and offer proposals for how society might look if we could just get it right. These works, in turn, have stimulated wide-ranging discussions among philosophers, literary critics, historians, sociologists, and others regarding the meanings and implications of the words utopia, utopian, and utopianism. Conceptually, does utopia belong to the world of political theory, or fiction, or social criticism, or something else? Are utopian works escapist fantasy or revolutionary activism? Does this genre deserve its pejorative connotation of "too good to be true," or can utopian works serve as valuable tools for social and political improvement? Or, must any tool that promulgates perfection—and, as such, must contend with imperfect humanity—necessarily lead to violence or totalitarianism?

The motto beneath the title of *Altneuland*, now one of Herzl's most quoted sentences—"If you will it, it is no fairy-tale"—wholly captures this dilemma of utopian thought: the intended relationship between image and reality. According to Herzl, the difference between fantasy and reality is will. His utopian vision of life in Palestine is meant to inspire action toward its concrete realization. Indeed, in the afterword to the novel, Herzl continues from the motto: "but if you don't will it, everything I have told you [here] is a fairy-tale, and a fairy-tale it shall remain." Still, we might ask: Did Herzl write this "fairy-tale" of a happy, peaceful Jewish polity characterized by good taste and social justice as a blueprint for social engineering, or as a general siren song to tempt the Jews to reject the status quo and take action to create a state for themselves? In other words, did he *really mean it* in all its concrete detail?

This question of purpose and intent, which I call "the utopian dilemma," has been a constant theme in utopian thought since ancient times. Jewish discourse regarding the ideal Jewish state can be seen as part of that literature. The question of the purpose and intent of the imaginary polity can be asked not only about *Altneuland*, but also about the Torah's depiction of life in the Promised Land, about prophetic visions of restoration, and about medieval and modern images of the desired and expected Jewish state.

Throughout the centuries, the vision of the Jewish state has been a utopian image in which collective memory, desire, hope, and faith will converge to create an ideal life for the Jewish people in the Land of Israel. But in the course of those centuries, I will show, "ideal" was not consistently understood; ambivalence and even discord entered into dreams of the Jewish state. There were different opinions and schools of thought regarding not only what we desired, but even what we remembered.

More significantly, I believe that there has always been a certain vagueness, or ambivalence, regarding the purpose of the vision. Exhortation and encouragement? Critique of the status quo? Call to action? Blueprint for implementation? In other words, to what extent was the vision a real hope, and to what extent was it recognized as an inspiring fantasy?

Thus, the key question that must be asked of any utopian plan must also be asked of the ideal of the Jewish state: What is our real intention in articulating this vision? Whereas this can be seen as a literary or philosophical question, in the case of the Jewish people, three millennia of theory have come crashing into the possibility—or the necessity—of concrete, practical implementation.

My thesis is that after three millennia of imagining an ideal Jewish polity, it is almost impossible to think about Israel without being influenced, often unconsciously, by these accumulated utopian images. This book aims to bring these images into consciousness, examine them, and sort them out, in order to help us think clearly about what we *really desire* Israel to be.

The Plan of the Book

Part 1 presents and explains basic concepts that can help us understand the images of a Jewish polity. Chapter 1 presents an overview of the utopia concept: its history, its power, and its weaknesses and even dangers. Chapter 2 explores the centrality of utopia in Jewish thought, from the Torah onward. Chapter 3 examines the distinction between utopian and apocalyptic thought, and their respective historical impacts.

Part 2 seeks to clarify controversies around key challenges facing the modern Jewish state by examining their roots in both traditional and modern utopian thought. A sequence of chapters, each devoted to a different Jewish utopian vision, builds a mosaic of how the Jews (and others) have imagined the State of Israel. These visions will be seen both to overlap and to conflict. Chapter 4 looks at how a Torah state utopia is implicated in the fraught relationship between the Jewish religion and the Jewish state. Chapter 5 considers what it means for the State of Israel to be seen as the fulfillment of the modern nostalgic longing for the premodern utopian, holy community. Chapter 6 weighs the idea of the Jewish national home—the utopia of the cultural Zionists—in the context of modern nationalism. Chapter 7 discusses the ambivalence present in Jewish political thought from the Bible to twentieth-century Zionist politics regarding whether the desert theocracy (theocratic anarchy—no state) or Solomon's monarchy (sovereign statehood) is the ideal. Is the latter essential—holy—or merely a necessity for survival? Chapter 8 studies the question of whether the Jewish state can be, solely, a normal state of all its citizens. Chapter 9 investigates the dream of the Jewish people to live within the borders of the Promised Land, over against the reality that there has never been consensus on where those borders lie (disparate maps are included). Chapter 10 explores the socialist Zionists' utopia—and how it can be seen to reflect the biblical prophets' vision of a just society.

Finally, Part 3 reflects on the relationship between Jewish utopian thinking through the ages and Israeli institutions and policies today and tomorrow. Chapter 11 presents case studies of currently controversial issues in Israel, showing how each reflects a collision of utopian visions—or a confusion between utopian dreams and human realities. Chapter 12 continues the utopian Zionist tradition, documenting an imaginary visit, in the indeterminate future, to an ideal Jewish state. This travelogue is an attempt to harmonize and prioritize among the various utopian visions examined in the preceding chapters. While it can be seen as a synthesis and a summary, I hope it will also serve as a stimulus for thought and discussion—and even as an inspiration to action.

I hope *Contested Utopia: Jewish Dreams and Israeli Realities* will inspire—and nourish—the kind of nuanced and constructive discourse about Israel we so urgently need.

How to Use This Book for Discussion

To further the purpose of this book—stimulating thoughtful discussion about readers' own visions of the Jewish state, based on their understanding of the utopian thinking that has influenced Israel's development to date—I have created a Study and Discussion Guide, available under the Resources tab at https://jps.org/books/contested-utopia/. While designed primarily for facilitators of classes and study groups, individuals will likely also find it helpful in clarifying their thinking about Israel.

The guide follows each chapter, section by section, offering open-ended questions around three foci:

1. **Unpacking the utopian authors' individual visions.** What do the central texts they wrote reveal about their views of the status quo? What were the gaps in their vision? What were the hidden questions? How do they meet us today, with our experience and values?

    For example, in relation to Zev Yavetz's "Torah State" utopia in chapter 4, the guide seeks to help the reader "read between the lines" to understand what truly bothered Yavetz about life in his community, and to find the unanswered questions about just how his utopia would function. Who has authority to interpret the Torah? How free is his ideal society? What exactly is the relationship among *halakhah*, governance, and the individual—is there enforcement of rules, or just general consensus? If some Jews reject the renewed and restored Torah law, what would likely happen to them? What might this reveal about how utopia needs to function?

2. **Comparing the utopian visions — over against one another and the realities of modern life.** What are the points of conflict between visions? Where might different visions be in harmony or even overlap? What obstacles do current realities pose to implementation of each vision?

   For example, the guide directs discussion of Herzl's utopia in chapter 8 to a fundamental problem: Wherein should lie the Jewishness of a modern, liberal, democratic Jewish state? Is there an inherent conflict in the attempt to envision such a combination? Can "the nation-state of the Jewish people" — reflecting the "Jewish national home" utopia examined in chapter 6 — and "a state of all its citizens" be one and the same state?

3. **Exploring our personal responses to the utopias.** Do we find them inspiring or scary or both? Would we want to live there? Are there components of each vision we can take with us? Are there components that must necessarily be rejected? What alternatives might we offer?

   Throughout, the guide pushes readers to build their own synthesis of utopian visions, to tailor a personal vision of a Jewish state to fit their hierarchy of values, and to understand how that vision converses with others — and with realities on the ground.

Contested Utopia

Part 1

Lands of Milk and Honey

Jewish Utopian Visions

1

The Eternal Quest for Utopia

Literary genre, folk belief, human need, political plan: the definitions and uses of "utopia" are many and often unclear. However, it has been a powerful enough concept in Western culture that it is worthwhile trying to understand the underlying ambivalences and dissonances that bedevil utopian thought. This exploration can serve as a basis for examining Jewish visions of the future through the ages, and their impact on the modern Jewish state.

Folklore

> In the Big Rock Candy Mountains
> All the cows have wooden legs
> And the bulldogs all have rubber teeth
> And the hens lay soft-boiled eggs.[1]

I grew up listening to Burl Ives singing "The Big Rock Candy Mountains," and later, at Jewish summer camp, we all sang Pete Seeger's version of "Oleanna," a land where beer flows from springs in the ground, and

> The cows all like to milk themselves,
> And the hens lay eggs ten times a day.[2]

I understood these two songs as whimsical exaggerations. I had no idea that they were part of a rich folk tradition dating back centuries, in which people of earlier eras imagined a place where the privations and tribulations of the present would be replaced by a life of Eden-like per-fiction—no suffering, no oppression, no scarcity, no work. This tradition, generally labeled as the "Land of Cockaigne" (a term of uncertain origin, found in several European languages), has found expression in poetry, music, and art since the Middle Ages. Examples include satirical descriptions of underworked and overfed priests in both the twelfth-century collection *Carmina Burana* and the fourteenth-century Irish poem "The Land of Cockaigne"; Pieter Brueghel's sixteenth-century painting *Het Luilekkerland*, where the inhabitants doze contentedly while roasted animals present themselves for carving; and the Brothers Grimm's "Story of Schlauraffenland," where, among various fantastic sights, honey flows from the ground like water.[3]

These paradisiacal imaginings were probably influenced by the biblical Eden and its interpretations, and may also owe some of their images to descriptions of imaginary voyages by Greek writers. Take, for example, *A True History*, the popular second-century Greek work by Lucian of Samosata (Turkey). Part science fiction, part satire on classical adventures like the *Odyssey*, *A True History* describes an imaginary journey west from Gibraltar, to fantastical lands where the rivers run with wine and other wonders abound. The popular imagination, it seems, has always been fascinated by the prospect of a better place, even as it knew such a place existed only as a fiction—indeed, as a humorous one, making fun of our own difficult lives and of any expectation that they might be different.

Prophecy and Plato

The propensity to dream of a better place extends considerably beyond the folklore of fantasy paradises. Prophets and philosophers have used the vehicle of utopia—a fictional community, island, state, or planet—in order to criticize the existing social, political, and economic order, and to imagine more perfect arrangements that would allow all members of society to live happy lives.

The work generally identified as the first, classic example of utopian social thought is Plato's *Republic* (ca. 360 BCE). Written in the form of a dialogue between Socrates and his companions, the book discusses various philosophical and educational topics, but its core is the presentation of a hypothetical ideal state, where justice—and therefore happiness—will be maximized. Beginning from the desire to define and implement justice, and working their way through a series of topics (education, governance, family, property, defense, etc.), the fictitious discussants agree on how each particular institution ought to be designed in order to achieve an ideally just state.

Both Cockaigne and *The Republic* were part of Europe's cultural heritage as the Renaissance dawned, together serving as a substrate for a new genre: utopian fiction. While Plato's analysis served as an inspiration for generations of utopian thinkers, *The Republic*'s structure would rarely be imitated. Almost all later descriptions of ideal polities took the form of an imaginary visit to a fully developed, functioning, perfect state.

The Renaissance

Sir Thomas More, the English Catholic scholar and statesman executed by Henry VIII in 1535 for refusing to recognize the king's authority over the Pope's, published his *Utopia* in 1516 in the Netherlands (in Latin; it would not be published in English until after his death). This was the age of exploration; the sudden exposure to the possibility of other worlds and other cultures served as important food for thought for anyone who, like More, harbored doubts about medieval European institutions. A decade earlier Amerigo Vespucci had published his report on his travels in the New World. This seems to have stimulated More's imagination, as the plot of *Utopia* involves a sailor from Vespucci's crew who is left behind in a heretofore unknown land; the book is his account of his adventures and discoveries there.

Thomas More brilliantly combined Lucian's humorous fantasy voyage, Vespucci's real voyages to new worlds, and Plato's thoughtful construction of an ideal state to create a model of utopian literature that became its own genre. His voyager discovers a democratically governed island state where people live simply, working according to their abilities and consuming according to their needs. There is no private property, idle nobility, conspicuous consumption, or waste. Utility and practicality are valued over glitz; iron, for example, essential for making tools, is highly valued, while gold is used to make chamber pots.[4] More's use of this imaginary better place to criticize the reality he experienced was pointed and often funny, aimed not only at specific institutions but at society's entire value system.

More coined the word "utopia" as a bilingual pun, based on two different but similar-sounding Greek words: *eutopia*—a good place; and *outopia*—no place. What did he really mean? *Utopia* was certainly more than escapist fantasy—but it was less than a call to violently overthrow the status quo and implement the proposed model. More could have published an angry screed condemning the greed, waste, and abuses of power he saw around him, or a set of constructive proposals for concrete changes in law and custom. Instead he chose to create an image of a different reality, unreachable perhaps, but possible: no lemonade springs, no lions consorting with lambs—just human beings behaving rationally. Neither fantastic nor apocalyptic, his *Utopia* suggested how we might live if only we could get it right. Thus he appears to have intended to awaken, to encourage, to inspire, to guide—but perhaps, first of all, to perform on himself the thought experiment of answering the challenge: stop complaining! If you had a magic wand, what would your ideal state look like?

Utopias became a popular Renaissance genre. The discovery of new lands and new scientific knowledge, the questioning of medieval institutions and beliefs, and the rise of secularism all contributed to the interest in imagining a better place—either across the sea or in a future time. The best known among dozens of such works were Tomas Campanella's *City of the Sun* (1623) and Francis Bacon's *New Atlantis* (1627). Notably, Thomas More published *Utopia* abroad, and in Latin. Bacon, whose utopia emphasized a science-based government, was written after his political enemies forced him out of public life and published posthumously. As for *City of the Sun*, which also envisioned rule by intellectuals, Campanella composed it in an Inquisition prison cell. It seems that however fanciful these utopias were, the powers-that-be still perceived the fantasies as at least potentially subversive. As one scholar of utopias put it, this literature was "an instrument of discreet protest in the hands of intellectuals excluded from the governing elite"[5] These books provided their authors with opportunities to articulate a coherent and convincing hierarchy of values different from the status quo, and to imagine its implementation—and thereby to inspire others to adopt these values and join the effort to apply them.

As the Renaissance gave way to the Enlightenment, the rising currents of dissatisfaction with medieval social structures found expression in many utopias published in France and England in the eighteenth century—these often envisioning a liberal monarchy ruling over a society characterized by liberty, equality, and fraternity. Both Jonathan Swift's traveler Gulliver (1726) and Voltaire's adventurer Candide (1759) discover fantastical societies that cast the contemporary European social and political reality in a most unflattering light.

Socialism

If the Renaissance gave rise to an outpouring of utopian works reflecting the new worlds—inner and outer—that were opening up in that era, the industrial revolution led to a similar burgeoning of utopias in the nineteenth century. The promise of rational and scientific industry engendered optimism about improvements in the quality of human life; but at the same time it aroused fears of the dehumanization associated with industrial capitalism.

Three best-selling and influential utopian socialist novels of the late nineteenth century were Nikolai Chernyshevsky's *What Is to Be Done?* (1863, Russia), Edward Bellamy's *Looking Backward* (1888, United States), and William Morris's *News from Nowhere* (1890, England). Bellamy's imagined visit to Boston in 2000—where travelers encounter a harmonious state in which private property has been abolished—stimulated the creation of dozens of "Bellamy clubs" across the country, to advance its vision. Morris, a prominent artist and designer, focused more on the aesthetic and spiritual benefits of socialism.

What distinguished many nineteenth-century socialist utopians from their Renaissance forerunners was a focus on practical implementation. They and their followers saw these works as blueprints for action, and, indeed, thousands of individuals abandoned their former lives in order to build, by the sweat of their brows, real-life utopian models. Most of these experiments took place in North America, where the wide-open spaces and sense of endless possibility provided a sympathetic environment. A few examples:

- Welsh industrialist Robert Owen sank most of his sizable fortune into founding and supporting a collectivist community, New Harmony, Indiana, in 1825, which reached a peak population of a thousand before collapsing into internal dissent and economic failure just two years later. Owen had hoped that this experiment would serve as a model and vanguard for the eventual reorganization of society.[6]
- Around thirty "phalanxes," ideal communities as envisioned by French socialist Charles Fourier, were founded in the eastern and midwestern states in the 1840s. Most disbanded within a few years; none lasted a decade. Journalist Horace Greeley was an enthusiastic backer.[7]
- Another French socialist theorist and activist, Etienne Cabet, inspired and led the establishment of a utopian community, Icaria, in Texas, in 1848. The community went through a series of reorganizations and migrations—to Illinois, Iowa, Missouri, and California—before eventually dissolving in 1898.[8]
- Thousands of followers of Austrian utopian writer Theodore Hertzka signed up to support and ultimately join his envisioned ideal community, "Freeland," in British East Africa. However,

the British were not supportive, and an 1894 fact-finding mission turned back in frustration. The project never came to fruition.[9]

· At around the same time, an American engineer, Albert Owen, organized a utopian cooperative colony in Topolobampo, on Mexico's west coast, which would reach a peak population of five hundred. It lasted from 1886 to 1895 before collapsing in debt and disorder.[10]

· Popular Norwegian violinist Ole Bull attempted to found a utopian community (New Norway) in Pennsylvania. Bull's colony attracted several hundred settlers in 1852 and lasted two years. Interestingly, Pete Seeger's "Oleanna" with its Cockaignian imagery is based on an 1853 Norwegian song satirizing this utopian attempt.[11]

Both Karl Marx and Friedrich Engels were outspoken in their criticism of utopian socialism. They admitted that utopian socialists were correct in understanding the evil of capitalism and in seeking to replace it, but avowed that the utopians' "castles in the air" only distracted the masses from the revolutionary task at hand. Investing energy in imagining—and implementing—ideal social models was in their eyes naïve, pointless, and indeed counterproductive, delaying the revolutionary overthrow of the old order.[12] It is probably due to Marxist influence that the term "utopian" acquired its pejorative connotation: if an idea is "utopian," it is detached from reality, hopeless of realization, not to be taken seriously.

The tension between the natural desire to imagine where an optimal world would take humanity and the rejection of such imaginings in favor of immediate revolutionary action has continued to be expressed in socialist—and scholarly—discourse until the present. It is an interesting irony that Vladimir Lenin took the title of his famous 1902 pamphlet arguing for militant revolutionary activism, *What Is to Be Done?*, from Chernyshevsky's utopian novel of that name. It seems that even among revolutionaries, utopia had its fascination.

The Future in the Past

An interesting feature of many utopian visions is that they explicitly reflect a nostalgia for the past. Of course, the past for which they yearn is generally an idealized one—but nevertheless, they imagine not a revolution but a restoration. Eden, the Greeks' golden age, Solomon's empire, Rousseau's state of nature—the projected perfect future is often a return to an idyllic past. If we could just throw off the accumulated distortions of centuries of sin, or oppression, or mistakes, or divine punishment, we could "renew our days as of old."

This nostalgic strand in utopian thought raises with particular intensity the question of intention mentioned above regarding More's *Utopia*: What do utopians *really mean to achieve*? Is the model of a happy and successful life in a past era meant to serve as an inspiration for a new and better future (e.g., Camelot for the Kennedy years)? Or is the goal the actual restoration of that past reality in all its detail (e.g., the age of chivalry for Don Quixote)? Is the dream of restoration an inspiration (to keep up hope and work toward a better future) or a concrete aspiration? As we shall see, these questions have had particular relevance to the movements struggling to create nationalist states since the eighteenth century—including, of course, Zionism.

The Purpose, Power, and Danger of Utopia

This brief survey makes clear that imagining a better place—even when we know it is really no place—has been an important theme in Western culture across the centuries.[13]

These imaginings can be grouped into the following categories, along a scale from the fantastical to the ostensibly practical:

Land of Cockaigne

Humorous fantasy

God's kingdom

Prophetic vision of a redeemed world

Utopian fiction

Secular visions of an ideal human society

Utopian communities

Blueprints for ideal models

However, these boundaries—and this order—are subjective and by no means clear-cut. There are images of God's kingdom on earth that contain elements as fantastical as some in the songs of Cockaigne—and secular utopian visions (and plans for utopian communities) that claim to establish God's kingdom. And then it can certainly be argued that aspects of some nineteenth-century "practical" utopian schemes seem about as realistic as the Land of Cockaigne. In this book, "utopia" refers to a fairly broad spectrum of efforts to imagine a better place, largely excluding the clearly humorous and fantastical images of the Cockaigne tradition.

A leading contemporary utopian studies scholar, Ruth Levitas, suggests the following characterization of utopia:

Utopia expresses and explores what is desired; under certain conditions it also contains the hope that these desires may be met in reality, rather than merely in fantasy. The essential element in utopia is not hope, but desire—the desire for a better way of being. It involves the imaginings of a state of being in which the problems which actually confront us are removed or resolved, often, but not necessarily, through the imagining of a state of the world in which the scarcity gap is closed or the "collective problem" solved.[14]

Sociologist Fred Polak concludes his massive survey of utopian thought thus:

The utopia is more than a fairy-tale expression of an eternal-human longing predestined never to be fulfilled. Rather, it demands and compels fulfilment. It is a knock at the door of Everyman, and even the ears of the deaf shall be opened by its insistent "why?" It is the incarnation of the questing Socratic spirit, the divine gadfly ever hovering over man and stinging him into wakefulness. "If you kill me," Socrates warned the tribunal and the people, "you will remain sleeping for the rest of your lives, unless God sends you another gadfly." The *other* gadfly, which took over the task of the eternal questioner, is the utopia.[15]

Notably, however, since the First World War utopia in literature has largely been replaced by dystopia: imagining terrifying future worlds so as to make concrete for us the horrors that await us if we continue on our present moral and technological course (*Brave New World*, *1984*, *2001: A Space Odyssey*, *Black Mirror*, *The Handmaid's Tale*). If the Renaissance stimulated the imagining of new, ideal worlds and the industrial revolution gave rise to attempts to engineer utopias in the here and now, it seems that the traumas of the twentieth century cast such imaginings and experiments in a Cockaignian light: as juvenile fantasies. After the First World War—and the Second—we know too much about the human potential for evil and its ability to harness technology for corrupt ends to find much encouragement in images of a better place. Indeed, we have learned to distrust such images, fearing they will lead us to the gulag or to Jonestown. We seem to have entered an era when prophecies of doom are deemed more appropriate and instructive than prophecies of redemption.

Thus, it is important to beware of romanticizing utopia; indeed, some believe that utopian thinking is fundamentally misleading and even dangerous. For example, philosopher Isaiah Berlin:

One belief, more than any other, is responsible for the slaughter of individuals on the altars of the great historical ideals—justice or progress or the happiness of future generations, or the sacred mission or emancipation of a nation or race or class, or even liberty itself, which demands the sacrifice of individuals for the freedom of society. This is the belief that somewhere, in the past, or in the future, in divine revelation, or in the mind of an individual thinker, in the pronouncements of history or science, or in the simple heart of an uncorrupted good man, there is a final solution. This ancient faith rests on the conviction that all the positive values in which men have believed must, in the end, be compatible, and perhaps even entail one another. "Nature binds truth, happiness, and virtue together as by an indissoluble chain," said one of the best men who ever lived [Condorcet], and spoke in similar terms of liberty, equality, and justice. But is this true?[16]

Berlin (among others) argues that it is inherently impossible to achieve harmony among conflicting values and goals, individual and social; any ideal place must indeed always be "no place."[17] Therefore, by trying to translate utopia into a real place, we ignore, if not sabotage, efforts to make the world just a little better here and now.

This is a powerful criticism, particularly relevant whenever utopian speculation has hardened into concrete action plans for immediate implementation—as in the creation of a modern Jewish state reflecting millennia of utopian dreaming. Thus, the "utopian dilemma" is always with us: what do we *really mean*? How can we preserve utopia's positive function, using the vision of an unattainable ideal society as a vehicle for articulating our value priorities, without losing control and imagining that we really have found the map to no-place?

The Tragedy of Icarus

It is ironic that Etienne Cabet called his utopian community Icaria. According to the Greek myth, the wise artisan Daedalus, imprisoned with his son Icarus by King Minos of Crete, crafted wings of feathers and wax, enabling the two of them to escape, airborne. However, Icarus, in his enthusiasm, ignored his father's warning against flying too close to the sun; the wax melted and he fell into the sea and drowned. Cabet's followers, like Icarus, learned the hard way that while lofty goals are a value, so is understanding their unattainability. Icarus's tragedy expresses a key aspect of utopia that is often ignored: even as the utopian ideal comes to inspire us, to move us to reflect on our reality and to direct our efforts to change it, utopia must necessarily always remain *outopia*, no-place, a guiding ideal that will always lie beyond our reach. It seems that when we refuse to accept utopia's unreachability, when we create systems and wage battles to translate utopian visions into concrete realities, we fall like Icarus.

Navigating between reality and utopia is not for the impulsive or the impatient. It requires the wisdom and perspective of a Daedalus — or a Plato, who in *The Republic* imagines this conversation between Socrates and Glaucon:

> Do you doubt an artist's competence if he paints a paradigmatically good-looking human being, and portrays everything perfectly well in the painting, but can't prove that a person like that could actually exist?
>
> I certainly do not, he protested.
>
> Well, aren't we saying that we're trying to construct a theoretical paradigm of a good community?
>
> Yes.
>
> Then do you doubt our competence as theoreticians in this context if we can't prove that a community with our theoretical constitution could actually exist?
>
> Of course not, he said.
>
> So that's how matters really stand.[18]

Here Plato clarifies that the exercise of imagining an ideal state is not rendered pointless by the realization that such a state is impossible; rather, the process helps us define and commit to ideals that can guide our actions in moving toward a more perfect state. Thus Plato's utopian vision is not a blueprint for revolution but a tool for education and social and political change, an articulation of the ideals that ought to drive our efforts to improve the polity in which we live, bringing it closer — even if only a little — to the ideal.

So Ruth Levitas's formulation seems a fitting summation: "The essential element in utopia is not hope, but desire — the desire for a better way of being." To envision utopia is to imagine and articulate — carefully, thoughtfully, convincingly — what we want, even though we know that we can never fully achieve it.

Further Reading

Jennings, Chris. *Paradise Now: The Story of American Utopianism*. New York: Random House, 2016.

Levitas, Ruth. *The Concept of Utopia*. Oxford: Peter Lang, 2011.

Manuel, Frank E., and Fritzie P. Manuel. *Utopian Thought in the Western World*. Cambridge MA: Belknap Press, 1979.

Pleij, Herman. *Dreaming of Cockaigne: Medieval Fantasies of the Perfect Life*. Translated by Diane Webb. New York: Columbia University Press, 2001.

2

Paradise Lost, Remembered, and Promised

The Torah can be seen as an ongoing story about finding and losing the perfect place: Eden, "the land that I will show you," the desert, the promised land. Imagining—and longing for—the lost utopia became a central theme in Jewish thought throughout the generations. This quest for a perfect place served as a substrate for the *halakhah*, the messianic hope, and Zionism.

Eden

In 1492, when Christopher Columbus approached the mouth of the Orinoco River (in Venezuela today), the landmarks and phenomena he observed convinced him that he was nearing Eden. Not wishing to encounter the fiery sword of divine disapproval, he turned his ships around and sailed away.[1] For Columbus, and generations of believers before and since, Eden was not no-place, but a concrete location from which humankind had been irrevocably expelled. On the other hand, looking at the biblical account not as history but as literature leads us to explore where the story came from, why it was written, and how the Jewish tradition has interpreted it.

Ancient Sumerian mythology describes the Land of Dilmun, a primeval place where there is no suffering or want.[2] And Hesiod, thought to have written his accounts of Greek mythology in the eighth century BCE (around the time the Torah narratives were developing in the Land of Israel), speaks of a "golden age" long ago, when humans lived in peace and prosperity, free of grief and pain.[3] Later Greek sources reported other perfect places, such as Calypso's island and Plato's Atlantis.[4] So far, no one has proven or disproven clear relationships among these various ancient perfect place myths. In any case, whether or not they influenced each other, their universal appeal is clear.

How can we explain this fascination? Some suggest that the Eden story has an anthropological root—that it is about the rise of agriculture: the idyllic hunter-gatherer paradise of equality and modest, simple self-sufficiency lost to the farmer's need to clear more land, beget more children, conquer more territory, and establish a patriarchic control mechanism.[5] Jungian psychology sees the expulsion from Eden as a reenactment of birth—the expulsion of every person from the perfect place of the womb.[6] A different psychological explanation argues that the story is about the tension between individual immortality and species immortality: until their sexual awakening, it seems that Adam and Eve could have expected to eat of the tree of life and live forever; but after eating of the tree of knowledge they were driven out of the garden into a world in which humans must seek immortality through perpetuation of their genes and not their physical bodies.[7]

However it is interpreted, this is a story of loss. Here is how the Talmud narrates the human experience in Eden:

> Said Rabbi Yochanan bar Chanina: that day lasted twelve hours: in the first, the dust was gathered; in the second a body was shaped; in the third his organs were formed; in the fourth a soul was injected; in the fifth he stood up; in the sixth he named the animals; in the seventh he had relations with Eve; in the eighth two sons were born; in the ninth he was commanded not to eat from the tree; in the tenth he sinned; in the eleventh he was judged; in the twelfth he was driven out.[8]

A perfect God made a perfect place and put humans in it; and had it not been for their bad choices, all of our present suffering would not have occurred. But here we are, in the universal human predicament, struggling to reproduce and to make a living, ending up as dust. We know it might have been otherwise, but all is lost, and the fiery sword is unrelenting. The Eden story seeks to explain the dissonance between

God's perfect creation and our pain-filled experience of it. It is an origin myth to help us make sense of the world.[9]

And yet, it seems we cannot let it go and walk away from Eden. The sword flames, but the dream of Eden continues to draw us. The Rabbis—and the Church Fathers—made a connection between their belief in the immortal life of the soul and the return to Paradise. Sometime after the first century CE it became commonplace to speak of the Garden of Eden as the abode of the righteous after death. Indeed, the rabbinic literature contains very little discussion of the location and characteristics of the original garden. Almost all rabbinic references to Paradise are in the context of often hyperbolic descriptions of the reward laid up for the righteous; for example:

> When a righteous one enters the Garden of Eden . . . they bring him to a place of streams of water, surrounded by eight hundred kinds of roses and myrtle, and each one has a canopy prepared just for him, and from each canopy flow four rivers, one of milk, one of wine, one of balsam, and one of honey; and over each canopy grows a golden vine hung with thirty gems . . . and under each canopy there is a table inlaid with precious stones and gems. Sixty angels accompany the new arrival and urge him: "Go and eat your honey with joy, and drink the wine made from the grapes of the six days of creation."[10]

The Rabbis thus spiritualized the Garden of Eden, removing it from history and reimagining it as the place where human souls go to be compensated for the sufferings and injustices they had experienced in the real, historical world.

However, the memory of Eden had a much broader cultural impact in Judaism than simply providing imagery to describe the world to come. Adam and Eve were driven from Paradise not because of squabbling among the gods, nor due to immutable fate; nor did their mistake (sin) reflect some kind of inherent, hereditary flaw in the human soul—an "original sin" according to Christian belief. Rather, endowed with free choice but inexperienced in the game, they made a bad choice. The world had been created perfect and might have continued so, but humanity was not content with the rules governing that perfection, and so lost it. If we have such power and responsibility, even in the imperfect place to which we have been exiled, then only we can make that place better. Even if we cannot aspire to Eden, we can be inspired by its image of perfection, and understand from our experience there the principle of humanity's responsibility for its fate. This concept of human agency is the basis for all utopian dreams and plans. This humanistic view of social change, essential to utopianism, is a central theme in Jewish thought.

The Sabbath

"Israel requested: Master of the universe, show us an example of the world to come! God said to them: The Sabbath; for it is one sixtieth of the world to come."[11]

An interesting manifestation of utopian influence on Jewish thought and practice can be seen in the remarkable institution of the Sabbath. A central, identity-defining observance in Judaism, the Sabbath is a weekly moratorium on the everyday routine, defined by an elaborate structure of law and custom. On the Sabbath, Jews are forbidden to work, to travel, or to handle money, merchandise, and tools; concomitantly they are commanded to rest, eat, drink, pray, study, and enjoy, at home in the community, with the family. Indeed, the Sabbath is seen as the ideal time for marital relations.[12]

The Rabbis describe the Sabbath as a taste of the world to come. In other words, spending a day each week in a place of plenty, harmony, and peace — a better place than the one inhabited on the other six days — was a simulation of Paradise, a brief, periodic enactment of life in utopia. Indeed, secular Zionist thinker Ahad Ha'am ("one of the people," the pen name of Asher Ginsberg, 1856–1927) famously stated, "More than Israel has kept the Sabbath, the Sabbath has kept Israel," suggesting that this regular, institutionalized taste of utopia has been a factor in the survival of the Jewish people, keeping the people loyal to their religion and identity even when that loyalty exacted a high price.[13]

The Sabbath is, of course, a universalistic Edenic vision, without the geographical dimension of the Land of Israel; it is experienced wherever the Jews live. Nevertheless, it seems reasonable to suggest that the Jews' persistence in keeping their eyes raised to a concrete, geographical utopia has been at least partly based on their experience of the Sabbath as a relatable model of what that better place might be like.

The Promised Land

The 1937 British proposal to partition Palestine into a Jewish and a Palestinian state gave rise to a stormy debate at the 1938 World Zionist Congress. The Orthodox Zionist Mizrachi party declared: "The people of Israel did not surrender its right to the land of its fathers during thousands of years of exile, and will not now concede even one inch of the Land of Israel. We staunchly declare the eternal, complete and full right of the nation to its homeland within its historic boundaries, and absolutely reject any attempt to agree to the partition of Eretz Israel."[14]

As of today, the debate over the relationship between biblical utopian dreams and modern political realities has not subsided, as we'll see in chapter 9. Here is the backstory. The first eleven chapters of Genesis trace world history from Creation through Cain and Abel, the Flood, and the Tower of Babel. All of these can be seen as origin myths explaining various aspects of human reality. But then the focus narrows: in Genesis 12:1–2, God suddenly speaks to one Abram, of whom nothing is known except his pedigree, saying:

> Go forth from your native land and from your father's house to the land that I will show you.
> I will make of you a great nation,
> And I will bless you;
> I will make your name great,

And you shall be a blessing.
I will bless those who bless you
And curse him that curses you;
And all the families of the earth
Shall bless themselves by you.

Abram (renamed Abraham in Genesis 17:5) chooses to obey this
call, and moves to Canaan. There, Genesis records a number of further
conversations between God and Abraham and, later, between God and
Isaac and Jacob, reaffirming, as in God's final conversation with Jacob,
the promise that their descendants will be a great nation, rooted in
their land, living a blessed life:

I am El Shaddai.
Be fertile and increase;
A nation, yea an assembly of nations,
Shall descend from you.
Kings shall issue from your loins.
The land that I assigned to Abraham and Isaac
I assign to you;
And to your offspring to come
Will I assign the land. (Gen. 35:11–12)

The Patriarchs indeed prosper, but their life is not one of pastoral
stability in the homeland. After famine necessitates that Abraham
sojourn in Egypt (Gen. 12:10–20), he engages in military operations
against marauding kingdoms (Gen. 14), and must cope with a branch
of his family (Lot) whose choices and experiences hardly qualify as
"blessed" (Gen. 18–19). For his part, Isaac must decamp to Philistine
Gerar on account of famine (Gen. 26:1–22). And Jacob spends decades
abroad in Haran building his wealth and family (Gen. 28–33) before
he finally returns—only to be forced by famine to migrate to Egypt,
where he dies (Gen. 46, 49).

Thus the dream of roots, peace, and prosperity in the Land of Israel (Canaan) was only unevenly realized for the Patriarchs' growing clan. And we don't know what this clan remembered and dreamed about their land during the 430 years of Egyptian slavery (Exod. 12:40). The Bible does not report what they were thinking, what they believed, or how they acted in Egypt. However, from their skeptical responses to Moses' intervention—"'I will bring you into the land which I swore to give to Abraham, Isaac, and Jacob, and I will give it to you for a possession, I the Lord.' But when Moses told this to the Israelites, they would not listen to Moses, their spirits crushed by cruel bondage," (Exod. 6:8–9)—the dream of national life in the land of Canaan does not seem to have been a powerful component of their identity. In any case, they were released, willy-nilly, from Egyptian bondage, only to spend the next forty years looking back nostalgically at the paradise (!) of Egypt: "the meat . . . the fish . . . the cucumbers, the melons, the leeks, the onions, and the garlic" (Num. 11:4–5).

Moses and God cope with this nostalgia for Egypt by projecting a better place ahead. In Moses' first encounter with God, at the burning bush, the program is set forth: "I have come down to rescue them from the Egyptians and to bring them out of that land to a good and spacious land, a land flowing with milk and honey" (Exod. 3:8). And later, just before entering the land, the description is elaborated:

And if you do obey these roles and observe them carefully, the Lord your God will maintain faithfully for you the covenant that He made on oath with your fathers: He will favor you and bless you and multiply you; He will bless the issue of your womb and the produce of your soil, your new grain and wine and oil, the calving of your herd and the lambing of your flock, in the land that He swore to your fathers to assign to you. You shall be blessed above all other peoples: there shall be no sterile male or female among you or among your livestock. The Lord will ward off from you all sickness. (Deut. 7:12–15)

This is the goal, the motivating dream, that Moses repeatedly calls up to move the reluctant nation to leave Egypt, to cross the sea, to accept the law, to keep going in the wilderness, to face the challenge of conquering Canaan. Throughout, the guiding vision is of a better place. Not Eden, of course—but resounding in the descriptions are the echoes of Paradise.

The Desert

In the harsh desert, the Israelites long for the lost paradise of Egypt. And—already from the moment of their hard-won arrival in the Promised Land—we begin to hear hints of nostalgia for . . . the "good old days" of the desert wandering! The Bible's description of the nation's early days in the land seems an ironic echo of the expulsion from Eden:

> On the day after the Passover offering, on that very day, they ate of the produce of the country, unleavened bread and parched grain. On that same day, when they ate of the produce of the land, the manna ceased. The Israelites got no more manna; that year they ate of the yield of the land of Canaan. (Josh. 5:11–12)

In the desert, no one had to work for a living: manna and quail appeared miraculously as needed. Now, in the land, sustenance requires labor. Moreover, the desert was the site of the key turning point—the sealing of the covenant at Mount Sinai—when the nation became a holy nation. Seeing Sinai as the "wedding" of Israel to God, the prophets will later express nostalgia for the desert honeymoon. For example:

> I accounted to your favor
> The devotion of your youth,
> Your love as a bride—
> How you followed Me in the wilderness,
> In a land not sown.

Israel was holy to the Lord,
The first fruits of His harvest.
All who ate of it were held guilty,
Disaster befell them. (Jer. 2:2–3)

So, it seems, these two conceptions of better places—the Promised Land and the wilderness—express a tension between two aspects of Israelite identity: nation and faith. For the Patriarchs, and then for Moses and the freed slaves, the dream of Canaan was a dream of being a great nation rooted in its land—powerful, prosperous, and tranquil. But for the nation in its land, the desert experience was recast as a kind of honeymoon period—a time of pure undistracted faith in which the people were free from the responsibilities and tensions of livelihood and nationhood and enjoyed unlimited divine favor.

These two utopias are integrated by the Sinai covenant, which links faith and nation. Judaism's central ideology, from Sinai onward, became the understanding that Jewish history reflects a covenant between Israel and God: Israel will live according to God's law—and in return, God will protect and prosper Israel in its land. However, since nothing is ever perfect in the here and now, the covenant has always been viewed with an eye to the future: when Israel finally succeeds in getting its act together and living by the law as a utopian community, then the national utopia of life in the land will be realized, and Israel will indeed be a great and holy nation.

Envisioning Life in the Good Land

If we take the Torah narrative at its face value, once the Israelites have crossed the Red Sea, they find themselves in the desert, liberated from Egyptian slavery, with no political structure, no economy, no real estate, no plan other than the promise that they will be brought into Canaan. A few months later at Mount Sinai, and continuing for forty years, God, through Moses, sketches a picture of the life they can expect once they arrive in their land. Indeed, the text that records this life-to-be, the

Torah, predominantly presents a forward-looking perspective, setting forth laws and social institutions that will provide the framework for the nation's new existence—one totally different from anything they have known either in Egypt or in the desert.

Most laws, guidelines, and promises are presented in two major assemblies: at Mount Sinai (in Exodus and Leviticus) and just before crossing the Jordan into Canaan (in Deuteronomy). Their organization is not systematic; some sections of the text give coherent, comprehensive coverage of particular topics, while others are compilations of disparate laws and exhortations. It is possible, however, to identify several broad categories: family law; social justice and welfare; criminal, real estate, and tort law; religious observance; and communal governance.

Up to this point, the Israelite nation has only known life under Pharaonic oppression. Freedom, responsibility, and how to live with them have not been part of the people's collective consciousness. The Torah provides them with a dream of an orderly life of peace and prosperity, where abstract concepts like justice, mercy, and holiness will be translated into concrete institutions. In the envisioned near future, priests will preside over majestic rituals, and an elaborate tithing system will support this priesthood. A hierarchy of courts will judge fairly. Land will be distributed according to a divinely ordained plan, and a reset mechanism every fifty years will prevent clans from losing—or amassing—real estate holdings. The social welfare safety net will take care of all in need. The sanctity of the family will be enshrined in laws defining prohibited relations, governing divorce, preventing adultery, and detailing child-parent obligations. The land and the farmer will rest one year of every seven. Indentured servitude will be limited. A network of cities of refuge will prevent blood vengeance against accidental killers. Furthermore, enemies will pose no threat, and the rain will fall at the right time.

Note that this is no dream of a land of Cockaigne. Unlike in the desert wandering, when the Israelites were freed from labor and fed manna and quail by God, in the Promised Land they will have to live a normal life, working for a living, subject to challenges and obligations, even wars. Nonetheless, the Torah's plan for national life in the Promised Land is understood as a utopia. The Torah's repeated expression in future tense, "When you enter the land," prefacing its sets of laws (e.g., Exod. 12:25; Lev. 19:23; Num. 10:9; Deut. 26:1), charges the people: Just wait, have faith, internalize these instructions — and the next generation will enter the "good land" — that is, *eutopia*.

The Jubilee Year and Cities of Refuge: Utopia and Reality

Once the Israelites entered the land, they would have had to confront the "utopian dilemma": What did God *really* intend for them? Were all the laws they had received meant to be actualized, or were some solely intended to convey a moral message?

We today have remarkably little information about their everyday life in their land, from Joshua's conquest through the period of the monarchy. There are only hints here and there, mostly in the form of the prophets' criticism of the people's (or their rulers') abandonment of particular commandments (e.g., Jer. 17:21–27; Amos 2:6–8). We don't really know how the Sabbath was observed, what social welfare institutions actually functioned, how the criminal courts worked, whether the sacrificial cult was or was not fully implemented. In fact, we have virtually no evidence from either the text or archaeology as to whether the people understood the Torah as a handbook, a code of law, or a manifesto setting forth the principle of the covenant along with examples to serve as guidelines.

Meanwhile, from our vantage point, some of the laws — such as for the jubilee year (Lev. 25:1–28) and for the cities of refuge for accidental killers (Num. 35) — seem more like theoretical constructs expressing value priorities than plans for real-life institutions.

Consider the jubilee year.[15] After seven sabbatical year cycles, the fiftieth year is declared a jubilee — functioning as another year of rest (agricultural labor is prohibited in both years forty-nine and fifty) — and any farmland sold since the last jubilee reverts to its original owner. Thus the jubilee law comes across as an impressive system for preventing the development of major economic inequality, based on a renunciation of private real-estate ownership. However, it is hard to imagine its actual implementation. For one thing, even living for a single year without working the soil would have been a challenge; enduring a double sabbatical seems unbearable. Furthermore, keeping track of leases and enforcing the jubilee reversion would seem to require a bureaucracy able to record and enforce land claims over half a century.

The Jerusalem Talmud contains an entire tractate, *Shevi'it*, spelling out the fine points of the sabbatical year laws, including historical and geographical detail. On the other hand, it seems that the Rabbis had questions, but no stories, no collective memory regarding observance of the jubilee — except a tradition that it had already ceased a millennium earlier, with the destruction of the kingdom of Israel in 722 BCE.[16]

As for the cities of refuge, this provision for asylum from blood vengeance for accidental killers recurs several times in the Torah: Exodus 21:13, Numbers 35:9–34, and Deuteronomy 19:1–13. This concept seems to be an important one, part of a transition from a system of personal revenge to one of institutional standards of justice.[17] However, the differences among the descriptions — and the Rabbis' attempts to reconstruct their details–suggest that here too we lack historical memory of how this concept was actually implemented.[18]

It thus seems reasonable to suggest that the descriptions of the jubilee year and the cities of refuge for unintentional killers to be observed in the future in the Promised Land were meant less as user manual and more as manifesto. As such, we are left to ask if, at that time, the Torah was itself seen primarily as an operative legal document (as rabbinical tradition holds) or as a utopian vision, an inspiring ideal. Could it not be that the Torah was at least partly utopian in its intent? Was it perhaps using a utopian image to express the principle of divine (not human) land ownership, and to criticize great disparities in wealth — as we have in the story of Joseph's converting all the peasants in Egypt to sharecroppers (Gen. 47)?

Many modern scholars question the traditional view of the Torah, arguing that it is actually a composite document, much of which may have been written, or at least edited, only during or after the era of the monarchy.[19] Such a scenario would strengthen the suggestion that the jubilee year was a utopian concept: expressing criticism of the existing social and economic order under the monarchy by offering a vision of a better future, an ideal system for preventing wide economic disparity.

These perspectives, moreover, raise questions about the entire enterprise. If certain laws in the Torah are only intended to convey a moral message and not to be implemented, how do we determine where to draw the line between exhortation — or social criticism — and legal obligation, between utopia and practice? If the jubilee year laws are only meant to inspire more equitable attitudes regarding property, one might ask whether, perhaps, the Sabbath laws are "only" meant to teach limits to materialism, to inspire a commitment to "being" as well as "doing." Could it be, then, that even the Sabbath was a utopian — ideal but unrealizable — construct, an expression of desire rather than a blueprint for action?

Halakhah — The Way to Utopia?

Jewish law as we know it today — the *halakhah* ("the way") — is a post-biblical phenomenon that looks back toward the Torah as a divine revelation, a sacred text serving as the basis for a living body of law for real people in real time. Thus, conventionally, the *halakhah* is not seen as a utopian aspiration but rather as a body of eternal norms for the here and now, for a way of life that fulfills Israel's covenant with God.

However, the ongoing development of Jewish law can also be seen as a constant effort to move toward the Torah's utopia by providing the laws that will define and sustain the perfect society.

It can be argued that the *halakhah*, like the Written Torah, is utopian. It can be understood as a law system based on a guiding, perhaps unattainable, vision of an ideal society. A case study:

The foundational document of the *halakhah*, the Mishnah (ca. 200 CE), was compiled under Roman rule, well after the destruction of the Temple and loss of sovereignty — and after the failed Bar Kokhba rebellion (132–35 CE), bloody proof that it was not timely or wise to anticipate national restoration any time soon. The Mishnah hardly ever speaks of a vision for national redemption, or of a Messiah. It does, on the other hand, devote significant attention to the details of the ideal life under king and priesthood—recollections of a past reality discussed as if it were present here and now. For example:

> The high priest may judge and may be judged, bears witness and may be testified against. . . . The king may not judge and may not be judged, does not bear witness and may not be testified against.[20]

The Mishnah is largely occupied with laws for a life which can only be remembered nostalgically or longed for in the future. Over the next three centuries, succeeding generations of rabbis developed and applied the Mishnah's statements to the historical reality in the Land of Israel and in Babylonia; their work was gathered into the Jerusalem and Babylonian Talmuds, which in turn served as the basis for all later development of Jewish law. Thus, wherever Jews lived, under whatever government, the laws that defined individual and communal life were explicitly based on the categories and concepts of the Mishnah. Jews lived in constant awareness of the dissonance between the Mishnah's ideal and their own reality.

The Babylonian Talmud states that the above Mishnah only excludes non-Davidic kings from being judged, and explains why by means of a story:

> Why . . . ? Because of the case of the slave of King Yannai who killed a man. [The rabbinic leader] Shimon ben Shetach said to the rabbis: Cast your eyes upon him that we may judge him. They sent word to the king: "Your slave has killed a man." The king sent the slave to them, but they responded, "You must come too, for in the case of a dangerous ox whose owner had been warned, the

Torah says (Exod. 21:29), 'the ox shall be stoned and its owner, too, shall be put to death'." So he came and sat at the trial.

Shimon ben Shetach said, "Stand up, King Yannai, and let the witnesses testify against you, and know that it is not before us that you are standing, but before Him who spoke and the world came into being, as it is written (Deut. 19:17): 'The two parties to the dispute shall appear before the Lord, before the priests or magistrates in authority at the time'." The King answered, "I will not obey you alone, but only what your colleagues decree." Shimon ben Shetach looked to the right—the rabbis were all staring at the ground; he looked left—they were all staring at the ground. "Cautious thinkers," he railed at them, "Let the Master of thoughts reward you for your thinking!" And the angel Gabriel appeared and struck them dead. From that moment it was decided, "The king may not judge and may not be judged, does not bear witness and may not be testified against."[21]

This talmudic discussion, taking place at least two centuries after the Roman destruction of Jerusalem in 70 CE, tells a (somewhat fantastical) story set in an earlier time, that of the Hasmonean king Alexander Yannai (127–76 BCE; of the Levite tribe, not a descendant of David). The legal principle being justified had no current practical relevance for the Rabbis discussing it, or for the nation. Rather, as much as the *halakhah* was aware of, and instructed by, history, it simultaneously stood above it, often legislating for a remembered—or envisioned— ideal world seemingly unrelated to real life.

But then, a millennium later, Rashi (Rabbi Shlomo Yitzchaki, 1040– 1105), the preeminent rabbinical scholar of eleventh-century France, was asked about the possibility of a defendant being represented in court by a spokesman (attorney). His answer referred to the Mishnah's aforementioned statement regarding the judicial immunity of kings and priests—representation that might have solved the awkward conflict of authority experienced in King Yannai's case.[22]

Thus even though the Jews studying the talmudic text in medieval Troyes, or Baghdad, or Cordoba, had no experience—and no prospects—of Jewish sovereignty, they never stopped thinking about how that sovereignty ought to be. And they never stopped measuring the distance between their own reality and the halakhic ideal.

A leading modern Orthodox thinker, Joseph Soloveitchik (1903–93), likens the *halakhah* to a mathematical ideal: "The present time is only a historical anomaly in the ongoing process of the actualization of the ideal Halakhah in the real world, and there is no need to elaborate about a period which is but a temporary aberration that has seized hold of our historical existence. The Halakhah remains in full force, and we hope for and eagerly await the day of Israel's redemption when the ideal world will triumph over the profane reality."[23]

I myself would suggest a different mathematical image: the *halakhah* is an algorithm whose inputs are (a) the Torah's ideal society and (b) the present reality in a given community. The output is a living, dynamic legal system dedicated to moving b towards a, while recognizing the impossibility of actually arriving there. As historian Lionel Kochan puts it:

> What is "utopian" about this arrangement? The fact that the Torah makes it its declared intent to bring men and society to such a state of perfection as lies within their respective natures to reach. The laws of the Torah apply to an existing man in an existing society— since somewhere they have to begin and would otherwise have no purchase on reality . . . with a view to transforming that status quo not only into an improved society but into the perfect society, characterised by its theocratic government, its universalism, its material plenitude and its peaceful nature, combined with the exalted position of Israel amongst the nations.[24]

This understanding of the *halakhah* suggests that the Jews' experience of utopia was not restricted to the weekly Sabbath "taste of Eden," but was all-encompassing. Living within the *halakhah* would have meant, then, not merely conforming to a sanctified code of behavior, but also living in awareness of an ultimate end-goal. Recognizing life's messy reality with its constant value conflicts, the *halakhah* sought to guide the individual and community toward justice, toward responsibility, toward mercy—toward creating a perfect society.

Are We There Yet?

If the Written Torah and the *halakhah* have a utopian aspect, imagining a perfect society just over the horizon, what happens when we sail so fast we reach the horizon? To what extent should Torah law, as interpreted by the *halakhah*, inspire, guide, or rule a modern Jewish state? For example:

- The Sabbath: The Torah contains only a few sentences indicating how the Sabbath is to be observed. However, later traditions and rabbinical interpretations erected a massive edifice of law and custom defining Sabbath observance, which established it as a central institution of Jewish life and identity throughout the Diaspora. The attempt to impose this structure on a modern state has led to endless and often bitter controversy. If the Torah's intention regarding the Sabbath is seen to have been utopian rather than technical, the way would be opened for a creative effort to explore how the values and social criticism expressed by the Sabbath can be institutionalized in the state context.

- Governance: The Torah envisions a hierarchy of courts but is somewhat vague about the roles of priests and judges within it. It also seems ambivalent on the question of monarchy: was a kingdom—a state—an ideal or a compromise with the popular demand to be like "all the nations" (Deut. 17:14)?

- Borders: The Torah contains several descriptions of the future borders of the Promised Land. Should these be seen as utopian—as expressions of desire for an unrealizable ideal—or are they divinely ordained maps, which the restored nation is obligated to translate into facts on the ground, at any cost?

Here we confront the utopian dilemma—the question of what the Torah "really meant": Where must we ourselves draw the line between a hypothetical ideal and real political, social, and economic institutions that assure plenty, justice, and peace? If the Torah is *not* simply a handbook for life in the land, then what *should* the relationship be between the Torah's utopian vision and the reality of a Jewish state in the here and now? What means of interpretation will allow us to extract practical guidance from the Torah's utopia?

In part 2, we will consider attempts to address this challenge.

Further Reading

Delumeau, Jean. *History of Paradise: The Garden of Eden in Myth and Tradition.* Translated by Matthew O'Connoll. New York: Continuum, 1995.

Gitelman, Zvi. *The Quest for Utopia: Jewish Political Ideas and Institutions through the Ages.* Armonk NY: M.E. Sharpe, 1992.

Higger, Michael. *The Jewish Utopia.* Baltimore MD: Lord Baltimore Press, 1932.

3

Utopia, Apocalypse, Messiah

During the Hellenistic period, apocalyptic thinkers projected not just national but cosmic restoration; however, at the same time they defused the covenant, seeing history as a process beyond human influence. Can the Jewish messianic hope be seen as utopian if it is driven by cosmic forces, not by the covenant?

The First Flowering of Our Redemption

Rabbi Abraham Isaac Hacohen Kook (1865–1935), an influential twentieth-century Jewish thinker (and first chief rabbi of Palestine), taught that the Zionist endeavor represents the first stage of the messianic redemption: "Our entire spiritual heritage is presently being absorbed within its source and is reappearing in a new guise, much reduced in material extent but qualitatively very rich and luxuriant and full of vital force. We are called to a new world suffused with the highest light, to an epoch the glory of which will surpass that of all the great ages which have preceded. All of our people believes that we are in the first stage of the Final Redemption."[1]

Zionism may have been a modern secular nationalist movement, but its roots clearly go much deeper. Beyond the utopian images from the Torah and the prophets that color how Jews (and most everyone else) see the possibility and reality of Israel, there is another, powerful set of ancient images that help shape our consciousness regarding the Jewish state: the apocalyptic literature. This literature continues to have a significant impact on public discourse—and political decision-making—in Israel.

Daniel's Visions

The biblical book of Daniel (in the third section of the Hebrew Bible, the "Writings") comprises a collection of stories and visions associated with a Jewish courtier in the Babylonian court (sixth century BCE). However, most scholars believe that the setting is anachronistic, and that this book is actually the latest in the Hebrew Bible, dating from the Hellenistic period (second century BCE — the time of the Hasmonean revolt and rule).[2] In chapter 9, Daniel records the following vision:

> [1]In the first year of Darius son of Ahasuerus, of Median descent, who was made king over the kingdom of the Chaldeans–[2]in the first year of his reign, I, Daniel, consulted the books concerning the number of years that, according to the word of the Lord that had come to Jeremiah the prophet, were to be the term of Jerusalem's desolation — seventy years. . . .

> [20]While I was speaking, praying, and confessing my sin and the sin of my people Israel, and laying my supplication before the Lord my God on behalf of the holy mountain of my God–[21]while I was uttering my prayer, the man Gabriel, whom I had previously seen in the vision, was sent forth in flight and reached me about the time of the evening offering. [22]He made me understand by speaking to me and saying, "Daniel, I have just come forth to give you understanding. [23]A word went forth as you began your plea, and I have come to tell it, for you are precious; so mark the word and understand the vision.

> [24]"Seventy weeks [of years] have been decreed for your people and your holy city until the measure of transgression is filled and that of sin complete, until iniquity is expiated, and eternal righteousness ushered in; and prophetic vision ratified, and the Holy of Holies anointed. [25]You must know and understand: from the

issuance of the word to restore and rebuild Jerusalem until the [time of the] anointed leader is seven weeks; and for sixty-two weeks it will be rebuilt, square and moat, but in a time of distress. [26]And after those sixty-two weeks, the anointed one will disappear and vanish. The army of a leader who is to come will destroy the city and the sanctuary, but its end will come through a flood. Desolation is decreed until the end of war. [27]During one week he will make a firm covenant with many. For half a week he will put a stop to the sacrifice and the meal offering. At the corner [of the altar] will be an appalling abomination until the decreed destruction will be poured down upon the appalling thing."

Chapters 7–12 of Daniel comprise a series of such cryptic visions, including imagery of the "four mighty beasts" (chapter 7), the ram and the goat (chapter 8), and the kings of north and south (chapters 10–11). These visions are unique within the Bible; they are the only clear-cut example in the Hebrew Bible of the genre known as apocalyptic literature.

Reading the Map of History

There is scholarly debate about the exact definition of the term apocalyptic (Greek for "uncovering" [of secret things]). It is used to refer to a literary genre, to a historical body of literature from the Hellenistic period, and to a worldview that finds expression in that literature.[3] For our purposes, what is relevant is a thematic definition, which includes several key elements (not all of which are present in every apocalyptic text):

· The existing social—and cosmic—order is about to be overthrown (Dan. 9:26–27).
· This upheaval is part of a preordained divine plan, for which cryptic evidence can be found in the prophets' teachings and in past events (Dan. 9:2; see Jer. 29:10).

- This upheaval will usher in God's kingdom on earth; the judgment (and reward and punishment) of the good and the evil among humankind, past and present (Dan. 9:24); and a return to Paradise.
- A royal personage will bring the plan to its denouement (Dan. 9:26; the term here is *Mashiaḥ* [messiah] = anointed one).
- Angelic messengers make this secret information known to the writer, often via cryptic terminology (Dan. 9:21–22).

Besides Daniel, other apocalyptic works that survived did so outside of the Bible, among them all or parts of 1 and 2 Enoch, 4 Ezra, 2 and 3 Baruch, Apocalypse of Abraham, Testament of Levi, Apocalypse of Zephaniah, and the New Testament book, Revelations. These books did not survive in Hebrew versions (either originals or translations) once they were excluded from the Hebrew canon. Thus they have not been found on the "Jewish bookshelf" until modern times. However, their ideas found their way into the Rabbis' interpretations of the Bible — especially of the prophets — and thus influenced later Jewish thought.

The key difference between prophetic and apocalyptic thinking lies in the understanding of history. For the prophets, history is a work in progress. The covenant is a mechanism that helps us understand it, and so free will plays a key role. The nation's behavior influences events, through God's response. We can't know what is going to happen until we have actually taken action. We may be able to make educated predictions (e.g., the people are weak-willed and easily tempted, so it is reasonable to predict that they will sin and thus experience punishment), but the future is open, and up to us. For apocalyptic writers, by contrast, history is a script that we are enacting. God knows what will happen, and to those with the gift of prophecy the plan is revealed. Human action affects the playing out of this plan minimally if at all. Prophecy warns what might happen. Apocalyptic understanding knows what must happen.

Utopia and Apocalypse

Clarifying the relationship between utopia and apocalypse provides further insight into just what characterizes utopian thinking. One key quality that emerges is humanism: Whether utopian imaginings come to criticize the social order, to exhort the reader to work for a better future, or to articulate the values that guide a good society, they relate to human activity in the real world. Whether driven by religious or secular values, they assume that people are free agents, and that if they were to act well, they could achieve utopia. Outside the gate of Eden, wandering in the desert, oppressed by venal kings, living in exile — it is always our own arrogance and weakness that have gotten us where we are, dreaming of a better place. And, therefore, utopian thinking is inherently optimistic; it is unrealistic but somehow realistic at the same time. Beneath the satire of present social failures and seemingly far-fetched images of life in utopia, utopianism is motivated by faith in the human potential to perfect the world.

Apocalyptic thinking despairs of human action for the good. It does not offer an ideal vision or a plan for achieving it, for the human role in history is to be strapped to a speeding locomotive, hurtling off a cliff. History is not conditional, and so our free will is irrelevant in the social and historical context. God is about to destroy us and our world, and create a new one that will presumably be perfect.

Moreover, while utopianism is a social perspective, dreaming of a better society or a better world, apocalyptic thinking often narrows the focus of the ideal future to the fate of the individual. Daniel, like other apocalyptic texts, devotes significant attention to individuals who will be meted out their just deserts: "At that time, your people will be rescued, all who are found inscribed in the book. Many of those that sleep in the dust of the earth will awake, some to eternal life, others to reproaches, to everlasting abhorrence. And the knowledgeable will be radiant like the bright expanse of the sky, and those who lead the many to righteousness will be like the stars forever and ever" (Dan. 12:1–2).

Inasmuch as apocalyptic thinking is pessimistic, seeing no hope for improving and sustaining society, it essentially encourages each individual to tend to his or her own behavior so as to merit personal reward, and not punishment, in the world to come. This way of thinking was part of the substrate out of which Christianity could arise — abandoning the hope of real-time national redemption in favor of ahistorical individual salvation.[4]

Interestingly, both utopian and apocalyptic worldviews can be seen as expressions of social criticism; they have in common the intense sense of disappointment with the status quo. Both see the current sociopolitical situation as shot through with injustice, oppression, and suffering. However, the utopian projects a better option that is at least in theory achievable by human effort; the apocalyptic sees the terrible present as proof that the world is on a downward spiral that can only end in catastrophe.

Apocalyptic Midrash

The Rabbis who closed the canon of the Bible around 100 CE left apocalyptic literature almost completely outside the gates. However, their own interpretation of the biblical text shows definite apocalyptic influences.[5] These do not add up to any kind of clear and consistent shared vision, but rather seem to have been proposed as speculative options among a variety of different views regarding the map of history and the dreams and expectations of the future. References and discussions that resonate with apocalyptic chords are scattered throughout rabbinic literature, but a concentrated collection is found in a few pages of Tractate *Sanhedrin* in the Babylonian Talmud.

For example, the debate over the value — or acceptability — of apocalyptic thinking finds clear expression in this conversation between two *tannaim* (rabbis of the Mishnah — second to third centuries CE). Rabbi Eliezer insists that the nation's suffering — and its redemption — are dependent on sin and repentance; Rabbi Joshua argues that the redemption is beyond the people's control, and will come in any event, according to God's plan.

R. Eliezer said: if Israel repent, they will be redeemed, as it is written (Jeremiah 3:22): "Turn, back, O rebellious children, / I will heal your afflictions."

R. Joshua said to him: But it has been written (Isaiah 52:3): "For thus said the Lord: / You were sold for no price / And shall be redeemed without money." "... sold for no price" refers to idolatry; "... redeemed without money" means without repentance and good deeds.

R. Eliezer said to R. Joshua: But it is written (Malachi 3:7): "Turn back to Me and I will turn back to you—said the Lord of Hosts."

R. Joshua responded: But what about this text (Jeremiah 3:14): "Since I have been lord over you, I will take you one from a town, and two from a clan, and bring you to Zion? ..."

R. Eliezer: It is written (Isaiah 30:15): "You shall triumph by stillness and quiet..." ["stillness" is a translation of *shuva*, a pun on *teshuva* = repentance].

R. Joshua: But it is written (Isaiah 49:7): "Thus says the Lord, / The Redeemer of Israel, his Holy One, / To the despised one, / To the abhorred nations, / To the slave of rulers: / Kings shall see and stand up; / Nobles, and they shall prostrate themselves—/ To the honor of the Lord, who is faithful, / To the Holy One of Israel who chose you."

R. Eliezer: But it is written (Jeremiah 4:1): "If you return, O Israel / ... Nations shall bless themselves by you ..."

R. Joshua: But it is written (Daniel 12:7): "Then I heard the man dressed in linen, who was above the water of the river, swear by the Ever-Living One as he lifted his right hand and his left hand to heaven: 'For a time, times, and half a time; and when the breaking of the power of the holy people comes to an end, then shall all these things be fulfilled'."

And Rabbi Eliezer was silent.[6]

Rabbi Eliezer is holding on to the classic prophetic understanding of the Sinai covenant: the fortunes of the nation are determined by their behavior. Rabbi Joshua's position reflects the "grant covenants" made with Abraham and then David: the promise of a glorious national future is eternal and unconditional. Both of them, of course, find support for their positions in the words of the prophets. Rabbi Joshua's final shot, from Daniel's vision, silences Rabbi Eliezer. Apocalypse gets the last word.

Future Visions

The rise of apocalyptic thinking in the Hellenistic period provided the Rabbis, who lived in a context of Roman and Babylonian rule, with a lens through which to view traditional utopian images that had come down to them: the Edenic golden age, the Torah's just society, the desert theocracy, and the divinely chosen monarchy. The result of this refraction was a number of different visions of the future that continued to influence Jewish thought, belief, prayer, and action in the ensuing centuries. Here are some examples of major strands (which have often been entangled with each other):

Kingdom of God, Davidic king, Temple cult:

Rabbi Shimon ben Manasiah said: Israel will never see a sign of blessing until they return and request three things, according to Hosea 3:5, "Afterward, the Israelites will turn back and will seek the Lord their God and David their king—and they will thrill over the Lord and over His bounty in the days to come": The kingdom of heaven, David their king, and the Temple [where they "will thrill over the Lord"].[7]

Miraculous rebuilding of the land and Jerusalem beyond any past experience:

"I will make your battlements of rubies, / Your gates of precious stones, / The whole encircling wall of gems" (Isaiah 54:12). Rabbi Johanan once explained this verse thus: In the future, The Holy One, blessed be He, will bring precious stones and pearls thirty by thirty cubits, will cut openings in them ten by twenty, and will erect them in the gates of Jerusalem.[8]

Restoration of a pure faith, as in the desert:

What is the meaning of (Psalms 42:3) "my soul thirsts for God, the living God; / O when will I come to appear before God!"? My soul thirsts for God who will wear His divinity as He wore it at Sinai. Bring near the End and enact the uniqueness of Your divinity in Your world, as in Zechariah 14:9: "And the Lord shall be king over all the earth; in that day there shall be one Lord with one name."[9]

Simple restoration of national sovereignty:

Samuel said: This world differs from [that of] the days of the Messiah only with respect to servitude to [foreign] powers, as it is written (Deuteronomy 15:11): "For there will never cease to be needy ones in your land."[10]

No future Messiah at all:

Rabbi Hillel said: There will be no Messiah for Israel, as they already experienced him in the days of Hezekiah [Ahaz's successor Hezekiah is depicted in the Bible as a righteous, reforming king].[11]

This brief sampling gives some idea of the wide range of concepts that are tangled together when the Rabbis speak of dreams and expectations for the future. A leading twentieth-century scholar of this literature, Ephraim Urbach, wrote: "At times this diversity exceeds the standards of normal differences of opinion and reaches down to fundaments. It is not confined to divergences within the framework of the generally accepted system of concepts, but reaches antitheses that imply the complete negation of one doctrine by the other.... The terms referred to are: 'end of days,' 'End,' 'days of the Messiah,' 'resurrection of the dead,' 'the world to come,' 'the future to come,' 'the new world.'"[12]

For the past two millennia, poets and legalists, rationalists and mystics, common folk and spiritual and communal leaders have tried to find within this spectrum of visions guidance and support appropriate for their particular historical context. The tension between utopianism based on free will and apocalypticism based on a deterministic view of history has informed these efforts, down to our own day.

Utopus and Messiah

We are left with the question: Is Jewish messianism an expression of utopianism?[13] Thomas More's fictitious seafarer, Raphael Hythloday, reported that Utopia was named for its founder, one Utopus, who conquered the land many centuries ago and established its unique culture and system of government. Hythloday relayed no further information about the man, his background, personality, or personal history. Apparently, he was blessed with great wisdom and leadership skill. He did not establish a dynasty; he created Utopia and left the stage. More doesn't seem to have been all that interested in Utopus or in imagining a historical process leading to Utopia; his focus was on the fully formed ideal, which he held up in order to mock his own reality and inspire his readers to seek something better. Nor does More offer a plan or even suggestions as to how to get from here to there, from present reality to a realized utopia. He simply describes what might be. He certainly does not present it as inevitable, nor does God play any role.

The Jewish expectation of a messianic kingdom in the future is similar to Utopia in that the Torah, and the prophets' visions of a better reality, are seen as descriptions of an ideal society—unlike the present—characterized by justice, peace, and prosperity, to which the nation can aspire. However, for the Jews, utopia is not an unknown, far-off island, but rather a known place, one they even experienced in the past. The Jewish messianic dream is bound up with a sense that the nation is engaged in a historical drama, that the dismal present is poised between an ideal past and an ideal future. The messianic kingdom is not just an interesting and instructive ideal; it is a key element in group and individual identity, a belief that gives meaning to everyday sufferings and actions and gives shape to the Jews' perception of historical time.

The covenantal thread in Jewish messianic thinking—Rabbi Eliezer's view that the redemption depends on the nation's behavior—seems a clear manifestation of utopianism. Rabbi Joshua's apocalyptic view—that redemption is beyond our influence, part of a divine plan—can be seen as an escape: utopia is something we have to work on; apocalypse is something we have to wait for. Since that utopian work often feels Sisyphean, a slow and painful trek toward a constantly receding horizon, the temptation is great to cast the burden elsewhere, to assume a passive role in history. Jewish messianism can be understood as an uneasy coexistence of these two strands.

Messianic Impatience

The conflict between covenantal and apocalyptic views of history, expressed in the debate between Rabbi Eliezer and Rabbi Joshua, echoed down through the Middle Ages. The covenantal view may be seen as the driving force behind the centrality of the *halakhah*. Even in their darkest times, the Jews lived their lives illuminated by the halakhic vision of a utopian society. Living and studying the *halakhah* afforded them the opportunity to experience aspects of utopia and to see their actions as moving the nation toward its full realization. *Halakhah* may be God-given, but it is intimately involved with the human, with the here and now.

If the halakhic utopia was a steady light to live by, apocalyptic traditions and speculations provided occasional brilliant—even blinding—

flashes that sought to light up the whole world. When Jews studied talmudic literature, as they sought guidance in halakhic decision-making, they could not avoid also reading the Rabbis' apocalyptic speculations and wondering how these might apply in their own time. Such wondering was an important component in the thinking of Jewish mystical schools and movements.

Thus, these ideas were ready and waiting in the Jews' minds and bookshelves when periods of uncertainty and upheaval suggested that the times were changing. From Jesus of Nazareth and Simon Bar Kokhba in Roman times down to Sabbetai Zevi (1626–76) in the Ottoman period, messianic pretenders and messianic movements were a recurring feature of Jewish life. Their adherents tended to see the new age dawning as a full restoration of Solomon's empire and Temple, coupled with the ingathering of the exiles and the destruction of Israel's enemies. Interestingly, some of these movements were distinctly antinomian (do we really need *halakhah* in Eden?). In any case, none of them ended well for the Jewish people.

The temptation of apocalyptic thinking did not fade away with premodern messianic movements. Even in the age of Enlightenment it continued to influence Jewish thought, and then found resurgent expression in both Marxism and in Orthodox Zionism. Just as Enlightenment enthusiasts of the eighteenth century and their Marxist heirs in the nineteenth century believed that they could read the map of history and pinpoint their location on it—"knowing" that rationalism was an unstoppable force about to turn the old world upside down—so Rabbi Kook and his disciples believed that current events were signs of an inevitable messianic process.

Policy decisions by those who believe they are actors in a drama beyond their control are generally different from the judgments of those who believe they are free to choose among courses of action. In other words, the two approaches—seeing Israel as an apocalyptic inevitability or understanding our vision of a Jewish state as a utopian ideal—yield different practical consequences. We will examine this tension in chapter 11.

Further Reading

Cook, Stephen L. *Prophecy and Apocalypticism: The Postexilic Social Setting*. Minneapolis MN: Fortress Press, 1995.

Gillman, Neil. *The Death of Death: Resurrection and Immortality in Jewish Thought*. Woodstock VT: Jewish Lights, 1997.

Murphy, Frederick J. *Apocalypticism in the Bible and Its World*. Grand Rapids MI: Baker Academic, 2012.

Scholem, Gershom. "Toward an Understanding of the Messianic Idea." In *The Messianic Idea in Judaism and Other Essays on Jewish Spirituality*, 1–36. New York: Schocken, 1971.

Part 2

A Jewish State

Zionist Utopian Visions

4

A Torah Society

As Judaism's foundational document, the Torah provided utopian images toward which Jewish eyes were raised over the millennia. In modern times, these images provided a substrate for thinking about renewed Jewish sovereignty in the Land of Israel. This interaction between ancient dreams and modern schemes helps explain the fraught relationship between the Jewish religion and the Jewish state.

Torah and the Utopian Dilemma

When my youngest son and his fiancée were planning their wedding several years ago, they wanted me to conduct the ceremony. However, as a Reform rabbi, my authority is not recognized by the Israeli Ministry of Interior, so the marriage could not be registered; moreover, I would be in violation of the law that prohibits rabbis unrecognized by the Orthodox Chief Rabbinate from officiating (indeed, in 2018 Conservative rabbi Dov Haiyun of Haifa was arrested for doing so). So the two were married in a private civil ceremony while vacationing in the United States—foreign civil marriages are recognized by Israel—and returned home for me to perform an unofficial Reform religious ceremony among family and friends.

We waited two thousand years to restore a Jewish state. How frustrating and ironic it is that in this state, of all places, so many Jews feel that they cannot live a full Jewish life on their own terms—among them my son and daughter-in-law, who had to fly to Las Vegas to have a marriage that Israel now recognizes. And this story is only the tip of the iceberg of conflicts generated by the religion-state relationship in Israel. Never out of the headlines, these conflicts—from enforcement of Sabbath work prohibitions to the funding of private religious schools, from religious draft exemptions to gender segregation at public events, from the sale and consumption of nonkosher food to the Orthodox monopoly on conversion—are often central issues in election campaigns and in the forming and collapsing of parliamentary coalitions. It seems that even after seven decades of statehood, Israel has made no progress in resolving the rather basic question: What should be the place of the Jewish religion in the governance of the Jewish state? It was not supposed to be this way.

Throughout Jewish history, not only did the Jews taste utopia each week, as they observed the Sabbath, but they were reminded of the outlines of the ideal Torah society year after year, as they studied the weekly Torah portion. Thus, when Zionism arose in the nineteenth century—even as a secular nationalist movement—for the great majority of Jews, the most familiar, available image of a Jewish polity in the Land of Israel was the Torah's utopia. Whether modern Jews saw the Torah as divine revelation and commandment, as national epic, or as collective historical memory, they had grown up on its stories, its landscapes, its descriptions of social and religious institutions; they could not avoid seeing the prospect of renewed life in the land through its lens. The Torah, in its own time, seems to have been a utopian document; however, after two millennia of longing for its realization, many Jews looked on it as a historical model, a blueprint for the renewed Jewish state.

Thus from its inception Zionism had to confront the utopian dilemma: the almost unbearable temptation to confuse utopian dreams with practical schemes. This confusion could not but lead to frustration and conflict.

Zev Yavetz's Torah Utopia: *New from the Not-Old*

Zev Yavetz (1847–1924) was a popular Hebrew author of both historical research and fiction, a pioneering educator in Palestine during a decade living there among the First Aliyah settlers (the first wave of Zionist immigration, 1881–1903), and a leader in the Mizrachi movement (the Orthodox faction founded in 1902 within Herzl's Zionist Organization). Yavetz was a product of what might be called "enlightened Orthodoxy" in late nineteenth-century Russia. He was raised in an Orthodox home and community, yet his father saw to it that he was tutored in Bible (traditional education focused almost exclusively on Talmud) as well as Hebrew and modern languages. He retained his Orthodox belief and practice, but sought throughout his life to define the appropriate interface of the tradition with such phenomena as Enlightenment, socialism, and Zionism.

Yavetz published a number of romantic stories about life in the new settlements in Palestine. Sometime around 1903 he started to write a utopian novel, which apparently was in part a dig at Theodor Herzl's 1902 utopian novel *Altneuland* (*Old New Land*), since Yavetz titled his manuscript *New from the Not-Old*. He never completed it, however; it was found among his papers and posthumously published in 2013.[1]

The unnamed narrator, living a few generations after the Jews' ingathering to the Land of Israel, has been living in Europe as a care-taker of now-abandoned synagogues and cemeteries. However, an organization of gentiles who have taken on Jewish customs and beliefs offers to replace him, and his employer arranges for his retirement to the Land of Israel. Touring the land in order to find a place to settle, he rejects Haifa as too bustling and cosmopolitan and Jericho (where he has cousins) because there too the focus is on industry and commerce (exporting perfumes and Dead Sea bitumen). His guide, Aminadav, even discourages him from considering Jerusalem, for it too is too cosmopolitan:

> The Sanhedrin there is the supreme court for all the nations of the world, and all the dwellers on earth raise their eyes to the results of its peaceful deliberations, set to bring an end to the conflict between the Mongols of eastern Asia and the Aryan nations. You want to experience the culture of Israel in its purity. If so, there is no better place than quiet Yavneh, the Torah center.[2] For when

God brought back the captivity of Jerusalem, the great matron [Jerusalem] remembered her little sister who had saved her treasures and guarded them like the apple of her eye, transmitting them fully to her progeny. Therefore she established her as the small Sanhedrin, concerned not with judgement but with Torah study in all its breadth, depth, and completeness. There the elite youth of Israel are trained to enter the service of the Sanhedrin.

There is no branch of Torah knowledge which is foreign to these respected wise men—nor any science or language. Just as it was the rule for our ancestors, in the time of the First and Second Temples, for the Sanhedrin to know every science and every language, so it is today when all the nations turn to it for judgement. . . . Half the population of Yavneh are scholars and their students. It is they who are creating and preserving the high culture you see all around you.

Arriving in Yavneh (by balloon), the visitor notes: "We passed through gardens with all kinds of trees, large and small, planted along the paths and on the lawns between the avenues of trees; spice beds and rose gardens, and among them small crystal-clear mirror-like pools bordered in marble."

Aminadav relates that two generations ago, at the time of mass emigration of Jews from Europe, Palestine was not prepared to absorb them all, so they scattered around the world. One group of a thousand young people formed a colony in Africa, called Jezreel, where by trial and error they created a successful industrial/agricultural commune. Their experience was used in building the new society in the Land of Israel:

Wherever there has been continuous habitation for thousands of years, it is very difficult to make changes in the social order and to innovate. But this is not the case in our land. All vestiges of our forefathers' settlement in Temple days have been lost for 1500 years, and the Arab settlement is as if it never was. And so since an organized society like those of Europe and America was lacking, commerce and professions were undeveloped in the land of Israel. This very absence became an advantage for us, enabling us to experiment and to establish a new system: the *Eruv*; God was with us and our experiment succeeded.

The *Eruv* is a socialist economic structure, based on rational planning, in which every member works at his or her chosen occupation, with the output belonging to the collective—and every member's needs are met by the collective. No middlemen, no hierarchy. When the narrator questions why the Jews have adopted a foreign system, Aminadav is indignant: "Foreign?! . . . The sabbatical and the jubilee, the core of the *Eruv* system, are foreign? The prohibition of interest . . . the prohibition of permanent land sale between Israelites, as in our kingdom of old; the division of the land among all the people—these are foreign customs? The repeated commandment 'one law, for you and for the stranger' (Num. 15:16) is foreign? It is these commandments alone that are the basis of the *Eruv* system."

Interestingly, perhaps the most obviously utopian law in the Torah, the jubilee year, appears as an exemplary institution of social justice in other Zionist utopias, including those of Herzl and Lewinsky, which we will discuss further on.

Aminadav continues: "In the days of the Exile, . . . our nation couldn't rule its members except in matters of the heart. . . . But now that it has regained its sovereignty in all matters, it can establish its rule according to the spirit [of the Torah]. . . . This was a cornerstone of our rabbis' moral teaching . . . : 'A person must never separate himself from the community.'[3] This served as the basis for building the Torah culture which has now been established in the land of Israel and in the far off colonies."

Aminadav explains that *eruv* (which means "mixing") refers to the familiar *halakhah* of creating a symbolic, temporary unification of a number of homes into a common space, thus allowing members of the community to carry items on the Sabbath from house to house, overcoming the prohibition of carrying from private to public domains.

The ritual for establishing an *eruv* involves exchanging symbolic items of food before the Sabbath. Thus, the *eruv* is the basis of socialism: "The Sabbath grants dominance to collective possession, by instructing individuals to join together and exchange bread—according to a consensus, for the benefit of all equally, so that no one has an advantage. The common bread makes the individual possessions into one common possession, the individual spaces into one common space, and more than that—the individual opinions into one common opinion, perfect and complete."

The manuscript ends after a description of how the new noncompetitive and egalitarian economy has effectuated a great reduction in sexual tension and immorality by enabling everyone to marry—for love—at the age of eighteen, without worrying about dowry, livelihood, or marrying for money.[4] Governance is not described (state? kingdom?). Peace prevails, and clearly Israel is a light unto the nations.

Yavetz's utopian travelogue gives beautiful expression to a major and highly influential idea running through Zionist thought: that the restoration of a Jewish state in the Land of Israel would lead not just to the expansion of the *halakhah* to all areas of life, but to the revitalization of the *halakhah* itself (see discussion of Moses Hess in chapter 10).[5] Yavetz's focus is not on a state that *enforces* the *halakhah*, but rather on a state that reestablishes the organic connection among Torah, land, nation, and life, so that *halakhah* can free itself from the distorting influences of oppression and economic injustice that have crippled it over centuries of exile. In Yavetz's utopia, the Torah lives in synergy with all the human experiences from which it was seen as estranged in Eastern European Jewry in 1900: aesthetic beauty, science, productive labor, socialism, romantic love, and the gentiles' respect.

The Torah State: Three Attempts

Yavetz's utopia remained unknown. However, its ideas and images found repeated expression in Zionist discourse and action. A few examples:

Reviving the Sanhedrin

One expression of the longing for a revitalized *halakhah* through the Zionist project was the effort to reestablish the Sanhedrin in the early years of statehood. The leading supporter of this effort, Rabbi Yehudah (Fishman) Maimon (1875–1962), a founder of Mizrachi who would later serve as Israel's first Minister of Religious Affairs, argued that restoring Jewish sovereignty invited the revival of the Sanhedrin. This assembly of the greatest halakhic authorities in the world would have the authority to solve the problems created by the encounter of *halakhah* with modern technology and with social, economic, and political developments. Like Yavetz, he envisioned a reestablished Sanhedrin that would "revive Torah Judaism, and increase its influence not by means of enforcement, fines, and punishments, but by ceaseless broad and deep explanation, by scholarship and education, by exposing all the beauty and the social justice and the holiness and the exaltation found in God's Torah, our written and oral Torah."[6]

Despite Rabbi Maimon's halakhic research demonstrating the basis for his proposal, his colleagues failed to support it.

The Religious Kibbutz

A more successful attempt to revitalize *halakhah* through Zionism was the Orthodox kibbutz movement. Originating simultaneously among Orthodox Zionist youth movement members in Germany and Russia in the 1930s, the vision of the religious kibbutz sought to integrate several goals:

- spiritual revival of an Orthodoxy that felt dry and ritualistic to these young activists;
- dynamic application of the *halakhah* to all of life;
- establishment of an intimate community characterized by a pervasive commitment to social justice;
- laying the foundation for a Torah state.[7]

The first religious kibbutz was Tirat Tzvi, established in the Bet Shean valley (southwest of the Sea of Galilee) in 1937. Here is one member's description of a Rosh Hashanah morning in 1950:

Five o'clock. . . . Slowly, the eastern sky begins to glow. . . . The chickens awake and the few roosters raise their voices in song . . . signaling the division between night and day.[8] From the distance may be heard the lowing of cows as they are turned out to pasture.

Nursing mothers, still sleepy, hurry to the children's houses to nurse their babies. For them this day is no different from any other. . . . The woman on kitchen duty wends her way . . . to work, denied the pleasure of sweet holiday sleep — but aware that yesterday, on the first day of the holiday, she had slept in while her colleague had cooked.

Six o'clock. . . . The surface of the water in the fishponds ripples. The members on duty are feeding the fish. Because it is a holiday, they do not use the rowboats to carry the bran to the center of the pond. Instead, they remove their clothes and enter the water themselves, dragging the sack of feed behind them. . . . This constitutes their ritual morning dip. . . .

It is 7:30, the hour of the morning service. From every direction the members converge on the dining hall (which doubles as the synagogue), tallit bags under their arms. . . . The members on livestock duty rush their tasks in order to finish and join those at prayer; likewise, the dairymen finish milking, the poultrymen finish tending their chickens, and the shepherd leads the herd to the barn and makes his way with the rest toward the showers, to change from working into festival clothes.

The children have finished their meal and hurry to prayer. . . . Some of the preschoolers, still too young to join the service, happily head for the swings outside their quarters. At last they go in for their breakfast and silence settles again over the settlement. Only the voice of the *hazzan* echoes through the air, giving voice to the heartfelt prayers of the congregation.

See how the profane has been abolished and the holiness of the day has spread over the whole settlement. For today is a festival to the Lord![9]

Spirituality, *halakhah*, the holy land, productivity, rootedness, social-ism: a Torah utopia, realized.

Of course, nothing is as simple as it seems. The relationship between halakhic and democratic authority in the kibbutz has often been fraught: What happens when the members vote to set a policy (for example, gender-mixed swimming hours at the kibbutz pool) that con-flicts with the rabbi's halakhic ruling? And the dream that the Orthodox kibbutz would serve as a model for the state has simply not material-ized. Today there are twenty-two Orthodox kibbutzim with about ten thousand members — about a tenth of the total kibbutz membership, which itself amounts to little more than one percent of Israel's popula-tion. Yet they represent an interesting and even inspiring experiment in creating a Torah-based utopian community.

Hebrew Law

From Zionism's earliest days down to the present, the idea that the Jew-ish state, even as a modern democracy, should somehow be governed according to "Hebrew law" has been a constant theme, a subject for both scholarly research and political debate. After two millennia living subject to other nations' laws, there was a widespread feeling that a restored Jewish state should finally liberate the Jews to live by their own lights, to reinstate the Torah as a living constitution. The Hebrew Law Society, founded in 1918 by Russian Zionist students who immigrated to Palestine soon thereafter, served as a focus for research and activism aimed at reviving and revising Hebrew law for the envisioned Jewish state. While some Zionists, like Yavetz, understood "Hebrew law" as a revitalized *halakhah* applied in a state framework, the Hebrew Law Society represented an approach rooted in secular culture. European romantic nationalism argued that just as a nation is characterized by a unique language and customs that organically express its "spirit," so too nations have their own unique legal systems. For these Jewish nationalists, an important goal—and challenge—in restoring Jewish statehood was extracting from Jewish sources the "spirit" of Hebrew law: the values and general principles that could inform a modern, secular legal system.[10]

By the mid-1930s this effort had stalled. Hebrew law activists were stymied by their own lack of clarity regarding the ideal relationship among biblical, talmudic, halakhic, and gentile legal systems. And in the meantime a legal reality in Palestine had been established: British government courts were the preferred authority for civil and criminal matters, while Orthodox rabbinical courts adjudicated matters of family law. Thus the old pattern that had long characterized diaspora Jewish life became the accepted norm in the "state-in-the-making."

From the Orthodox Zionist perspective, too, the ideal of a Torah state receded toward the messianic horizon. Rabbi Isaac Herzog (1888–1959), the first Ashkenazic chief rabbi of the state, wrote a detailed analysis examining how the halakhic concept of *ger toshav* (resident alien) would impact the status of gentiles in a Jewish state. The Rabbis of the Talmud had created the category of *ger toshav* to explain how it was possible to allow gentiles to continue to live in the land in view of the commandment to expel the Canaanites (Exod. 23:33). The solution was that gentiles who formally committed to a set of basic moral principles (the "Noahide laws") would be allowed to remain, and afforded certain limited protections, while not being part of the nation.[11] But Rabbi Herzog then neutralized his entire argument by explicitly placing it in a messianic context:

> We . . . could not have conquered the land against the will of the United Nations and without their consent, and there is no doubt that until our Messiah comes we will need their support to defend ourselves against the sea of national enemies surrounding us and even reaching inside the state; and there is also no doubt that they will not grant us a Jewish state unless we guarantee, in law and

in judgement, the rights of minorities. . . . Moreover, it is certain that preventing discrimination and unfair treatment of Muslims and Christians will serve as a key foundation of the right to a state that we shall be granted. . . . Shall we respond that our holy Torah forbids a Jewish government from granting them freedom of worship and the right to purchase land? I would say that there is no rabbi in Israel with a brain in his head, with common sense, who would . . . claim that that is our obligation according to the holy Torah.[12]

Utopia is important to study, but it is not where we live.

Today, the Israeli Justice Ministry's Jewish Law Department (which advises the ministry and the Knesset on the halakhic background and implications of pending legislation and legal decisions) displays on its website a catalog of judicial decisions that are at least partly based on halakhic concepts and precedents.[13] And, indeed, there are some impressive cases in which legislators have succeeded in translating Torah ideals into modern laws. One example is the law requiring that all salaried workers be paid promptly at the end of their pay period, based on Deuteronomy 24:15: "You must pay him his wages on the same day, before the sun sets, for he is needy and urgently depends on it; else he will cry to the Lord against you and you will incur guilt." This law, proposed by Orthodox Zionist MK Moshe Una (1902–89, a founder of Kibbutz Tirat Tzvi), achieved an easy consensus, and was enacted in 1955.

Now and then Orthodox and nationalist political figures call for legislation to establish the formal dominance of Torah law—or Hebrew law—in the Jewish state. However, these proposals are declaratory, without concrete detail. What they actually envision remains unclear, more slogan than practical plan. As we have seen, the Orthodox kibbutz struggles with the conflict between rabbinic and democratic authority, "Hebrew Law" never found a clear definition, and Rabbi Herzog felt compelled to put the *halakhah* of *ger toshav* on hold until messianic times.

In essence, it is one thing for a Torah state utopia to inspire legislation based on ideas of social justice found in the Torah, such as fair treatment of workers or observance of the sabbatical year (see below); it is quite another to imagine that the Written Torah, as is — or its rabbinic interpretation (the *halakhah*) — can serve as the constitution of a real state. Seeing the Torah's utopian vision, even filtered through rabbinical interpretation, as an obligatory blueprint, would in all likelihood:

- violate its own utopian nature;
- give rise to overwhelming problems of interpretation and application inherent in the attempt to return to a past which never was (as seems to have been the case with the jubilee year, for example);
- lead to conflict with other utopian visions of a Jewish state.

This "utopian dilemma," the tension between the Torah as inspiration and the Torah as binding constitution, lurks in the background whenever we invoke imagery of the Jewish state as a return not just to a place, but to the lost utopia of life in that place as envisioned in the Torah.

Utopia Now — or Apocalypse Later?

I adjure you, O daughters of Jerusalem . . . that you awaken not, nor stir up love, until it please.

This text occurs three times in Song of Songs (2:7, 3:5, 8:4). The Rabbis explain why:

The text refers to three [different] oaths:
One: Israel shall not go up [to the land] as a wall [by force];
Two: the Holy One blessed be He, adjured Israel not to rebel against the nations of the world;

Three: the Holy One, blessed be He, adjured the idolators not to oppress Israel too much.[14]

At the turn of the twentieth century, Zionism was becoming a popular movement — but the majority of the Orthodox world, and its rabbinical leaders, rejected it as a form of "forcing the end," violating the first two of these three oaths. Moreover, not only was the attempt to take history into the Jews' own hands seen as impudent interference in God's plan, but also, the movement's secular nature was perceived as a threat to the traditional community and its leaders' authority. In this respect, Zionism appeared to be just one more in a series — Haskalah (Jewish Enlightenment), Reform, socialism — of rebellions against *halakhah*. If anything, Zionism was more sinister, due to its successionist element: the implication (or open claim) that Jewish national restoration was a return to a more perfect past existence — before Judaism was "distorted" by the focus on religion and *halakhah* in Exile. In other words, Zionism threatened to make the *halakhah* obsolete.

In 1912, six hundred Orthodox rabbis and communal leaders, convening in Kattowitz (Prussian Poland; today Katowice) founded the organization Agudat Israel (the Union of Israel), dedicated to Orthodox opposition to Zionism. They declared: "The Jewish people stands outside the framework of the political peoples of the world, and differs essentially from them: the Sovereign of the Jewish people is the Almighty, the Torah is the Law that governs them, and the Holy Land has been at all times destined for the Jewish people."[15]

Agudat Israel became associated with the "Old Yishuv"[16] in Palestine, the Orthodox communities that had been living for generations in the "holy cities" of Jerusalem, Hebron, Safed, and Tiberias, supported primarily by philanthropy from abroad. It sought to advance a vision of the Jewish polity in the Land of Israel as essentially just another Jewish community, similar to those of the Diaspora except for the sanctity of the land itself. When establishment of the state was imminent, Agudat Israel's proposal for a constitution comprised the following elements:

The Jewish state is based on the recognition of the authority of the Torah in public life. This principle is an immutable constitutional law. The authority to interpret and implement this principle lies with the chief rabbinate of the Land of Israel. The following religious foundations are part of the constitution:

- Prohibition of all commercial activity, public transport, and public works on Sabbath and holidays (except, of course, where danger to life is involved).
- Prohibition of slaughter or sale, by Jews, of non-kosher meat; requirement of kosher food in all public institutions.
- Control of marriage and divorce by the chief rabbinate.
- Requirement of ritual circumcision for male Jewish babies.
- Requirement to teach basics of Judaism in all schools.
- Requirement that all courts operate according to basic principles of Torah law.
- Tax exemption for Torah scholars.
- Tax exemption for Jewish farmers observing the sabbatical year.
- Establishment of government-sanctioned, Torah-based communities in every locality, with powers of taxation and enforcement.

And in cases where any of the above is not politically possible, the following safeguards will be in place:

- Guarantee of the option of forming an autonomous local community.
- Guarantee of the option to be judged in a rabbinical court.
- Guarantee of full funding for independent educational frameworks.[17]

Note that this proposed constitution is not a vision of a Torah state, but a defense mechanism for a religious minority in a secular state:

it aims to protect and preserve life according to *halakhah*, or at least to guarantee the rights of those who are committed to it. Beyond the principle of rabbinical authority, it contains no discussion of governance, criminal and tort law, defense, social welfare, general education, or minorities. The Jewish state is seen not only as not utopian (and certainly not messianic!), but as a potential danger to the traditional community, so that its powers must be carefully circumscribed.

Secular Zionists dreamed of Hebrew law; Orthodox Zionists dreamed of a Torah state; Old Yishuv Jews had nightmares about the breakdown of their community, rabbinic authority, and way of life under the modernizing assault of the Jewish national revival. Agudat Israel's defensive vision might have been swept away by the successful creation of a modern state, but two factors have kept it in play: one political, one spiritual and utopian.

1. For the Zionist leadership to obtain United Nations support for establishing a Jewish state in 1947, they needed to show that the entire Jewish population of Palestine favored this resolution. However, the anti-Zionist Orthodox community, a significant "native" population, would only assent to this proposal if their needs were met. They did not envision, or demand, or even want a Torah state. They insisted on a state in which halakhic authority would be enforced by the state in certain specific areas of life (primarily family law, public Sabbath observance, and dietary laws). In order to prevent Agudat Israel from undermining the Zionist negotiations with the United Nations, a compromise agreement was reached in June 1947. On the one hand, equal rights and freedom from religious coercion were guaranteed for all citizens. On the other, Saturday would be an official day of rest, all efforts would be made to insure adherence to the dietary laws in public institutions, all efforts would be made to maintain a unitary authority in family law, and all educational "streams" would have autonomy.[18]

This agreement can be seen as the precedent for the coalition agreements that have been standard in every Israeli government since independence. Small Orthodox parties join together with larger parties, enabling them to cobble together a majority coalition, in return for the maintenance of key guarantees of religious enforcement and autonomy. It is often argued that such "extortion" is the basis of the continued power of the chief rabbinate and the Orthodox bureaucracy to force halakhic norms on a population that is in large part opposed, or at least indifferent, to them. That said, it can also be argued that the "extortion" argument is somewhat of an oversimplification, which brings us to the second point.

2. The utopian notion of a Torah state also influences public perceptions of the role of rabbinical authority. A good example is Prime Minister David Ben Gurion's 1952 meeting with Rabbi Abraham Karelitz (1878–1953), one of the most widely respected rabbinic leaders and halakhic authorities of his generation. To Ben Gurion's query regarding how religious and secular Jews could reach a modus vivendi in the state, Rabbi Karelitz famously referred to a talmudic discussion: if two camels are trying to pass on a narrow path, the one carrying the heavier load has the right of way.[19] "We, the religious Jews, are analogous to the camel with the load—we carry a burden of hundreds of commandments. You have to give way."[20] While Ben Gurion objected that secular Jews had their own important commandments— building and defending the state—the image of the Orthodox and secular camels (or, as the story was later told, carts) on the narrow path became a commonplace in the popular imagination. Thus, while no one has ever succeeded in translating the Torah state utopia into a real-life constitution and, furthermore, it's not even clear what a Torah state utopia is, the common—often unspoken—assumption of many secular Jews is that if anyone does know, it must be the Orthodox rabbis, with their knowledge

of and loyalty to *halakhah*, so we should defer to them. If the *halakhah* itself is utopian, then those who adhere to and study it should be granted the authority to lead the Jewish state on its utopian quest.

The Sabbatical Year: A Case Study

While a number of Zionist utopians suggested the reinstitution of the jubilee year as emblematic of the new state's commitment to social justice, no proposals or efforts have been made in that direction (except for a symbolic expression: over 90 percent of the land area of Israel is owned by the state, and in most cases cannot be sold but only leased by means of a renewable forty-nine-year lease). On the other hand, the biblical commandment of *shemitah* (from the root *sh-m-t*, to let go), a "Sabbath of the land," according to which the land is to lie fallow every seventh year (Lev. 25:1–7), has been the focus of serious attempts at implementation—and of serious controversy.[21]

The modern consideration of *shemitah* began in 1889, the first sabbatical year (according to rabbinical calculations) to occur since the beginning of modern agricultural settlement in Palestine. Since these early settlements were struggling to survive, it was clear that proper *shemitah* observance might well cause them to go under. A halakhic solution to this emergency was approved by a leading authority of the time, Rabbi Isaac Elchanan Spector of Kovno (1817–96): the agricultural land would be sold temporarily to a gentile for the duration of the sabbatical year, so that it could be worked without technically violating the prohibition of working "Jewish land." While there was rabbinic opposition to this arrangement, and ultimately some communities rejected it, it saved the struggling settlements and became the commonly accepted response to the strictures of *shemitah*.[22] After the establishment of Israel, the chief rabbinate continued to support this practice, despite the irony in the symbolism of essentially selling the Jewish state to a gentile in order to adhere to Torah law.

The motivation for the practice has since evolved. Today, individual farmers wishing to observe the *halakhah* can do so without fear of economic collapse, by utilizing modern methods of storage and preservation, developing nonagricultural sources of income, consuming imported produce, and other work-arounds. However, fully observing the sabbatical on a national scale would not be economically sustainable. In addition, since the large majority of Israel's farmers and consumers do not feel obligated to obey the *halakhah*, an enforcement of national *shemitah* observance would be a massively unpopular bureaucratic undertaking. Thus, the simple legal fiction of selling the land to a gentile neutralizes the entire issue—but highlights the gap between the utopia of a Torah state and the frustrating reality of trying to operate a real state within a halakhic framework.

What else could be done with regard to *shemitah*? A simple response, of course, would be to say that *shemitah* is just irrelevant now in a modern state with industrialized agriculture, and therefore should be seen as a historical memory—or, perhaps, a messianic fantasy of a return to a life of biblical proportions and institutions. Thus, with or without a legal fiction, it should be set aside. However, another approach that has gained some traction in recent years is to see *shemitah* as a utopian concept that can guide us in creating new institutions and practices that reflect its moral content rather than its halakhic technicalities. For example, all workers might benefit from a sabbatical every seven years, as is currently the practice in many educational institutions. This approach sees *shemitah* laws as inspiration, not as a technical manual, and it generalizes the concept to relevance beyond the small sector of the population engaged in agriculture.

The 2015–16 *shemitah* year saw a flowering of initiatives to try to translate the sabbatical concept into relevant terms for our times. A number of organizations and Israel's Ministry of Education sponsored educational endeavors on the environmental implications of abstaining from exploiting the land. And the sabbatical remission of debts (Deut. 15:1–2), traditionally circumvented by a legal fiction, was creatively revived in a cooperative effort by government and philanthropy: thousands of Israeli families suffering under cruel debt burdens were given the opportunity to renegotiate their obligations, obtain partial remission, and benefit from ongoing counseling aimed at economic recovery.

There is something romantic, heartwarming, and inspiring about seeing in the restoration of Jewish sovereignty the renewal of the simple, natural, authentic, agrarian life described in the Torah. But, again, a utopia is not a blueprint. Nor is a sovereign state a halakhic community, as we shall see in the next chapter.

Apocalypse Now

For Orthodox Jews who were drawn to Zionism, the answer to Agudat Israel's insistence on awaiting the Messiah was the belief that the present moment is indeed an early phase in the messianic redemption. The belief that the modern Jewish state is the "first blossoming" of the messianic redemption became a cornerstone of Orthodox Zionism, making possible active, constructive Orthodox participation in the Zionist endeavor and in Israeli public life. At the same time, however, it opened the door to messianic speculation and activism, both of which had long been suppressed in Judaism because of negative historical experiences (e.g., Bar Kokhba, Sabbetai Zvi). Once Jews accept that certain current historical events, such as the Balfour Declaration, the establishment of the state, or the victory in the 1967 Six-Day War, are recognizable milestones on the apocalyptic timeline, then all other events—and thus also decisions—are open to interpretation in this context. Since the 1967 conquest of the West Bank (the ancient heartland of the Israelite empire) and the Old City of Jerusalem (containing the site of Solomon's Temple), such interpretation has gained an important foothold in Orthodox Zionist thought and political activity.

An influential rabbinic spokesman for this view of history was Rabbi Tzvi Yehudah Kook (1891–1982), son of Rabbi Abraham Isaac Kook. The younger Rabbi Kook would recollect that after the United Nations vote to partition Palestine in 1947, Jews around the world burst into spontaneous dances of joy, but his own response was a sense of bereavement:

They divided my land! And where is our Hevron? Do we forget this? And where is our Shechem? Do we forget about this? And where is our Jericho? Do we forget this too? And where is our other side of the Jordan? Where is each block of earth? Each part and parcel, and four cubits of God's land? Is it in our hand to relinquish any millimeter of this? God forbid![23]

And after 1967, he declared:

Any coercion to transgress this command (that the Land of Israel be under our sovereignty)–whether on the part of the Israeli government or on the part of a gentile government, obligates us to rise up against it with all of our life and souls . . . and all "decisions" which come to steal away parts of this land . . . are null and void.[24]

A key feature of this ideology is the conflation of biblical events with current ones: living during the incipient messianic restoration implies that biblical concepts such as conquering the land, rebuilding the Temple, and driving out the Canaanites are relevant, and actionable, today. Agudat Israel's apocalyptic approach dictated passivity: the redemption will come in God's good time; mundane events such as the victories of 1948 and 1967 are mere distractions; if anything, setting up a modern Jewish state is a rebellion, a sin that will delay redemption. Rabbi Tzvi Yehudah Kook's apocalyptic Zionism, on the other hand, interprets the same events differently—as evidence of a redemptive process that has begun and with which Jews must cooperate in order to move it along in accord with God's plan.

Alas, trying to translate utopia into reality by force is a violation of the nature of utopia, and has usually been a recipe for disappointment, if not suffering. "Knowing" the plan of the apocalypse and seeking to further its progress by force is even more fraught with disastrous potential, as we will see in chapter 11.

Further Reading

Abramov, S. Zalman. *Perpetual Dilemma: Jewish Religion in the Jewish State*. Rutherford NJ: Fairleigh Dickinson University Press, 1976.

Elon, Menachem. *Jewish Law: History, Sources, Principles*. Philadelphia: The Jewish Publication Society, 1994.

Inbari, Motti. *Messianic Religious Zionism Confronts Israeli Territorial Compromises*. Cambridge: Cambridge University Press, 2012.

Sapir, Gideon, and Daniel Statman. *State and Religion in Israel: A Philosophical-Legal Inquiry*. Cambridge: Cambridge University Press, 2019.

5

Holy Community

What does it mean for Israel to be the fulfillment of the modern longing for community?

The Ideal Jewish Community

Some years ago I attended a group bar/bat mitzvah ceremony for a
dozen young people from a North American synagogue. A windowed
hall overlooking the walls of Jerusalem's Old City provided a golden
backdrop for the ceremony. Each participant had prepared a brief
sermonette, and several mentioned how exciting it was for them to
celebrate this milestone in Israel—a place where "everybody is Jewish!"
It was hard to miss the dissonance between the words and the setting:
if there is one place in Israel where *not* everybody is Jewish, it is the
Old City of Jerusalem.

About a decade earlier, the year 1999 saw the birth of "the largest
educational tourism project in the world." A coalition of individuals and
agencies (including the Israeli government) created Taglit-Birthright,
providing free ten-day educational tours of Israel to young (eighteen- to
twenty-six-year-old) Jews from around the world. As of 2019, 650,000
Jews have participated—including a hundred thousand Israelis. The
stated goal of this effort: "Birthright Israel seeks to ensure the future
of the Jewish people by strengthening Jewish identity, Jewish communities, and connection with Israel via a trip to Israel."[1]

Taglit-Birthright takes seriously the old popular notion that the cure
for Jewish identity "issues"—or any issues—of young diaspora Jews is
to send them to Israel, preferably to a kibbutz. Not because, I suggest,
Israel is seen as a Torah state; indeed, neither Torah nor statehood are

considerations. Rather, Israel is seen as the Jewish supercommunity—where "everybody is Jewish"; where the street (the 'hood) is Jewish; where both the police and the criminals are Jewish; where Jews take care of each other; where everything is closed on Yom Kippur, not Christmas; where even sports heroes and supermodels are Jewish. This experience of a "fully Jewish" existence is seen as therapeutic for those growing up in an open society where Jews are a minority and where "Jewish community" is a pale reflection of what it was a few generations ago.

Moreover, this perception of Israel as a community is not only held by diaspora Jews; it has been a trope in Israeli culture as well. In *The Sabra* (2003), an examination of Israeli identity in the years 1930–60, sociologist Oz Almog writes: "The familial, communal culture of the kibbutz affected not only the Sabra organizations but also society as a whole—including urban society. . . . Jewish identity with its historical baggage, the cultural and economic isolation in a hostile environment, the common traumas, and the mourning rituals that united the entire nation all reinforced the intimate character of life in the country and granted the Yishuv and the young state the nature, sociologically, of one large kibbutz."[2]

Israel as a utopian Jewish community would solve all of the Jews' modern ambivalences and conflicts about identity and belonging. But can a state be a community?

Community and Modernity

With the destruction of the Judean kingdom in 586 BCE, Jewish political life evolved into a format that became standard up until emancipation in the nineteenth century (and in Eastern Europe, up to the Russian revolution): the semiautonomous community. Sometimes in self-contained villages, more often in the "Jewish street"—neighborhood or ghetto—in a Christian- or Muslim-majority city, the Jews functioned as one of many corporate entities in medieval society (e.g., clergy, burghers, craftsmen, nobles, etc.). They were subject to the local ruler in diplomacy, defense, criminal justice, and public works, while ruling themselves—according to *halakhah*—in all matters internal to the community: business, torts, family, education, welfare, ritual. Typically, a dual leadership structure consisting of rabbis (expert in Torah) and lay leaders (with wealth and connections)—echoing priests and kings—governed the community.

In the eighteenth and nineteenth centuries, modernization upset this equilibrium. Increasing numbers of Jews now came to see the same autonomous community that had provided support, protection, belonging, and a framework for living according to the Torah as confining and segregating—and Jewish otherness as the key obstacle to Jewish emancipation from medieval strictures and persecutions. The process of the dissolution of the medieval community began in Western Europe. In the New World, such communities were absent from the beginning, so there was nothing to dissolve. In much of Eastern Europe and the Middle East, the process came later—in the first decades of the twentieth century.

The steamroller of the modern state flattened not only the traditional Jewish community, but all communities. Whether it was an absolute monarchy, a democracy, or a fascist dictatorship, the state demanded the individual's direct allegiance, with no intervening loyalties and authorities. Clan, guild, church, union, local and regional government—all had to be weak for the state to be strong. As the rights of the individual became supreme, and the focus of all struggle, the authority and thus the relevance of all these smaller-scale associations diminished in proportion.

The accumulation of centralized loyalty and power had clear advantages—and not only in the realm of military power. Public health, universal education, the welfare state, fair taxation—in these and other spheres the efficiency of the state made life more equitable and better for just about everyone. And yet . . .

A constant theme in Western thought, art, literature, and politics over the past two centuries has been the longing for the lost community of the past. Despite the many benefits of the Enlightenment and the modern state, one doesn't have to be a starry-eyed romantic to sense that something's gained, but something's lost in the transition. Alienation, atomization, anomie, disempowerment, loneliness: these are just some of the terms used to characterize the life of the individual in modern mass society, absent the support and meaning provided by community. In fact, a number of phenomena in contemporary social and political life—from nationalism to fascism to gangs to Facebook— have been described as attempts to restore or replace the function of community in human life.[3]

Not surprisingly, historians and sociologists continue to debate the degree to which the ideal community was ever so ideal—or even real; to what extent did Norman Rockwell's America—or Tevye's Anatevka— ever really exist in their remembered stability, simplicity, and happiness?[4] Indeed, even if we filter out obvious aspects of the good old days that were not good, such as racial and religious persecution, disease, and poverty, we don't have to dig too deeply to uncover not-so-romantic aspects of the traditional community. The stultifying effects of community life depicted in Sinclair Lewis's *Main Street* (1920) were documented centuries earlier in halakhic responsa written by rabbis throughout the Diaspora: rigid class hierarchies, power struggles, the power of shame, petty disputes, family feuds, resistance to new ideas. It seems that it is much easier to feel nostalgia for the old-time community if you have never lived in one yourself.

However, when it comes to utopian visions, what matters is not what really was, but what is imagined to have been. So it is that throughout the past two centuries, visions of the future utopia that progress will enable humankind to reach have existed alongside nostalgic visions of utopian communities of the past.

The Shtetl Remembered: *Life Is with People*

The traditional Jewish community survived in the form of the Eastern European shtetl (Yiddish for "little town") until the Russian Revolution, and in some cases until the Holocaust. In Middle Eastern and North

African settings, the traditional *mellah* (walled Jewish quarter) lasted until the mass migrations following Israel's birth in 1948.

In 1952, anthropologists Mark Zborowski and Elizabeth Herzog published *Life Is with People*, a study of the shtetl based on interviews, memoirs, and literary sources. It became a best-seller and was reprinted several times; parts of it even found their way into the text of *Fiddler on the Roof*. Despite the book's professed intent of academic objectivity, it conveyed a certain nostalgia for the lost world it described. While the authors portrayed unsavory elements (class hierarchy, the power of gossip and shame), on the whole the shtetl came across as a warm, moral, even holy community — utopia. The book gave academic reinforcement to the popular literature in Yiddish and English (e.g., of Sholom Aleichem and I. L. Peretz) that despite irony and satire, tended to romanticize the shtetl. For generations of American Jews, this vision of the lost community provided an image of what they thought they were missing:[5]

> The synagogue as House of Assembly is the town hall of the shtetl. Here community business is conducted, whether in the main central shul for the whole shtetl, or in a smaller shul in connection with welfare activities of that one congregation. All important announcements are made in the synagogue, from new decrees of the local or national government to announcements of a marriage, a birth, a death, involving some member of the congregation. No clear-cut distinction is made between religious and secular functions, since for the shtetl Judaism is not a religion but a way of life. . . .
>
> Within the area of shtetl autonomy the highest legal authority is the rabbi, who is also the highest religious and scholastic authority. . . . The rabbi's decision will be enforced only by the pressure of public opinion. A salient feature of the civil machinery is that lack of enforcing power for the functions that are delegated to the shtetl. There are no police to implement the verdict of the rabbi or the decisions of the other officials. Enforcement is solely

by the combined authority of God and of man. As long as belief in the Almighty is effective, the Holy Books are the Law and the rabbi's interpretation of the Law carries weight. As long as concern about what people think is strong, the popularly accepted arbiter keeps his authority—and such concern is extremely strong in the shtetl. . . .

There is systematic provision for meeting needs connected with problems and crises of the individual life cycle—the continuing needs of food, shelter, clothing, the critical needs of birth, marriage, illness, death, and education. . . .

[T]he shtetl is run by the men who know and the men who give. Their leadership, like their earthly honor and their heavenly merits, must constantly be validated. If they want to preserve their status, they must respond to any appeal of their fellows. . . .

Whenever possible one "goes a little bit among people," the men to shul, the women to gossip with their neighbors. You dart into the house next door to relay the latest tidbit, and perhaps to borrow an onion. The door is never locked and nobody stops to knock. . . .

The freedom to observe and to pass judgment on one's fellows, the need to communicate and share events and emotions is inseparable from a strong feeling that individuals are responsible to and for each other. Collective responsibility is imposed by outside pressures on a minority group, but these pressures combine with and re-enforce the basic tenets of religious faith. The Covenant solemnized on Mount Sinai is with all Jews and with each Jew. . . . Again and again in the books studied from early childhood until old age, it is repeated, "All Jews are responsible each for the other." . . .

Within this community where each person is linked and identified with the group and all its members, the individual is never lost. He is merged but not submerged. In the shtetl crowd, each person has his own face, and his own voice. "Nearly everyone in the shtetl was a separate character—a 'type' all for himself." Each one has a name, a nickname, a specialty or at least a distinctive trait. . . .

The community, a whole made up of many closely welded parts, is felt as an extension of the family. "My shtetl" means all the Jews who live in it and the bond persists even when members meet in distant lands. . . .

The shtetl folk feel themselves united not only by bonds of blood, belief and usage, but also by their common burden and reward. In accepting the Covenant the Jews accepted the tremendous *ol fun Yiddishkayt,* "yoke of Jewishness." The burden is the complement to the rewards of belonging to the Chosen People.[6]

Is the holy community lost forever? Can we go back? Do we want to? Can we salvage aspects of it? Could it be that what we dream of when we dream of Israel is actually a utopian *community*? And if so, perhaps we need to be aware that the inherent tension between state and community is not going to go away.

Reconstructing Community

In September 1908, at the peak of the great wave of Russian Jewish immigration to the United States, New York's police commissioner published an article claiming that "perhaps half of the criminals" in the city were Jewish.[7] No sooner had the outrage died down (and the commissioner apologized) than the city's widely diverse and disparate Jewish groups, factions, and organizations founded an all-inclusive representative organization, the New York "Kehillah" (Hebrew for "community"), led by Rabbi Judah Magnes. This experiment in a limited resurrection of a semiautonomous Jewish community survived until 1922. During its existence, perhaps its most noteworthy achievement was to create a Bureau of Education that united a broad swath (but not all) of the Jewish population. Almost all sectors of the Jewish population agreed that the American utopia posed a daunting educational challenge: how to educate Jews for both solid Jewish rootedness and full integration into the open society. However, even in the face of this clear need—and a degree of success—the centrifugal forces and the very incongruity of creating a Jewish "sectarian" community in the American context ultimately doomed the Kehillah. It was succeeded by a number of much less comprehensive and authoritative structures throughout North America, such as Jewish federations and boards of Jewish education.

A leading figure in the Kehillah was Rabbi Mordecai Kaplan (1881–1983), a professor at the Jewish Theological Seminary who would go on to become known as a leading twentieth-century Jewish thinker. Kaplan proposed a "reconstruction" of the classic Jewish community, adapted to the American reality. In his monumental *Judaism as a Civilization: Toward a Reconstruction of Jewish Life*, published in 1934 (twelve years after the disbanding of the New York Kehillah), he argued that a Kehillah-like Jewish polity was essential:

> The familiar fact that before the emancipation the Jews were organized into self-governing communities is usually viewed as having had merely political significance. Its implications for the cultural and spiritual life of the Jew have been entirely ignored. Yet it was by virtue of that autonomy that the community was able to make itself needed in the everyday life of the individual Jew. Without that concrete service which the community rendered to every Jew, rich or poor, learned or ignorant, Judaism would long ago have disappeared.[8]

The old communal ideal may be unreproducible in our time, but, Kaplan stressed, it is essential to retrieve its essence and create a reconstructed community:

> In the very ghettos where the Jews suffered persecution, Judaism helped the Jew in his work and in his play. It gave him the language of social intercourse; it had a voice in the activities he

pursued for the purpose of making a livelihood; and it provided him with the means of amusement and entertainment. Emancipation and industrialism have practically made it impossible for Judaism to influence the Jew in his work. All the more imperative, therefore, has it become for Judaism to influence the Jew in his leisure activities.[9]

Kaplan imagined reconstructing the congregational synagogue into a more all-encompassing community, reflecting (even if somewhat palely) the premodern Jewish communal utopia:

> In olden times, the synagogue was like a dynamo near a waterfall. As the power of the waterfall develops electric current in the dynamo, so did the social life that surged about the synagogue develop the spiritual power within the synagogue. The condition of the synagogue at the present time is similar to that of a dynamo when its water power is cut off and it has to resort to a fuel like coal or oil, which is kept within the power house itself. Now that the stream of Jewish social life has dried up, the problem consists in finding ways and means of storing up a substitute social energy within the synagogue itself.

In America, the synagogue had been relegated to the function of "house of prayer" in a context in which secularism was dominant. Kaplan suggested reimagining the synagogue as the center of a multidimensional community (like the shtetl) — in addition to a house of prayer, a house of culture and social welfare, education and recreation.

> The synagogue should not be displaced by, but it should evolve into, the *bet am*, or Jewish neighborhood center. Each center should be placed under the joint auspices of the kehillah, and of the Jews of the neighborhood where it is located . . . The *bet am* should have all of the spiritual sanction that formerly rendered the

synagogue dear to the heart of the Jew, and, in addition, should deliberately be developed to meet the broader humanist-cultural needs that are included in a modern civilization . . .[10]

The idea of trying to regain at least some aspects of the lost utopian, idealized community has had a powerful influence in North American Jewish life, from synagogues constituting themselves as "Jewish Centers" to immersive Jewish summer camps to Jewish Community Centers. *The Jewish Catalog*, the popular expression of "Jewish Renewal" published in 1973, stated:

> A new idea [has] developed among Jews disenchanted with the synagogue . . . that it [is] possible, here in the Diaspora, to resurrect in some way the old Jewish idea of community and join together to work, learn, pray, and live. . . . [S]omething new, exciting, and creative is happening—something good.[11]

Intentional Communities

The universal nostalgia for lost community—not only among the Jews—has often been entangled with concrete efforts to create small-scale "utopias," living models of an ideal society in present time.

In sixteenth-century Mexico, Vasco de Quiroga, the first bishop of Michoacan, was inspired by Thomas More's just-published *Utopia* to establish native American communities in his diocese, organized according to More's description. This seems to have been the first attempt to translate a utopian vision into a real community. However, while de Quiroga was venerated by the local populace in subsequent centuries as a benefactor, his intention was not to build a model society, but rather to create a framework for efficient, humane, and stable colonial rule over the native population.[12] The Michoacan experience raises two questions that apply to the hundreds of "utopian" communities that would be established in the modern period:

1. Is any attempt to create a community as an island of better life, protected from the oppression and corruption of the larger society, ipso facto a utopia? Utopia, after all, implies vision; a conscious effort to design an imaginary society that solves—or rises above—the ills of present social reality. Utopia is an exercise in thinking about the priority of moral values and how that priority, ideally, should determine reality. Perhaps a distinction needs to be made between communities that are indeed guided by some sort of articulated vision, and those whose goal is simply withdrawal to a protected place.

2. The utopian dilemma: Is it not a contradiction in terms to call any real community "utopian," as utopia, as we saw in chapter 1, is by its nature "no-place," unattainable? Its power lies in its pure idealism, in its ability to inspire and guide. As such, it is able to sustain a degree of unresolved internal contradiction, or unanswered questions. The moment it is read as a blueprint for concrete action, these cracks either cause the vision to crumble, or require authoritarian, even violent, means to hold it together.

The term "utopian community" has been widely and indiscriminately used to refer to any attempt to create a community where there was none before—as though any community, by virtue of its having been formed as an alternative to non-community, is by definition utopian.

It seems fair to label as utopian many of the intentional communities established in the eighteenth and nineteenth centuries in England and America (see chapter 1). They set out with a clearly articulated social and economic vision, and saw themselves as pioneers, creating by example the building blocks of a new reality. As "utopian communities," of course, these all exemplify the utopian dilemma: the inherent conflict between a pure vision and messy reality. Perhaps that is why most of these experiments were so short-lived—and why none of them gave rise to a mass movement or even left much of an echo.

In 1825 Jewish activist and entrepreneur Mordecai Manuel Noah assembled investors to purchase part of Grand Island in the Niagara River to establish a Jewish colony, "Ararat." The venture never progressed beyond the corner-stone laying. It seems that Noah's project was in the tradition of Enlightenment efforts to "improve" the Jews—a temporary refuge that would provide modernization and social, linguistic, and vocational preparation for Jewish integration into American society—while at the same time clearly a capitalist venture. This example of a non-utopian community typified many later efforts. As the Jewish historian Jonathan Sarna has written: "All over the western world, reformers came to view colonies—especially, but not exclusively, American frontier colonies—as the best solution to the problems posed by minority, deviant, and oppressed groups. Rather than attempting to create an equitable pluralistic state, they proposed to create insulated communities where each individual group could flourish on its own."[13]

This description fits the many communities established before the Civil War, throughout the Midwest and Canada, for training free Blacks for economic integration and self-sufficiency.[14] Similarly, during the mass migration of Jews from Russia, 1880–1914, at least a dozen Jewish agricultural communities were planted, from Louisiana to South Dakota to Oregon. Sponsored by philanthropies (e.g., the *Alliance Israelite Universelle*), and populated by immigrants with no farming experience, they were driven less by a social vision than by established, veteran immigrants' desire to "normalize" and productivize their "green" brethren, to prevent their becoming a burden or an embarrassment.[15] Most of these agrarian communities disbanded within a year or two. The residents lacked a shared idealistic motivation and were unsuited to the hard, isolated way of life.

The Kibbutz

In terms of longevity and reach, the most successful modern intentional community with a claim to utopianism has been the kibbutz. In

1909 twelve young immigrants from Russia established the first kibbutz, Degania, situated just southwest of the Sea of Galilee. They were driven by a multifaceted utopian vision: to implement socialism locally and to model it for the world; to claim—and reclaim—the Land of Israel for the Jewish people; to create a community to replace the Orthodox shtetl from which they were alienated; and to "improve" themselves as authentic Jewish peasants rooted in the soil. This conjunction of goals turned out to be well-suited to the needs of the Yishuv in Palestine—and to the needs of many idealistic young immigrants—so the model was widely replicated. Over the years, the kibbutz model evolved and diversified: Whereas communal child-rearing ("children's houses" staffed by professionals) was the original norm, today all kibbutzim have closed their children's houses and restored the centrality of the nuclear family. Whereas private property was once anathema, most of today's kibbutzim allow a degree of economic freedom—and, hence, inequality. Whereas the original kibbutz saw agriculture as crucial for personal renewal and national development, most kibbutzim have moved to mixed economies, including industry and services like tourism. Despite these and other changes, the kibbutz has produced stable communities. Today more than a hundred thousand Israelis live on 270 kibbutzim, a large majority of which were founded before 1960.

The Jewish philosopher Martin Buber (1878–1965) was fascinated by the kibbutz idea, and influenced its development. In 1945 he wrote the following evaluation:

> Nowhere else in the history of communal settlements is there this tireless groping for the form of community-life best suited to this particular human group, nowhere else this continual trying and trying again, this going to it and getting down to it, this critical awareness, this sprouting of new branches from the same stem and out of the same formative impulse. . . . Thus on the soberest survey and on the soberest reflection one can say that, in this one spot in a world of partial failures, we can recognize a non-failure—and such as it is, a signal non-failure. . . . In the spirit of

the members of the first Palestinian Communes ideal motives joined hands with the dictates of the hour; and in the motives there was a curious mixture of memories of the Russian *Artel* [informal workers' cooperatives common in Russia before the rise of modern socialism], impressions left over from reading the so-called "utopian" Socialists, and the half-unconscious after-effects of the Bible's teachings about social justice.[16]

Buber observes that the kibbutz was sustained not just by a utopian plan for a community, but by other needs and ideals—to return to the land, to reclaim it, to survive on it. The evolving socialistic model of the kibbutz was a response not to a fixed communal vision, but to a complex interplay of fragments of vision and a harsh reality: "The important thing is that this ideal motive remained loose and pliable in almost every respect. . . . These men did not, as everywhere else in the history of cooperative settlements, bring a plan with them, a plan which the concrete situation could only fill out, not modify; the ideal gave an impetus but no dogma, it stimulated but did not dictate."[17]

It is interesting to consider Buber's evaluation in the light of the ideological development of the early kibbutzim, in which Buber himself had played a role. Peter Kropotkin, a Russian anarchist thinker and activist (1842–1921; he spent half his life in exile in Switzerland), believed in a human instinct for mutual aid, and taught that the small, local community with a mixed economy was the proper venue for developing an organic socialism—as opposed to the centralized state. On the one hand, his thought showed a romantic nostalgia for the pre-modern community; on the other hand, he refused to try to articulate a utopian blueprint: "There will be full freedom for the development of new forms of production, invention and organization; individual initiative will be encouraged and the tendency towards uniformity and centralization will be discouraged. Moreover, the society will not be crystallized into certain unchangeable forms, but will continually modify its aspects, because it will be a living, evolving organism; no need of government will be felt, because free agreements and feder-ation take its place."[18]

This approach differed significantly from that of Owen, Fourier, Cabet, and the many others whose visions were complete to the small-est detail.

Notice how Buber's description above echoes Kropotkin's emphasis on constant evolution. In popularizing Kropotkin's work, the German Jewish anarchist Gustav Landauer (1870–1919) caught Buber's attention. Buber invited Landauer to speak at a Zionist conference, and spread his ideas in Zionist circles.

Kropotkin, Buber, and the kibbutz experiment seemingly have in common the insistence that the utopian dream must be held as a dream. It must serve as inspiration and motivation, but must not be crystallized into a rigid, compulsory, absolute plan. Only thus can it remain utopia—and be effective in moving its ideals toward realiza-tion.

The kibbutz utopia also had a nostalgic root. The young pioneers may have rebelled against their bourgeois—and Orthodox—diaspora upbringing, but (influenced by Russian populist socialists of their time, who idealized the traditional peasant village community), they missed and sought to reconstruct the intimate, holy community of the shtetl on their own terms. New ritual traditions replaced old ones: chanting in synagogue gave way to community singing and holiday agricultural pageants; Hasidic dance gave way to exuberant folk dancing until the wee hours; intimate yeshivah Torah study gave way to soul-baring "gen-eral assembly" meetings where members endlessly debated ideals and their applications.

Community or State

The Balfour Declaration of 1917 has always been celebrated as the first official recognition of Zionism's claim that the Jews are entitled to national self-determination in the Land of Israel. However, the declaration is actually notoriously vague: "His Majesty's government view with favour the establishment in Palestine of a national home for the Jewish people, and will use their best endeavours to facilitate the achievement of this object, it being clearly understood that nothing shall be done which may prejudice the civil and religious rights of existing non-Jewish communities in Palestine, or the rights and political status enjoyed by Jews in any other country."

The word "state" does not appear; and borders are not specified by "in Palestine." Later, when the League of Nations Mandate granted Britain control of Palestine and charged the nation with temporary rule of the area in order to bring it toward independence, how British officials imagined the outcome of this process is not clear. Throughout their thirty years' governance they struggled to contain the conflicting nationalist forces, and ultimately, in frustration, they gave up. Early on, however (1928), they promulgated the "Religious Communities Organization Ordinance," which established the Jewish community (including both the Zionist New Yishuv and the Orthodox Old Yishuv) as a religious one parallel to and coequal with the Muslims and various Christian denominations in the area. Both Yishuvs opposed this designation, for quite different reasons. The Old Yishuv did not want to be part of a secular communal organization. The New Yishuv was moving toward national self-determination, and certainly not toward a return to a diaspora-style Jewish community.

Nevertheless, Britain ruled, and the chief rabbinate, with its central and local bureaucracies, was established (and the Jewish community made responsible for its funding). As in a typical diaspora community, its powers were limited to matters of Jewish family law and ritual (e.g., dietary law); all other aspects of life were subject to the jurisdiction of the British government courts and bureaucracy. With the transition from Mandate to State in 1948, the State assumed the entire structure of the chief rabbinate, and this division of powers, unchanged. Thus, ironically, the independent, sovereign State of Israel, from its beginning, maintained the very diaspora political structure that Zionism had dreamed of undoing.

The Jewish state made no pretension of being a Torah state—rather, it was, in a sense, an oversized Jewish community: a very big shtetl. Why did Zionism miss the historic opportunity to redirect Jewish history? The usual answer is that in the rush to prepare for the sudden end of the Mandate, there wasn't time to build new institutions. I would suggest a variation on this answer: no one had a plan. Between the utopia of the idyllic agrarian Torah state and the utopia of the warm, enveloping, holy community, there was no practical proposal for a real Jewish state—so Israel ended up with a distortion of the latter as a stand-in for the former.

What's wrong with this picture? The problem is a fundamental mismatch between a modern state and a traditional Jewish community. A state is associated with a specific territory, with borders, its authority applying to everyone living within those borders. It is, ipso facto, "a state of all its citizens," regardless of their identities and beliefs. A Jewish community, on the other hand, comprises an assembly of people who identify as Jews, and its authority applies only to them. A Jewish community exists alongside other religious communities, under an overarching state authority.

Moreover, *halakhah* is a system of religious law, based on the community's belief in its divine origin. It is, essentially, voluntary: any individual is free to decide at any time that he or she no longer believes in the divinity of the law, and hence to withdraw from the community. Enforcing *halakhah* by means of secular state power violates the very nature of *halakhah* as an expression of the individual's free relationship with God.[19]

Rabbi Isaac Herzog, Israel's first Ashkenazic chief rabbi, devoted considerable attention to this problem. As we saw in chapter 4, he recognized the distance that must obtain between a modern democratic state and a halakhic community. However, the very existence of his position—state chief rabbi—represented (and continues to represent) a blurring of boundaries, a conflation of two utopian visions.

The unattainability of both utopias, the Torah state and the premodern community, gave rise to a third powerful, new, and very influential utopian conception: the national home — as we shall see in chapter 6.

Further Reading

Bauman, Zygmunt. *Community: Seeking Safety in an Insecure World*. Malden MA: Polity Press, 2001.

Ben-Rafael, Eliezer. *Crisis and Transformation: The Kibbutz at Century's End*. Albany NY: SUNY Press, 1997.

Buber, Martin. *Paths in Utopia*. Translated by R. F. C. Hull. London: Routledge and Kegan Paul, 1949.

Delanty, Gerard. *Community*. New York: Routledge, 2003.

6

A National Home

Zionism represents the encounter of modern nationalism with Jewish collective memory preserved in sacred texts. We have seen one possible outcome of this meeting: a Torah state utopia. Another is a secular nationalistic vision where "national culture" serves as the value substrate.

The Nation-State of the Jewish People

In 2018 the Knesset passed, by a margin of 62 to 55, new legislation: Basic Law: Israel—the Nation-State of the Jewish People. It includes the following declarations:

1. Basic Principles
   a. The Land of Israel is the historical homeland of the Jewish people, in which the State of Israel was established.
   b. The State of Israel is the nation state of the Jewish People, in which it realizes its natural, cultural, religious and historical right to self-determination.
   c. The exercise of the right to national self-determination in the State of Israel is unique to the Jewish People....
5. Ingathering of the Exiles: The State shall be open for Jewish immigration, and for the Ingathering of the Exiles....
7. Jewish Settlement: The State views the development of Jewish settlement as a national value, and shall act to encourage and promote its establishment and strengthening.

In addition, the law specifies the symbols, capital, calendar, and languages of the state, and the state's responsibility for the welfare — and cultural heritage — of diaspora Jewry.[1]

Meanwhile, the Declaration of Independence published in 1948 contained the following paragraphs:

> On the 29th of November, 1947, the United Nations General Assembly passed a resolution calling for the establishment of a Jewish State in Eretz-Israel; the General Assembly required the inhabitants of Eretz-Israel to take such steps as were necessary on their part for the implementation of that resolution. This recognition by the United Nations of the right of the Jewish people to establish their State is irrevocable.
>
> This right is the natural right of the Jewish people to be masters of their own fate, like all other nations, in their own sovereign State. . . .
>
> The State of Israel will be open for Jewish immigration and for the Ingathering of the Exiles; it will foster the development of the country for the benefit of all its inhabitants; it will be based on freedom, justice and peace as envisaged by the prophets of Israel; it will ensure complete equality of social and political rights to all its inhabitants irrespective of religion, race or sex; it will guarantee freedom of religion, conscience, language, education and culture; it will safeguard the Holy Places of all religions; and it will be faithful to the principles of the Charter of the United Nations.[2]

The new nation-state law became the focus of a strident public debate (ongoing). Some argued that it was a deliberate provocation: its restating of (selected) principles from the Declaration of Independence served no purpose other than to distance and humiliate the Arab minority. Others claimed it was necessary (1) to counter a perceived rising chorus of voices both inside and outside Israel questioning the justification for a "Jewish state" or (2) to put a check on "liberal judicial activism" on the part of Israel's judiciary, which was seen as prioritizing universal human rights over Jewish national interests. On the other side, some were vexed by the idea that the right to a Jewish nation-state needed reaffirming while the commitment to freedom and justice for all did not, and feared that the endorsement of Jewish settlement was a legal cover for ethnic discrimination in housing. And many wondered why the law was necessary in the first place, as it was already obvious that Israel is the nation-state of the Jewish people.

But what does it mean to be the "nation-state of the Jewish people?" It seems to me that before we can argue intelligently about the law's significance, some clarifications are needed. What is a nation? What is a state? What is a nation-state? And what is "the Jewish people?" In this chapter we will consider, historically, the concept of peoplehood, and visit nationalist utopias; in chapter 7 we will explore Judaism's long and fraught relationship with the ideal of statehood. Then in chapter 8, we will reflect on the modern encounter—the hyphen—between these two visions.

Jewish Peoplehood

To convey something of the complexity of this concept, I offer a few illustrations.

1. When I became an Israeli citizen in 1993, I received an official identity card, which citizens are required to carry at all times. It includes a photograph, my country of birth, my Hebrew and Gregorian birth dates, my parents' names, my gender, and my nationality (*le'om*—in the sense of ethno-cultural identity), which is listed as Jewish. Among the over 130 recognized nationalities besides Jewish are Arab, Druze, and Circassian. A decade later the "nationality" entry was dropped from new ID cards, because of a dispute between the courts and the Orthodox minister of the interior as to whether Reform converts should be listed as of Jewish nationality.

2. In 1885 the Central Conference of American Rabbis (Reform rabbinic organization), convening in Pittsburgh, declared in the "Pittsburgh Platform":

We recognize, in the modern era of universal culture of heart and intellect, the approaching of the realization of Israel's great Messianic hope for the establishment of the kingdom of truth, justice, and peace among all men. We consider ourselves no longer a nation, but a religious community, and therefore expect neither a return to Palestine, nor a sacrificial worship under the sons of Aaron, nor the restoration of any of the laws concerning the Jewish state.[3]

3. A decade later, Theodor Herzl wrote: "I think the Jewish question is no more a social than a religious one, notwithstanding that it sometimes takes these and other forms. It is a national question, which can only be solved by making it a political world-question to be discussed and controlled by the civilized nations of the world in council. We are a people (*Volk*)—One people."[4]

4. About ten years ago, a group of imams from villages in the Galilee visited our community's synagogue in Moshav Shorashim. I described for them various Jewish customs and beliefs, and demonstrated chanting from the Torah. "Any questions?," I concluded. There was one: "I don't get it; are the Jews a religion or a nationality?"

Indeed, what are the Jews? The Jews' anomalous nature as both a nation and a religion has given rise to the use in English of the term "people," which fudges the distinction. Confounding the attempt to label the Jews as either just an ethno-cultural group or solely a community of faith is the memory of the covenant at Mt. Sinai. There, God revealed to the Israelite nation that the redemption, which was so far only partial (the completion would come with the entrance into the land), was conditional: God's strong hand would continue to support and protect the Israelites as a nation only if they lived according to the elaborate code of laws that God, through Moses, revealed to the assembled masses.

This covenant between God and the nation became the central theme of Jewish life, thought, and law ever after. It established that Jewish nationhood and the Jewish religion are inseparable. The biblical text emphasizes that both of these formative experiences happened to the entire group. No Jews can claim that they were not included in the Exodus, and in the Sinai revelation. All Israelites, and all of their descendants for all time, are expected to keep the memory of the redemption—and the attendant commitment to the commandments—alive. Thus a nation, with a shared historical memory, a shared language, and (soon) a shared land. Thus a religion, committed to a life according to a code of divinely ordained laws, enriched and given meaning by a set of symbols and beliefs.

Two interconnected utopias: the Torah's ideal society, realized in the context of a "great nation" living according to its own particular culture, in peace and prosperity, in its Promised Land. The Torah state utopia, discussed in chapter 4, sought to maintain the linkage, anchored in the covenant, between nation and religion. But as the passages above indicate, in the modern period other Jewish utopian visions have denied or reinterpreted the covenant to give primacy—or exclusivity—either to nationhood (Herzl) or to faith (the Pittsburgh Platform). The contemporary stream in Zionism usually labeled "cultural Zionism" sees the Jewish nation as parallel to other modern nations like the French or Hungarian or Italian in being defined by culture and territory—and thereby designates religious belief as a private affair. However, it has not (yet?) succeeded in truly disentangling nationality from religion. Perhaps the most striking evidence of this is the fact that secular Zionists have never seriously proposed changing the traditional procedure for joining the Jewish nation—which, from the perspective of Israeli law, remains Orthodox religious conversion.

Nationalism and Utopia

> Belonging together, preferably in groupings with visible badges
> of membership and recognition signs, is more important than
> ever in societies in which everything combines to destroy what
> binds human beings together into communities.... For those who
> can no longer rely on belonging anywhere else, there is at least
> one other imagined community to which one can belong: which
> is permanent, indestructible, and whose membership is certain:
> ... "the nation," or the ethnic group, "appears as the ultimate
> guarantee" when society fails.[5]

Many scholars have suggested that one of the phenomena that grew out
of the loss (or sense of loss) of the pre-Enlightenment, preindustrial
community discussed in chapter 5 was nationalism. Indeed, sociologist Benedict Anderson's important 1983 work on nationalism is titled
Imagined Communities. In the absence of a safe and supportive local
community providing norms, meaning, and a feeling of belonging,
people turn to ethnic or national identity. Homogeneity—of language,
customs, historical memory—promises to replace or restore what has
been lost. The collective memory of the nation's mythic primordial
golden age—heroic, unconflicted, and culturally pure—comes to provide a utopian image, a present aspiration.

Thus, over the past two centuries, in response to feelings of rootlessness in the mass society of lonely individuals, new-old roots have been
found or invented: languages revived; historical heroes and sagas discovered, recovered, or invented; folksongs composed and folkdances
choreographed. And, of course, such conceived communities have
had clear boundaries: defining a nation involves delineating who is in
it and who is outside it. This can be seen in the rise of Italy, Germany,
Greece, Hungary, and Finland in the nineteenth century, and in the
splintering of Europe into ever smaller national units in the twentieth.
A nostalgic utopia fueled ethnic homogeneity as an ideal—which in
turn often led to unimaginable violence.

Following the 1881 pogroms in Russia and intensifying political and economic oppression, many Jews despaired of a future for themselves—or for the traditional Jewish community—in Russia. The universalistic, individualistic, cosmopolitan utopia of the New World beckoned, and the vast majority of the two million Russian Jews who emigrated over the next four decades made their way to the United States. A tiny minority went to Palestine. This minority, and those who encouraged and supported them back home, became known as the *Chovevei Tzion* (Lovers of Zion), scattered local groups that organized themselves into a movement in 1884. Their choice of Palestine (against all odds: settling there was fraught with dangers and discomforts) was explicitly romantic and nationalistic—a return to primordial roots, a rejection of assimilation. Far beyond a focus on escape, they departed holding aloft a shared vision of living in their ancestral land, speaking their ancestral tongue, reclaiming and renewing their national culture.

Their leading spokesman, the writer Ahad Ha'am, opposed Theodor Herzl's diplomatic efforts to secure a Jewish state as well as his vision of mass immigration. Ahad Ha'am believed that the current task was to create a cultural center in the Land of Israel that would facilitate the revival of Jewish culture and pride, and thereby renew a healthy Jewish ethno-cultural (national) identity. Judaism as a culture is sustainable, indeed eternal, and independent of religious belief, he argued: cultural symbols and behaviors are sanctified by the "spirit of the nation," not by God. Thus, a modern atheist is in no way excluded from the Jewish nation. Even when the Jewish holidays celebrate God's acts in history, they also represent values, folkways, and historical memories that are the possessions of all Jews, believers or not.

Elchanan Lewinsky's *Journey to the Land of Israel in 2040*

Ahad Ha'am and his "school" envisioned the reestablishment of authentic, natural, secular Jewish life rooted in the ancient homeland, reconnecting with the nation's youth when it had been robust, productive, creative, and independent.[6] Elchanan Leib Lewinsky (1857–1910), a leader of *Chovevei Tzion* in Odessa and a popular Hebrew writer, sought to translate this general vision into a concrete description—a utopia. In 1892 he published *A Journey to the Land of Israel in the Year 5800* (the Hebrew year 5800 corresponding to 2040, 150 years in the future). Serialized in the journal *Pardes* (and, given its popularity, soon republished in book form), it purports to be a travelogue by an anonymous young Hebrew teacher who, with some difficulty, convinces his new wife to honeymoon in the Land of Israel instead of Paris. They end up spending three months in the land.

Two themes stand out throughout the account of the tour: criticism (generally with a satirical smile) of the decadence and oppression Lewinsky observed in the Jewish and general society around him; and extravagantly romantic descriptions of the Jews' return to their cultural roots. For example, here is the traveler's impression of Jaffa, the couple's port of entry:

> Jaffa is like any port city, but . . . in this it is different: it stands on Hebrew soil, the vernacular is Hebrew, the laws are Hebrew laws, the way of life is a bit different from that in other lands. There is complete freedom in the city; no one will ask you who you are, what you are doing, where you came from and where you are going. No one will ask to see your passport; you won't see police, or weapons, or uniforms. The coast is open to all goods from abroad, and traders from other lands come to trade freely, and no one questions them, for the Jews have no reason to fear competition.[7]

In contrast to the experience of the nineteenth-century Russian Jew, there is freedom of occupation and freedom of movement, for everyone.

Further on, the traveler is thrilled to discover the revival of ancient customs, like the celebration of the Fifteenth of Av as a festival of romantic love (and he is even happy to see that it has been commercialized).[8]

The sense of a return to a mythical past is very strong. Lewinsky's traveler is moved by the feeling that he is back in the Bible, when the Jews lived a healthy agrarian life, speaking Hebrew, governed by Torah law—but of course, with all the conveniences of modern technology and even global capitalism. Among his observations about the countryside:

> Every person is required to learn a skill (craft) beyond the primary and central profession of agriculture. There is no school that does not teach agriculture. Working the soil, the one natural human labor, has become a national possession—of the entire nation with no exception. Israel has now returned to its origins, as it was in the days of the patriarchs—a people of peasants; and peasants they are now, from the greatest to the least of them. . . .
>
> I couldn't get enough of seeing the life of the Jew on his land. Whole portions of the Bible came alive before me. . . . For the Jews try in everything to imitate the life of their ancestors, in their purity and simplicity, and in addition, they have accepted the power and the glory of modern customs. All the good ascribed in the Bible to their forefathers, and all the beauty, all the practices and customs and practical laws of Europe, are combined together in the life of the Hebrew.[9]

Like other Zionist utopians from different "schools," Lewinsky looks to the Torah's utopian vision for a model of social justice. Once again we encounter the jubilee year:

> The land is divided equally per capita, and if occasionally there are conflicts, or accumulation of land by an individual, the jubilee year comes around and resets all to equality. Thus there is no one without land, and there are no slaves. And the [biblical] laws of gleaning are maintained. . . . All is according to the Torah of Moses according to rabbinic interpretation. . . . Thus there is no issue

of workers or of property in the land of Israel, for there are no workers and no masters, as all are workers and all are masters.[10]

For cultural Zionists, a common theme was the connection of Jewish cultural renewal with the renewal of the individual Jew—the creation of "new Jews." For example:

> The young men are all robust as oaks, healthy and solid, the dew of youth, strength and courage on their faces, and vigor flashing in their eyes. . . . It is pleasant to see these giants, whose faces are also illuminated with wisdom, and who carry themselves with nobility. And the daughters of Israel? They are certainly beautiful; their stature like the date palm, their cheeks pure and ruddy, their figures like sapphire, their curls raven black; and their eyes? God of my father! One would give half the world for those eyes!
>
> The daughters of Israel had always been beautiful, but poverty, exile, suffering, false education, and ugly clothes had caused them to wither; now their beauty has been restored.[11]

Moving on to the capital, Jerusalem, the traveler notes that on the one hand, Ezekiel's messianic prophecy (Ezek. 47) has been fulfilled: "The Kidron Valley is now a powerful river, as blocked springs have been opened."

But on the other hand, he makes it clear that the messianic time has not arrived; this is a human, historical utopia: "The Temple has not yet been built, and the Western Wall stands in ruins. It is a sign to Israel that the day of its redemption has not yet arrived, and that he must wait—and wait—even if it be delayed."

Indeed, Lewinsky's traveler repeatedly emphasizes that Jewish life in the land does not represent the ingathering of all the exiles. On the contrary, just as he himself sees the Jewish national home as a cultural center (part of his motivation for making the trip was his hope to improve his skills as a Hebrew teacher in the Diaspora), he finds this relationship to be normative: While millions of Jews live in Lewinsky's utopia, Jewish life continues around the world, not only in the old centers but in new colonies like Argentina. The center in the Land of Israel sustains these communities, spiritually and culturally.

The traveler gives short shrift to the institutions he finds in the capital; he mentions a ruler (*nasi*, traditionally referring to a nonmonarchic leader; he uses "King" here to refer to divine providence), and a "National Council," but gives no details. Peace—within and without—is a recurring theme; it seems that finally, with authenticity in their own culture and security in their own land, the Jews have become a member in good standing of the family of nations. "Since they came to the land they have lived in peace with all the nations, every man under his vine and fig-tree with none to make them afraid, under the wing of the great King who protects them."[12]

In Lewinsky's utopia all the evils of the centuries of exile have been washed away: poverty, illness, ugliness, weakness, alienation from physical work and from the soil. Jews are strong, productive, steeped in their own authentic culture but open to the world. If utopia is a critique of the status quo, Lewinsky's reveals how *Chovevei Tzion* viewed the reality of nineteenth-century Jewish life. We saw Yavetz's Torah utopia in chapter 4 echo much of this critique.

Lewinsky's descriptions of the strength and beauty of his utopia's inhabitants may come across as a bit over-the-top, but they reflect a common theme in cultural Zionism and in Israeli culture: the vision of the New Jew. In mocking the sickly, decadent, hypochondriacal culture of Europe—and the stooped, pale-faced, obsequious stereotype of the Jew, he carries forward an important concept from the Enlightenment: that in order for the Jews to be emancipated, they must be "improved," productivized, cured of their medieval ills. To many Zionists, agriculture, working the soil to which they had a mystical attachment, was the key to returning the Jews to their origins and restoring their moral backbone.

The New Man

The Zionist image of the New Jew can be seen as a particular expression of a more general cultural vision: the Enlightenment idea that progress toward utopia is contingent on educating better people. Thus, a vision of utopia was not enough; utopians needed a vision of the ideal person in order to engineer their educational efforts toward an agreed-upon goal. The macro utopian vision had to be translated to the micro, to the level of the individual. And, indeed, "the new man"[13] became a recurrent theme in different cultural contexts from the eighteenth into the twentieth centuries.

Already in 1783, French immigrant St. John Crevecoeur, in his *Letters from an American Farmer*, enthused about the new American man:

> What then is the American, this new man? . . . *He* is an American, who leaving behind him all his ancient prejudices and manners, receives new ones from the new mode of life he has embraced, the new government he obeys, and the new rank he holds. . . . He becomes an American by being received in the broad lap of our great *Alma Mater*. Here individuals of all nations are melted into a new race of men, whose labours and posterity will one day cause great changes in the world.[14]

Crevecoeur's book became a best-seller in Europe, where the dream of a new human type unencumbered by all the old strictures of ancestry, class, and nationality fit well with how many Europeans imagined the American utopia.[15] And this image of the new, classless individual, cut off from the oppressive past, self-reliant, independent, optimistic, rooted in and mastering nature, facing an open future with courage and joy—"the sky's the limit!"—became a central theme in the mythology of and about American society.[16]

Nearly a century later, in 1863, Nikolai Chernyshevsky (1828–89) published his novel *What Is to Be Done? Tales of the New People* (written in a Tsarist prison; apparently the author was framed as a way to silence his progressive views). Rapidly achieving great popularity in Russia, it inspired two generations of populist socialists. The narrator explains that each of the leading characters—the strong-spirited feminist and utopian dreamer Vera Pavlova; the two men who love her, Lopukhov and Kirsanov; and the "extraordinary" wise, honest, strong, and ascetic Rakhmatov—exemplifies

> a different type. Every one of them is . . . dauntless, firm, unwavering, capable of undertaking any matter; and if he undertakes it, he sticks so resolutely to it that it cannot slip out of his grasp. This is one side of their nature. Another side: each one of them is a man of irreproachable integrity, so much so that the question never even enters our mind, "Is it possible to rely on this person unconditionally?" . . . These general features are so prominent that the personal peculiarities are covered over by them. It is not long that this type has been in existence among us.[17]

Chernyshevsky's vision of the "new people" who would overthrow the old, decadent, and corrupt social order was decidedly not a Marxist, materialistic, apocalyptic vision, but rather one based on a belief in the human spirit, on the perfectibility of the individual.

In the ensuing decades, a similar fascination with the image of the "new man" found expression in Western European literature. A sense that the old Europe—decadent, passive, passionless, even sickly—was about to pass away led to the anticipation of a new human type bearing a revitalized cultural vision. Like the American and Russian new man, the European image of the new ideal was vital, brave, natural, and self-reliant. But in Europe the longing for something primal or primeval led not to idealizing the conquest of an untamed continent or to a new, rational, classless society, but to a romantic nostalgia for ancient heroes, for a golden age when men were men, faith was faith, war was war, and life thus had meaning. In the European imagination, these new men were brave and strong risk-takers, but eager to submit to and exercise authority. Intellect—bookishness, philosophizing—represented the decadent old Europe, to be smashed or at least left behind. Though often subject to polemical, oversimplified interpretations, the works of German philosopher Friedrich Nietzsche (1844–1900) were widely seen, in his own time, as giving voice of the spirit of this era.

The First World War experience confirmed for many the disillusionment with the dying old Europe—and validated the image of the vital new man.[18] This image can be seen to have influenced such phenomena as the back-to-nature youth movements (*Wandervogel*), which glorified romantic national rootedness in nature and homeland and, ultimately, fascist nationalist movements between the wars.[19]

Old Jews and New Jews

The idea of "improving" individual Jews to make them worthy of emancipation had been in the air since Mendelssohn's time, in eighteenth-century Enlightenment Germany. Later, a different formulation of this same idea, "productivization," became a popular aspiration among Zionists. As Zionist pioneers began to found agricultural settlements in Palestine, from 1882, the dichotomy Old Jew/New Jew became a familiar theme both in the Diaspora and in Palestine. It found political manifestation in the tensions between the Old Yishuv and the New Yishuv all the way until 1948 (and, essentially, until the present).

The Old Yishuv comprised the Orthodox communities who opposed Zionism (see chapter 5) and any form of modernization. In Zionist eyes, its members were typical Old Jews, characterized by apocalyptic passivity, blind faith, dry ritualism, and economic dependency.

The New Yishuv comprised the Zionist immigrants, both urban and rural. Religious and secular, liberals and socialists, farmers and shopkeepers shared a dream—albeit often vague—of an independent, democratic, modern Jewish polity in the Land of Israel. A widely held belief was the important role of education in realizing this dream. One had to educate the immigrants' children to create a New Jew, possessing the skills and characteristics needed to build utopia.

Imagining the New Jew was an enduring theme in literature, art, and music, as well as in educational practice, from 1882 until the 1970s. The New Jew—a.k.a. the New Hebrew, the Sabra—was seen (often enthusiastically, sometimes critically) as epitomizing the Zionist project—a symbol of and a necessity for its success.[20]

Siegfried Lehmann's New Jew

Many Zionist educators tried to describe their goal in creating the New Jew. A typical and comprehensive example appears in a brief essay by Siegfried Lehmann (1892–1958). A physician and Zionist activist who had established progressive Jewish orphanages in Berlin and Kovno (Lithuania) during and after World War I, he is best known as the founder of the Ben Shemen Youth Village in Palestine in 1927 (near today's Ben Gurion Airport). Interestingly, he entitled his original fundraising brochure for the project "Utopia."

In the Ben Shemen model, children lived away from their families in a communal "youth society," learning—by doing—to work the soil of the homeland. The model was widely imitated: today there are over forty such residential schools throughout the country. Over the years, though, the centrality of agriculture waned. Many of the schools adopted a more therapeutic emphasis, often serving youth at risk or children who cannot live with their families.

Early in his tenure at Ben Shemen, Lehmann articulated his vision of his educational goal, the New Jew:

The image hovering before our eyes as educators is that of the new man of the land of Israel . . . [characterized by] freedom and confidence in his behavior, natural directness, and dignity. We find [in] him . . . characteristic simplicity in his standard of living, his dress and his living quarters . . . [a] new physical type, so foreign to the Jew up to now, nourished by creative work in the fresh air and sunshine. The body, for him, is not secondary to the spirit, simply a necessity for life, but rather it is his direct expression, representing him faithfully. As he always sees before him the broad foundation lines of free nature, he gains rootedness. Without fear he will confront all that is truly essential, even in areas of life that are distant from him, for no essential human connection is foreign to him. . . . His language is simple, devoid of froth and empty words; glibness arouses his distrust, as does the political hack whose words do not match his actions. . . .

His social quality—in the context of cooperative belonging—stems from an empathy able to rise above petty bourgeois egotism, so common in interpersonal relationships; and his ability to understand what is in the heart of members of another nation. Despite physical labor his soul is not dulled, even as he rejects from the depths of his heart "education" directed toward social status, which is merely empty, cosmetic. . . . Wealth makes no impression on him, and extreme and sickly intellectualism is no better in his eyes than any other disfigurement caused by the hypertrophy of a particular organ. . . .

To all the treasures of culture—especially of his own people—his heart is wide open, on the condition that they have the ability truly to enrich his working life and to bring spiritual inspiration to his leisure hours. . . .

The image cannot yet be compared in its clarity and concreteness to the ideal images projected by educators in other nations; for example, the image of the gentleman in English educational institutions. It may be that some of the lines are still incomplete and blurry. Still, the basic outline is valid for our education, which sees the redemptive act as the creation of a new working man, rooted in the soil of the homeland.[21]

For Lehmann and many other Zionist educators, the vision of the national home they were building was inseparable from the New Jew they were creating. They saw "the redemptive act as the creation of a new working man, rooted in the soil of the homeland." That is, they would rebuild the Jewish nation one Jew at a time.

The Jewish National Home

And so, from Lewinsky the utopian novelist to Lehmann the utopian and practical educator, the vision of the New Jews and their national home comprised a number of salient qualities:

- Strength, courage, self-reliance
- Naturalness, directness, unpretentiousness
- Rootedness in the soil of the homeland
- Commitment to physical labor, especially agricultural labor
- Commitment to social justice
- Disdain for bookishness
- Natural connection to Jewish culture; a sense of belonging to the nation

As Yishuv—and then Israeli—society developed over the years, in the ongoing attempt to translate the national home utopia into reality, these qualities found concrete expression in a number of different spheres. Needless to say, as in all such attempts at translation, "it's complicated." For example:

Rootedness: To be rooted in the soil of the homeland can certainly be seen as a noble aspiration for the Jews, who for centuries had felt (and been seen by others as) detached from their geographical roots— eternal wanderers. Thus the exuberance with which the Zionist settlers hiked the length and breadth of the land, and studied its geology, flora, and fauna, is understandable and inspiring (to this day, high school biology majors must pass a test in Israeli wildflower identification).

But the ideal of agricultural rootedness—that of the peasant who works the land—is about exploiting the land, not just knowing or even loving it. And then there is the question of defining just where the homeland's borders are situated, and how "rootedness" might affect the Jews' actions regarding claiming, conquering, and relinquishing land. Moreover, how does it fit with "startup nation"? Thus, the utopian ideal of rootedness is by no means free of ambivalence, an ambivalence we'll be discussing in more detail.

Tradition: Ahad Ha'am's secularization of traditional symbols has dominated Israeli education and culture for over a century. It can be seen in kibbutz Passover *Haggadot* which omit God; or in the reclaiming of obscure holidays like Tu b'Av (Fifteenth of Av), Tu b'Shevat (Fifteenth of Shevat, "new year of the trees"), and Lag ba-Omer (thirty-third day of the forty-nine days between Passover and Shavuot); or in teaching the Bible as a national historical epic.

However, a sense of dissatisfaction with the result has been present from the beginning. The debate over how and why to study classic Jewish texts, from the Bible onward, is ongoing: Without religious belief—without the covenant—what is the point of studying the rabbinic literature—or even the Bible? Yet the question nags: How can one be an educated Jew without knowledge of these texts? And the deeper question remains: Does Jewish secular culture indeed contain moral values, as Ahad Ha'am argued, if it is severed from the Jewish religious belief system? Every few decades the Ministry of Education establishes a commission to review these questions or a project to address them (e.g., the Shenhar Commission in 1994 and the "Jewish-Israeli Culture" curriculum inaugurated in 2016). What, indeed, is *Jewish* about New Jews? About the renewed Jewish nation?

Hebrew: One answer to this question, of course, is the revival of the Hebrew language. If language is central to any national culture, then rebuilding the Jew and the Jewish nation can be seen first and foremost as the creation of a society in which Hebrew is the dominant language. Hebrew, it was imagined, could reunite the Jews scattered among other nations speaking other languages. Hebrew could reconnect the Jews with their cultural roots: they would speak, write, sing, even curse and write graffiti in Hebrew. Led by lexicographer—and fanatic—Eliezer Ben-Yehuda (1858–1922), generations of scholars, artists, and educators took up this challenge and succeeded.

And yet, Ben-Yehuda's dream was not fulfilled in full. For many, if not most, diaspora Jews, Hebrew is not a bridge to Israel, but an obstacle to connection; communication happens mostly through the global lingua franca of English. And today (since the vast majority of research literature in most fields appears in English) many parents of Hebrew-speaking New Jews feel compelled to hire English tutors to prepare their children for university—and for life.

Military might: Levinsky's "giants . . . robust as oaks" and Lehmann's "new physical type" have never left the Zionist imagination. They gave rise to the stereotype of the Sabra (Arabic for the prickly pear cactus)—the native-born Israeli who is tough and prickly on the outside, sweet on the inside. (Think Ari ben Canaan, the hero of Leon Uris's 1958 novel *Exodus*, played in the movie version by a young Paul Newman.) Old Jews were seen as weak and timid; New Jews would know how to take care of themselves and their nation. In a Jewish national home, pale yeshivah students praying for divine protection would become tanned soldiers risking their lives to protect their homeland. And so it came to pass.

But can a nation which places such a premium on strength and courage—which sees army service as a compulsory rite of passage and a condition for full citizenship, and whose political elite is dominated by ex-generals—have the wisdom and breadth of vision to make its way in a complicated, interconnected world? This is an issue we will take up in the next chapter.

Palestinian Arabs: Perhaps the most daunting challenge facing the national home utopia is the presence in the Land of Israel of members of another nation, who constituted the majority until 1948. Utopians like Lewinsky tended to overlook this population. The actual settlers were of different minds about the Palestinians. To many European immigrants during the colonialist era, they were primitive natives, to be feared and exploited; to some socialists they were potential proletarian partners; to many Jewish nationalists, they were role models. They were living rooted in the land, just as the Jews imagined themselves. They were native, natural, and authentic, living just as (so it seemed) the ancient Israelites had lived on their land. Indeed, the *Shomrim* fighters in the early Jewish self-defense organization in Palestine (1909–20) donned Bedouin *jalabiyas* and *kefiyas* (robes and headscarves), baked pita over the fire, and brewed bitter Bedouin coffee. The appropriation in the arena of cuisine carried over into mainstream culture: hummus and falafel—not chicken soup and kneidlach—became the Israeli national foods.

However, the reality of two nations claiming the same homeland is not just a matter of cultural competition, blending, or appropriation. The problem is similar to the one we encountered in the last chapter, with the vision of Israel as an opportunity to establish authentic community. A nation—an "imagined community"—is a group of people defined by an ethno-cultural identity that comprises language, calendar, art, music, literature, food, folkways, historical memory, and often, attachment to a particular landscape. However, it is rare indeed to find a place in the world larger than a village that is ethno-culturally homogeneous. Thus, the dream of a place where "it is just us" is utopian, a lovely no-place.

Attempts over the past century to create a one-to-one correlation between national identity and sovereign borders have often resulted, to varying degrees, in oppression, ethnic cleansing, civil war, and even mass murder. It seems that nations have a tendency to see their natural right to self-determination as inherently superior to the same right of other nations. One nation's utopia thus becomes the other's dystopia. Rabbi Herzog's conclusion was perceptive: the full expression of the Torah-community nation-state will have to wait for the Messiah. For the present, everybody has to play by the same rules, which explicitly limit the right of a nation to exert state power to disenfranchise (or worse) other nations or their members.

In a nationalist utopia, the world would be neatly divided into states, each inhabited by—and only by—members of a distinct nation. Nation-states. But we do not and never will live in such a world. No-place. In fact, this utopia directly clashes with another that colors our view of Israel, which we will encounter in chapter 8: the vision of a pluralistic, cosmopolitan society. But first we will examine the other side of the hyphen: the state.

Further Reading

Almog, Oz. *The Sabra: The Creation of the New Jew*. Translated by Haim Watzman. Berkeley: University of California Press, 2000.

Anderson, Benedict. *Imagined Communities*. New York: Verso, 2006.

Tamir, Yael. *Why Nationalism*. Princeton NJ: Princeton University Press, 2019.

Zerubavel, Yael. *Recovered Roots: Collective Memory and the Making of Israeli National Tradition*. Chicago: University of Chicago Press, 1995.

7

Statehood and Power

The tension between divine and human monarchy, a recurring theme in the Bible, has occupied Jewish thinkers through the generations. Ambivalence over the monarchy — and the idealization of its memory — raises a question about the imagined ideal polity that echoes still: Is the state essential — or merely instrumental? Is Jewish coercive power (i.e., military power) an ideal — or merely a necessity for survival? To put it more sharply: Is a Jewish *state* a utopian dream, or is it rather a compromise with a dystopian reality?

Emergence from Powerlessness

In 1976 my wife and I led an Israel summer tour for teenagers from the suburban Reform synagogue which I served as assistant rabbi. For our three weeks in Jerusalem, the teens worked every morning at the Southern Wall archaeological excavation. On July 4, after the diggers had left for work, I went downtown to meet with our tour bus operator. On the way I encountered crowds in front of appliance stores, glued to the TV screens in the display windows. The Entebbe rescue was just being reported. Jews in Israel and around the world were moved by relief and pride. The promise of the Jewish state had become palpably true: no Jew, anywhere in the world, would ever have to fear again on account of his or her Jewishness — the Jewish people have a state and an army — and a long arm! It felt a bit ironic when the bus company manager suggested moving from our small hotel in the Old City to a hotel on the Jewish side of the city, for who knew what the Palestinian reaction might be to this Israeli demonstration of military ingenuity and chutzpah?

For most Jews who lived through 1948, the establishment of a Jewish state was a formative experience, giving rise to feelings of pride, relief, self-confidence, and solidarity. That the Jews — eternally powerless — gained state sovereignty and military power changed the whole nature of Jewish identity. The philosopher Emil Fackenheim wrote:

There are times in history when spirit is broken and impotent, and all that counts is power. But what is power? Money is power. So is influence. So is prudence. So is genius. Jews in their centuries of statelessness have used all these attributes, and sometimes one has helped, sometimes another. But during the Nazi regime none of them counted. The plain truth is that during the twelve years of the Third Reich, that were like unto a thousand to its Jewish victims, only one form of power counted, and that the Jewish people lacked. In the first period of the twelve years — persecution, expulsion — Jewish victims needed havens, but those only states could provide. In the second period — mass torture and murder — only a state that considered Jewish lives to be a top priority could have mustered planes, bombs, armies, and the other implements of state power that could have made a large difference.

It was therefore an act of world-historical significance when, on 14 May 1948, David Ben-Gurion, on behalf of an ad hoc government of the Jews of Palestine, proclaimed the first Jewish state in 1878 years.[1]

A quarter century later, we attended our youngest son's graduation from basic training in the Israeli paratroopers. I blogged about the experience:

Looking over the crowd, I was reminded again what a great leveler the army is here. The families represented every [Jewish] ethnic and socio-economic grouping, from professors to executives to laborers, religious and non, city and kibbutz, left and right. We were jockeying for camera angles, annoyed in a good natured way by each others' umbrellas. Our kids were learning to depend on each other and support each other, to take on responsibility for each other and for all of us in ways that seem unimaginable to me.

As a rite of passage and a leveler, the army with its silly ceremonies can make one feel proud. You find yourself *kvelling* to the taped military march music, and eagerly photographing your kid with his beret and rifle. And you know "we have no choice." You know we have a right to exist. You know history. You know we live in a violent world. And yet you wonder what you are doing, and if it has to be this way. You wonder how our democracy might be if it weren't led by generals. You wonder about the effect of learning how to kill as a rite of passage, as the one thing that unites us. And you wonder how it is that you decided to move to a place where your child is learning hand-to-hand combat while his classmates from elementary school in Philadelphia are learning liberal arts.[2]

Since I wrote that, I have discovered that ambivalence about Jewish power—its costs, benefits, and collateral damage—is as old as the Jewish people. In planning this book, I assumed that "state" would fit my neat categorization of Jewish utopian types, alongside Torah society, community, and nation. It seemed obvious that the dream of a sovereign Jewish state, both before and after Herzl's momentous manifesto *The Jewish State*, could be seen as one more among the various Jewish conceptions of an ideal existence: a utopia. However, it seems that from biblical to modern times, while the Jews dreamed of having the power to protect themselves and take responsibility for their own fate, they tended to see the possession and use of this power as a necessary evil, not as a utopian vision. They longed to be strong and thus (presumably) secure, to be independent—to be like "all the nations." And yet, built into their identity and collective memory, post-covenant, was that the whole point of their existence was *not* to be like all the nations.

In the fifth century BCE the prophet Zechariah admonished Zerubbabel, the governor of the restored Jewish polity in the Land of Israel, "Not by might and not by power, but by My spirit" (Zech. 4:6). And twenty-five hundred years later, Martin Buber wrote: "The free development of the latent power of the nation without a supreme value to give it purpose and direction does not mean regeneration, but the mere sport of a common self-deception behind which spiritual death lurks in ambush. If Israel desires less than it is intended to fulfil, then it will even fail to achieve the lesser goal."[3]

The Jews' relationship to statehood—and power—is complex, as we shall see in this chapter and the next. Perhaps the dream of statehood should be seen not as a utopia, but as a means for avoiding dystopia.

Zev Jabotinsky's "Tristan da Runha"

When the term "Jewish power" is mentioned, perhaps the first name to come to mind is Zev Jabotinsky (1880–1940), one of the most complex and influential leaders in the Zionist pantheon. And yet, as we shall see, "state" and "power" were not the same thing in his view. A product of a secular education in Odessa, Jabotinsky was not particularly interested in the Jewish tradition, or even in cultural Zionism. His approach to Zionism placed a strong emphasis on the acquisition and use of physical power (he spearheaded the effort to establish Jewish units in the British army in the First World War), and on an ideal of dignity, strength, order, and unity (elements of the New Jew discussed in the preceding chapter). Indeed, his opponents accused him of fascist tendencies; others described him as "hypernationalist." His ideas were embodied in the Betar youth movement (Betar was the site of the final bloody battle of the doomed revolt against the Romans in 135 CE, led by Simon Bar Kokhba) and the Revisionist Zionist Alliance he founded in 1925. The Revisionists remained the opposition to the dominant labor Zionist parties in the World Zionist Organization, and then in the state—until 1977, when they ascended to power, with Jabotinsky's disciple Menachem Begin as prime minister.

In the same year he founded the Revisionist Alliance, Jabotinsky published the utopian novella "Tristan da Runha," in which a fictitious British journalist reports on his visit to Tristan da Runha, an isolated island in the south Atlantic. According to the backstory, after the First World War the nations all agreed on a treaty abolishing capital punishment, and the most despicable criminals are now sent to this island, where no contact with the outside world is allowed. New arrivals are dropped off with minimal supplies, and an international naval patrol ensures that no one ever leaves or visits. The island is fertile and temperate. It has no mineral resources, and no metal of any kind is allowed ashore. The original native inhabitants opposed this plan, but British public opinion strongly favored it, so the League of Nations evacuated them, along with any remnants of their material culture. Today there are four thousand inhabitants, in scattered homesteads and twelve large camps, representing many different nationalities and religions. The journalist is unwilling, of course, to reveal how he managed to visit.

He begins by expressing his surprise at seeing how such a "problematic" population has developed a modus vivendi:

It was a mistake to think that the type so described had an absolute leaning to cruelty and violence. What they really needed was congenial surroundings, sterner conditions of existence and the company of men similarly disposed. In Civilisation, it was the meekness, the unresisting effeminacy of the average that lured and provoked the atavistic man to take advantage of his dangerous powers, either brutal force or brutal cunning. Jammed into the society of neighbors as tough as himself, he became as well balanced as a peg driven between two hard rocks.[4]

Recounting the history of this development, he expands on the idea that mutual deterrence is superior to a constitutional government:

Gradually . . . as the scanty wealth of the community grew and methods of work were perfected, a certain division of labour became necessary. The arrival of a few specialists, such as mechanics, carpenters, a master-builder, a medical student, facilitated the differentiation between the working mass and the few organizing or supervising individuals. It was at this time that the tendency of the "philosophers"—the nickname is still common use on the island, as a sort of vernacular for dodger—became apparent. Men who were by no means "specialists" in any branch of useful activity began to look for what is commonly known as soft jobs. They could only do it by advocating the necessity of permanent organization, hierarchy, offices and officials. In political terminology, they were the constitutionalists of the island, they wanted to convert the settlement into a municipality or even a state.

Charles Landree, a serial killer, was the first to stand up to the "philosophers":

In reply to their state-doctrine, he evolved the opposite theory, . . . giving articulate expression to the genuine feeling of the island's great majority. Landree proclaimed that permanent organization was a drug or a medicine necessary only to a sick or dying society, not to a community so brimful of vital force. He was the first man to declare what is today an article of faith with every islander—that the settlement of criminals in Tristan da Runha was a superior, better world than the one left behind. He framed the theory that order was a state of things as natural, as inherent in a healthy agglomeration of men as it was in Nature itself; that the best way of ensuring the permanency of order was to abstain from any interference with it under the form of fixed institutions. . . . The "philosophers" and a good many of their followers were lynched under his personal direction.

After this violent rejection of statehood, a stable and happy equilibrium was reached, as the visitor goes on to describe:

There is nothing which could even remotely be construed a government, either general or municipal. Popular meetings attended by all the male settlers seem to have been a fashion in the middle period of the colony, at the time of Landree's reform activities. But . . . for the last twenty years its life has been developing regularly without breaks or jumps, every today a natural outcome of yesterday, with no problems and no need for assemblies. . . . All the rest is custom; a rather interesting motley of customs collected from the wisdom of twenty nations and five religions. . . .

Their economy is strictly individualistic. Land is parceled out and the landmarks never infringed, simply because any attempt would be resisted. Every household, even that of an unmarried settler, is practically self-contained; the settler must build his own hut, make his own tools, mend his own clothes. The tendency towards division of labour, which had been noticeable among the first settlers, seems to have died together with the "philosophers."[5]

A new language, Anganari, has developed from a synthesis of all the languages spoken by the arriving convicts; and one Pastor Aho undertook to create a literary culture:

He framed a school-programme, adapted to the needs of the island and therefore strikingly different from the one usual with us. These children of a non-trading community would never have to deal with numbers beyond counting calves and eggs; he reduced the curriculum of mathematics to the manipulation of two figures. He excluded geography and history: the island was the only world worth knowing, its annals the only chronology. . . . His aim was to prevent the inborn generation from feeling eternal exiles like their fathers, to concentrate their interest and enthusiasm on the island as their home, not as their prison. He taught the children the names of the stars, the ways of the beasts and birds and plants and fish; boys and girls of ten were his assistants in extracting salt and bromides from sea-water; he trained them in choir-singing so popular in his own country; and he composed for them a prayer, American fashion, suitable for Christian, Mahommedan, Jew, Buddhist and Confucian alike. . . .

Pastor Aho led the effort, with some others . . . to create a literature from memory—writing down what they remembered of the Bible and then of all the world's great literature. . . .

They had infinite difficulties in translating, but they did what every young nationality does—they coined or adapted new words. After five years' toil—late evenings snatched from rest after days of ploughing and hewing—there was hardly any real genius of all times and races who was not represented by a page in the little library of Anganari. And if it was only one page, it was just therefore one of the best.[6]

Another of the colony's intellectuals, Joseph Verba, presents a manuscript to the visitor reviewing the colony's advantages, including

the absence of metal. Metal is the cause of all evil. I do not only mean iron swords and golden coin. I mean even peaceful productive machinery. It is dangerous for man to become so absolute a master of Nature. It is unnatural, and will be avenged. He was born to be Nature's son, not her lord. A son may feed from his mother's body, may claim her help and care; but if he makes of his mother a slave, he will degenerate, at first morally, and in the end materially. . . .

It is the absence of metal that forces us to stick to the role of humble toilers whose only gold is their sweat, who can never dream of riches. We who were born in the world of iron shall soon die; and the generations conceived on this island will never know the morbid ambitions, the lust of pawing new things which poison that world. This is why their life will be one of stable equilibrium; they will never need a government, any more than the trees of the forest.[7]

Though the novel is not about Jews, some Zionist hints can be found in it. For example, the narrator's conclusion that even the most despicable criminals could be "improved" by transfer to a more disciplined environment echoes the Enlightenment thesis that if the Jews could be taken out of their "sick" surroundings and allowed to develop naturally, on their own, they would "fulfil most brilliant promises,... reach great heights of refinement." Note, too, that the League of Nations, responding to British public opinion, ousts the natives of Tristan da Runha, who object to the colony's founding. Here Jabotinsky's vision reflects Herzl's assumption, passed on to the next generation of Zionists, that the Great Powers are free to dispose of their colonies as they see fit, regardless of the natives' opinions.

Jabotinsky may have been a "hypernationalist," but in his reading and writing he was a polyglot cosmopolitan. His book was written and published in English, and within it, he has Pastor Aho's Tristanian literary curriculum comprise the very best passages of all the world's literatures.

Most to the point, it seems that Jabotinsky's ideal was not a state, but a stable balance of power among strong individuals. No bureaucracy, no hierarchy, no systems of social control—rather, a permanent truce, based on mutual deterrence, would reign. Jabotinsky famously argued both for equal rights for the Arab minority in the envisioned Jewish polity and for the "iron wall," the expectation of a constant state of tension between the two nations, requiring eternal deterrence.[8] The key to a better place, according to Jabotinsky, seems not to be the apparatus of statehood, but the reality of power. Statehood is not an ideal, but a compromise, a temporary, utilitarian framework through which the nation can assert its power.

Interestingly, a year after publishing "Tristan da Runha," Jabotinsky published *Samson the Nazirite*, a novel based on the biblical figure who battled the powerful Philistines (Judg. 13–16). The Philistines had both a king and a monopoly on ironwork (1 Sam. 13:19). Jabotinsky imagines Samson's last words to the Israelites: "Two things... The first is: iron. Get hold of iron. Give whatever you have for it: money, wheat, olive oil, wine, your flocks, your wives and daughters.... The second thing is: a king. Tell Dan, tell Benjamin, tell Judah and Ephraim: a king! One person at a signal from whom thousands will raise their arms all at once. That's how the Philistines do it and that's why they're the lords of Canaan."[9]

For Jabotinsky, it seems that in utopia there will be no iron and no kings, but for real Jews in real time, both are indispensable. This suspicious, utilitarian view of statehood has deep Jewish roots.

Judges and Kings

Traditionally, the journey from the Red Sea shore to the Temple and palace in Jerusalem has been understood as a divinely guided progression toward an ideal, from a ragtag mob of liberated slaves to a world-class empire with all the accoutrements thereof. Ever since Solomon's death and the kingdom's breakup, the Jews have looked back with nostalgic longing toward the lost pinnacle of national greatness and divine favor, when a wise king ruled justly, the Temple and its service were inspiring and majestic, and the kingdom's boundaries lay far beyond the horizon. This memory (whether factually based or not) became the dominant utopian image in traditional Jewish thought.

However, when we examine this story more closely, it seems that nostalgia has smoothed over some rough patches. Looking back from a dark place of powerlessness in exile, the empire appears as a shining star. But it looked very different at the time. Several episodes in the biblical books of Judges and Samuel reveal strident disagreement over the ideal political structure for the Israelites in their land.

The book of Judges does not purport to be a unified chronological narrative; it is rather a series of stories describing the exploits of twelve *shofetim*—usually translated as "judges" (its modern Hebrew meaning), but actually a term referring to military, not judicial leadership (warlords?). Some of the tales are as brief as a sentence or two, such as the accounts of Shamgar, son of Anath (3:31) and Tola, son of Puah (10:1–2); others are quite detailed and dramatic, such as the accounts of Deborah (4–5), Gideon (6–8), Jephthah (11–12), and Samson (13–16). Interestingly, when a judge's details are given, she or he usually turns out to be one who, by birth or by character, would not be expected to achieve a leadership position. Deborah is a woman. Gideon is not only the youngest son of the humblest clan, but also a skeptic regarding God's power (6:13–18). Jephthah is the son of a prostitute (11) and Samson suffers from a recurrent and ultimately fatal attraction to Philistine women (14–16).

It is possible to see the book of Judges as expressing the ideology stated explicitly in the story of the judge Gideon.[10] After Gideon leads the tribes Naphtali, Asher, Manasseh, and Ephraim to victory over the Midianites, the "men of Israel" seek to establish him as king: "Rule over us—you, your son, and your grandson as well." But he responds, "I will not rule over you myself, nor shall my son rule over you; the Lord alone shall rule over you" (8:22–23). Later, Gideon's son Abimelech does set himself up, violently, as king; in response, his brother Jotham tells the "parable of the trees" (9:8–15), suggesting that only a useless, base person would be interested in being a king. The text seems to be advocating an anarcho-theocracy: no centralized government, but a patchwork of autonomous tribes, obedient to no king but God.

The Torah, after all, prescribes priests, judges, and tribal chieftains—but devotes only a few verses to the possibility of a monarchy, and even then seems to offer it as an option, not an ideal:

> If, after you have entered the land that the Lord your God has assigned to you, and taken possession of it and settled in it, you decide, "I will set a king over me, as do all the nations about me," you shall be free to set a king over yourself, one chosen by the Lord your God. Be sure to set as king over yourself one of your own people; you must not set a foreigner over you, one who is not your kinsman. Moreover, he shall not keep many horses or send people back to Egypt to add to his horses, since the Lord has warned you, "You must not go back that way again." And he shall not have many wives, lest his heart go astray; nor shall he amass silver and gold to excess. (Deut. 17:14–17)

A centralized state governed by a monarchy does not appear to be a key element of the Torah's vision. The ambivalence in Deuteronomy is echoed in 1 Samuel 8, when after years of living as autonomous tribes, "all the elders of Israel" gather and demand that the judge Samuel "appoint a king for us, to govern us like all other nations. Samuel was displeased that they said 'Give us a king to govern us.' Samuel prayed to the Lord, and the Lord replied to Samuel, 'Heed the demand of the people in everything they say to you. For it is not you that they have rejected; it is Me they have rejected as their king'" (1 Sam. 8:6–7).

So Samuel goes back to the people, and offers this daunting vision of a monarchy:

> This will be the practice of the king who will rule over you: He will take your sons and appoint them as his charioteers and horsemen, and they will serve as outrunners for his chariots. He will appoint them as his chiefs of thousands and of fifties; or they will have to plow his fields, reap his harvest, and make his weapons and the equipment for his chariots. He will take your daughters as perfumers, cooks, and bakers. He will seize your choice fields, vineyards, and olive groves, and give them to his courtiers. He will take a tenth part of your grain and vintage and give it to his eunuchs and courtiers. He will take your male and female slaves, your choice young men, and your asses, and put them to work for him. He will take a tenth part of your flocks, and you shall become his slaves. The day will come when you cry out because of the king whom you yourselves have chosen; and the Lord will not answer you on that day. (1 Sam. 8:11–18)

The "monarchists" are not dissuaded; perhaps because they have their own dystopian vision: of life with no king. The brutal story in Judges 19–21, the infamous tale of "the concubine of Gibeah," purports to be a description of the decentralized, disunited status quo. It begins with the phrase: "In those days, when there was no king in Israel" (19:1) and ends with the sentence: "In those days there was no king in Israel, everyone did as he pleased" (21:25). In between we read a blood-curdling tale of rape, murder, and tribal revenge that contains not-at-all subtle echoes of the story of Lot's visitors in Sodom (Gen. 19:1–11).

The author's message is clear: theocratic anarchy is still anarchy, and the collapse of moral standards and social cohesion under a regime of local tribal autonomy is beyond that found even in Sodom, that most horrendous model of a failed society.

So, which dystopian nightmare is preferable: the depredations of an oriental monarch, or the Sodom-like moral chaos of local autonomy?

Three Views of a Jewish State: Forbidden, Utilitarian, Essential

These competing dystopian predictions depict, in their mirror images, two ideals: an anarchic pure theocracy (reminiscent of life in the desert) and a proper centralized monarchy with its bureaucracy, "that we may be like all the other nations." We know, of course, the outcome according to the Bible: a hereditary monarchy was indeed established and did succeed in uniting the tribes, pushing back enemies on all sides, and creating a respectable empire. However, as predicted, the costs were daunting (1 Kings 4–5), and it wasn't long before the people grew tired of the burden and rebelled (1 Kings 12), permanently dividing the kingdom along tribal lines. The ten northern tribes remained united in the somewhat unstable kingdom of Israel (with many rebellions and succession struggles) for two centuries, until the Assyrian conquest in 722 BCE. This political entity then disappeared from Jewish history.

David's descendants continued to rule over the kingdom of Judah until the Babylonian conquest in 586 BCE. As a result, the Judahites transmitted the literature that was ultimately canonized as the Bible. Therefore, unsurprisingly, the Bible tends to view the Davidic dynasty favorably. Indeed, certain passages discussing David and Solomon express an ideology familiar from other ancient Near Eastern monarchies: the king is God's representative on earth.[11] For example, here is God's promise to David through the prophet Nathan:

The Lord declares to you that He, the Lord, will establish a house for you. When your days are done and you lie with your fathers, I will raise up your offspring after you, one of your own issue, and I will establish his kingship. He shall build a house for My name, and I will establish his royal throne forever. I will be a father to him, and he shall be a son to Me. When he does wrong, I will chastise him with the rod of men and the affliction of mortals; but I will never withdraw My favor from him as I withdrew it from Saul, whom I removed to make room for you. Your house and your kingship shall ever be secure before you; your throne shall be established forever. (2 Sam. 7:11–16)

This assertion of divine-right monarchy, "I will be a father to him and he shall be a son to Me ... [his] throne shall be established forever," is quite a leap from Deuteronomy's utilitarian "If ... you decide 'I will set a king over me, as do all the nations about me'," with its restrictions (not too many horses — or wives), and the lament in Judges 21:16: "In those days there was no king in Israel; everyone did as he pleased." We can find three models of governance in these texts:[12]

- Theocracy: Gideon argues for an ideal of direct theocracy, and rejects human monarchy outright;
- Limited monarchy: The practical position of Deuteronomy 17 that monarchic rule is an imperfect option, sometimes necessary to achieve military might and social order;
- Sacred monarchy: The Davidic ideal of a divinely ordained dynasty.

Translating these views, loosely, into a more modern language, we can articulate these three positions:

- A Jewish state is unnecessary and, indeed, spiritually undesirable. Judaism is about the Jews' relationship to God and God's laws. A state, however governed, is merely a compromise, or even a distraction, from perfecting that relationship.

- The Jewish state, like all states, is a human institution, arising out of the needs of the hour and subject to the forces of history. It may serve as a useful tool in furthering the Jews' national interests, and in fulfilling God's commandments.
- The state is essential, sacred, a manifestation of God's will in and beyond history.

Once Judah was destroyed and the Davidic dynasty cut off, this polemic was not silenced, but continued as the people looked with nostalgia toward the receding past, and with hope towards a future restoration. Regardless of one's views, the basic questions remained: What did we have—and what do we want? Living under the dominion of kings not their own, Jewish leaders and scholars continued to analyze and debate their ideal polity, past and future.[13]

The Rabbis' Ideal Kingdom

As we saw above, the Torah devotes just a few sentences to the monarchy, setting limits to the king's authority. The halakhic literature is similarly laconic: the Mishnah contains just one short chapter dealing with laws defining the king's powers and restrictions, enriched by a few parallels and expansions in the Midrash and the Talmud. However, even within this minimal framework, the tension between the different views of the monarchic imperative find expression in the interpretations of Deuteronomy 17 by two second-century Palestinian rabbis, Judah and Nehorai:

Rabbi Judah said: Israel received three commandments when they entered the land: to appoint a king, to build the Temple, and to wipe out the Amalekites. . . .

Rabbi Nehorai said: The text is a response to the people's [future] complaint [in 1 Samuel 8], as it is written, "If . . . *you decide*: 'I shall set a king over me'."[14]

The key question is the significance of "if" in Deuteronomy 17:14. According to Rabbi Judah, it could better be translated as "when"; that is, the time will come when you will appoint a king—as intended, and commanded, by God. The king's authority and its limitations will derive from this commandment. Rabbi Nehorai, on the other hand, sees appointing a king not as a divine imperative, but as a possibility, dependent on the people's choice: *if* you should so decide, then here are the rules. Thus, the text in Deuteronomy comes to support Samuel in his attempt to dissuade the people from insisting on a king. Elsewhere, Rabbi Nehorai emphasizes the negative significance of the people's request:

They only requested a king so that he would lead them in idol worship, as it is written, ". . . that we may be like all the other nations [I Sam. 8:19]."[15]

Another midrash ascribes the antimonarchic view to the Rabbis in general: "The rabbis said: the Holy One said to Israel, 'My children, I hoped that you would be free of monarchic rule, as it is written (Jer. 2:24) "Like a wild ass used to the desert": just as the wild ass grows up in the desert, with no fear of humanity, so I hoped that you would fear no monarch—but that is not what you wanted.'"[16]

A major theme in the traditional liturgy is the hope for restoration of the Davidic monarchy and the Temple sacrifices; these are the images of the future better place for which Jews prayed every day. Exile meant distance not only from Jerusalem, but from God; it meant powerlessness in a world ruled by power. The Jewish collective dream was of ingathering, return, and empowerment. But at the same time, as the Jews studied the Bible and the commentaries, they could not miss the ambivalence about what was *really* the ideal: state (David's monarchy) or no-state (anarcho-theocracy).

A Jewish State?

In 1902, six years after Theodor Herzl published his famous and influential manifesto, *Der Judenstaat* (*The Jewish State*), he published *Altneuland* (*Old New Land*), a utopian novel set twenty years in the future. There, a visitor to the imaginary Jewish polity is surprised to discover that there is no army. His host explains, "We have no state, like the Europeans of your time. We are merely a society of citizens seeking to enjoy life through work and culture."[17]

On the one hand, Herzl may have penned this surprising passage in an attempt to avoid riling the Ottoman Sultan, from whom he hoped to obtain a charter permitting mass Jewish settlement in Palestine. On the other hand, it is one of a great many similar expressions by Zionist thinkers and leaders—not least among them Zev Jabotinsky and David Ben Gurion—especially during the first four decades of the twentieth century.

As we saw in chapter 6, for Ahad Ha'am and the cultural Zionists, Jewish revitalization, a cultural center, a national home did not necessarily imply statehood. Political sovereignty was a secondary goal, and in any case should be delayed until the nation had indeed been culturally revitalized and was ready for statehood.

Under the British Mandate, the Zionists (in Palestine and elsewhere) could not avoid addressing the challenge of how Jewish national aspirations and the newly coalescing Palestinian national movement could find a stable modus vivendi in the same land. And so the Zionist leadership devoted countless pages of proposals and hours of debate to defining the ideal—and the realistically possible—relationship between national self-determination and state sovereignty. The one-to-one mapping of national identity onto the borders of a sovereign state that we of the twenty-first century tend to take for granted when we think about Zionism was by no means so obvious to the founding fathers of the State of Israel before the Holocaust.[18]

In 1925, a small group of intellectuals calling themselves Brit Shalom (covenant of peace) proposed the creation of a binational state. Among the activists were the prominent American Reform Rabbi Judah Magnes and the philosopher Martin Buber, who described the goal in these words: "Our return to Eretz Yisrael, which is to take place in the form of an ever-increasing immigration, is not intended to encroach upon the rights of others. In a just union with the Arab people we wish to make the common homeland an economically and culturally flourishing community whose structure will guarantee each of its national groups an undisturbed autonomous development."[19]

Many Zionists disparaged the binational idea as a betrayal of the ideal of national self-determination. However, throughout the 1920s and 1930s, the mainstream Zionist leadership also put forward serious proposals (in a variety of formats and timetables) for a state that would comprise two national autonomies.

Ahad Ha'am, whose main concern was culture, made a distinction between national self-determination and the utilitarian need for state power to keep order. If the Jews and Palestinians could cooperate to create a functioning polity, well and good; if not, foreign rule would be required: "National homes of different peoples in the same land can each claim national freedom only in their internal affairs, while the control of countrywide matters, common to all the inhabitants, must be entrusted to all the householders together, assuming that the relations between them and their cultural condition qualify them for this. If this condition is not met, control must be granted to an outside trustee, who will insure that no one's rights are infringed."[20]

Two of the outstanding political leaders of the prestate and early state periods, Chaim Weizmann (first president of the state) and David Ben-Gurion (first prime minister), emphasized the Zionist aim of mass return—but rejected political domination of the Palestinians. If the Jews could immigrate freely and control their own cultural institutions, Jewish statehood per se was not necessary. As Weizmann said in 1930:

Certainly we have a right over Palestine, but also the Arabs have a claim over the land. Certainly we are a state-forming element in Palestine, but so are they. We will certainly try to bring the maximum number of persons to Palestine and when we shall be the majority there, we will not dominate the Arabs, just as we will not allow ourselves to be dominated while we are the minority. That is the contents of the Balfour Declaration and the Palestine Mandate. Perhaps one can arrive at an understanding with the Arabs if our set aim were formulated. This set aim is, however, not the Jewish State, nor a majority which will administer the minority in the land.[21]

And Ben Gurion, in 1934, explicitly suggested a federal state of autonomous cantons:

I see the future of Palestine in the political constitutional sense as a federal state of cantons. . . . We must take this approach not because of political tactics but because this is the political reality of our Zionism: non-domination of the Jews over the Arabs and non-domination of the Arabs over the Jews.[22]

The model of Switzerland—one state comprising a federation of culturally distinctive cantons—then appealed to many Zionists as a means of resolving the problem of two nations in one land. Why not create a federation? This approach would respect each nation's need for self-determination, within the context of a shared state structure that would meet common needs.

Jabotinsky even brought the American model into the discussion, by pointing out that there are states—and then, there are states: "France is a state and Kentucky is a state. . . . When I speak about a state, I am not . . . actually interested in the exact extent or scope of its independence. I believe that the crucial minimum status of statehood is enough self-rule to administer internal affairs."[23]

For these leaders, state sovereignty in and of itself was not the point. At this stage in the development of Zionist thought (into the 1930s), what mattered most was to find a framework that allowed free Jewish immigration, with sufficient autonomy to be able to build Jewish national culture in the Jewish homeland. However, also key for mainstream Zionism was mutual nondomination—upholding a liberal nationalism that respected the national aspirations of all nations, including the Palestinians.

Alas, these leaders couldn't really know it at the time, but the uplifting, republican nationalist model of Garibaldi, the renowned leader of the Italian national revolution of the mid-nineteenth century, was shifting toward the dark nationalism of Adolph Hitler. Herzl's image of an enlightened world of nations, which we'll look at in more detail in the next chapter, of mutually respectful self-determination, was about to go up in smoke, casting models of shared sovereignty in a very different light.

Ein Breirah (We Have No Choice)

Alongside this ongoing process of trying to reconcile moral values with national aspirations and political realities in Palestine, the first half of the twentieth century saw a horrendous crescendo in Jewish suffering. Throughout the Middle Ages, the Jewish sense of powerlessness was tempered by the belief that the political reality was part of an apocalyptic drama—that Jewish suffering at gentile hands had a meaning, and would lead, ultimately, to repentance, forgiveness, and redemption. But in a context of encroaching secularism, the escalation of violence perpetrated against the Jews—in the 1881 and 1903 pogroms, the Russian civil war, the violent resistance in Palestine to Jewish immigration, and then the Holocaust—gave rise to ever-increasing frustration and outrage, and ultimately to active rebellion against Jewish powerlessness. In the eyes of many, fielding a Jewish army became a key element of the Zionist dream—even if all of the Zionist utopias downplayed or ignored the details of governance and defense.

Meanwhile, as we see in the thought of Jabotinsky, this rebellion against powerlessness (and its corollaries of cowardice, weakness, paleness, lack of dignity and of self-respect) dovetailed with the image of the New Jew. In the utopian national home, built and populated by New Jews, powerlessness would be overcome. Thus the desperate need for power and the vision of the New Jew converged with the dream of a state that would protect the Jews, and of a revitalization of Jewish culture that would produce soldiers for its army.

With this convergence, the image of the national home became firmly bound to the call for a state. And by the 1940s, it became progressively harder to advocate for any solution that did not include sovereign statehood for the Jewish nation—that is, the nation-state of the Jewish people. Binational and federated models, with no iron and no kings, were inspiring utopian visions, but as Fackenheim put it, "There are times in history when spirit is broken and impotent, and all that counts is power."

In 1942, an "Extraordinary Zionist Conference" was held at New York's Biltmore Hotel (in place of the World Zionist Conference that couldn't be held in Europe). The "Biltmore Program" that emerged explicitly linked the national home and the demand for statehood:

The Conference declares that the new world order that will follow victory cannot be established on foundations of peace, justice and equality, unless the problem of Jewish homelessness is finally solved. The Conference urges that the gates of Palestine be opened; that the Jewish Agency be vested with control of immigration into Palestine and with the necessary authority for upbuilding the country, including the development of its unoccupied and uncultivated lands; and that Palestine be established as a Jewish Commonwealth integrated in the structure of the new democratic world. Then and only then will the age old wrong to the Jewish people be righted.[24]

A half-dozen years later, Israel's Declaration of Independence articulated a sweeping vision of the Jewish nation-state. Standing behind it was this very linkage between the utopian vision of a national home and the perception that the Jews were victims of an "age-old wrong" that could only be righted by sovereign statehood: "This right is the natural right of the Jewish people to be masters of their own fate, like all other nations, in their own sovereign State."

The Jewish declaration that nation and state must be one—that the nation has the natural right to have a state—was, of course, not unique. It seems fair to say that the felt need to create nation-states, in which utopian dreams of ethnic homogeneity are linked to state boundaries and state power, has been the driving force of world history for over a century, a key force in—and expression of—modernization. Its benefits have been manifold. In the words of Israeli political scientist (and former government minister) Yael Tamir: "In seeking to build a more decent social and political regime, one that provides all citizens better protection and better life chances, it is important to remember that no institution did it better than the nation-state. . . . [No] international organization . . . is able to replace the state in its most important social and democratic roles: allowing individuals to be self-governing, meeting the political challenge of "no taxation without representation," and developing distributive tools and a social support system for those who need it."[25]

At the same time, the beneficial process of dividing the world up in this way has also been a major cause of bloodshed for the past century (from the First World War to the breakup of the British Raj to the disintegration of Yugoslavia). It seems that the nation-state is neither inherently good nor inherently evil. No outcome can be taken for granted. So, if Israel is to be the nation-state of the Jewish people, it must grapple with the difficult questions that beset any nation-state:

- If the state and the nation are the same thing, then what becomes of citizens of the state who are not members of the nation (i.e., Palestinian Arabs)?

- What is the status of members of the nation who are not citizens of the state (i.e., diaspora Jews)?
- Is the state sacred, apocalyptic, messianic—or just a temporary necessity, enabling its citizenry to live a normal life during the endless slog towards utopia? Is military might a regrettable means to a utopian end—or a sacred end in itself?

Moreover, because of the covenant—the unique Jewish relationship between nation and religion—further questions arise in Israel's case regarding the relationship between religious law and state law, between religious belief and state power, between religious teachings and state policy.

Looking back on the twentieth century, it is reasonable to argue that a Jewish state is necessary. However, necessity does not imply sanctity—or utopia. Furthermore, the attempt to use state power to translate utopian visions—Torah, community, nation, normalcy, the Promised Land, social justice—into practical realities comes up against the utopian dilemma we have been encountering throughout this discussion. Employing force to implement a utopian dream violates the very nature of utopia, and risks unintended consequences (resentment, oppression, and suffering among them). A state is what we need; utopia is what we desire. The challenge is keeping our categories straight.

Further Reading

Gans, Chaim. *A Just Zionism*. New York: Oxford University Press, 2008.

Gorni, Yosef. *From Binational Society to Jewish State: Federal Concepts in Zionist Political Thought, 1920-1990, and the Jewish People*. Leiden, Neth.: Brill, 2006.

Kugel, James. *How to Read the Bible: A Guide to the Scripture, Then and Now*. New York: Free Press, 2007, pp. 387–416, 437–57.

Lorberbaum, Yair. *Disempowered King: Monarchy in Classical Jewish Literature*. London: Continuum, 2011.

Shumsky, Dmitry. *Beyond the Nation-State: The Zionist Political Imagination from Pinsker to Ben-Gurion*. New Haven CT: Yale University Press, 2018.

8

Enlightenment and Normalization

Another Jewish utopian model that strongly influenced Zionism had its roots in the Enlightenment. In an enlightened world, all persons — and all nations — would be equals; there would be no exceptionalism based on religious belief, ethnic belonging, or anything else. But normalization — the integration of the Jews as equals into general humanity and of the Jewish polity into the family of nations — does not easily square with Torah, community, and nationalist utopian dreams. Achieving equality of all citizens is a daunting challenge for any state — how much more so in a state with a declared ethnic or religious identity.

A State of All Its Citizens

Three illustrations of the problem:

1. In the Bedouin town of Lakia, not far from Beersheba, there is a center for women's employment, education, and empowerment. On a visit there with a group of Jewish educators, I heard a talk by social worker and activist Amal Elsana Alh'jooj. A native of the town with degrees from Ben Gurion and McGill Universities, charismatic and articulate in several languages, she spoke of her efforts to help her community take responsibility for itself, despite all the obstacles facing a premodern Muslim minority population in a modern Jewish state. Very impressive would be an understatement. On the way out, I exclaimed, "Wow, she has my vote for prime minister!" — to which a colleague standing nearby responded, "Well, that would be the end of the Jewish state!"

2. In 2018, in the city of Afula in the Jezreel Valley (population 42,000), the new city council was inducted with an oath of office that, in addition to the required clauses swearing allegiance to the state and promising to uphold its laws, included a pledge to "maintain the Jewish character" of the city. This was on the heels of popular demonstrations protesting Palestinian Israelis' purchase of home sites in Afula. Later, the Attorney General of Israel declared the revised oath invalid.

3. From the Israel Declaration of Independence: "The State of Israel will . . . foster the development of the country for the benefit of all its inhabitants; it will be based on freedom, justice and peace as envisaged by the prophets of Israel; it will ensure complete equality of social and political rights to all its inhabitants irrespective of religion, race or sex."

In popular—and political—discourse in Israel, it is generally taken for granted that "the nation-state of the Jewish people" makes impossible "the state of all its citizens" and vice versa. In other words, if the state is defined as Jewish, there must be two classes of citizens: Jews, to whom the state belongs, and others, to whom it does not. If the state were to belong equally to all its citizens, then it would no longer be Jewish. This understanding appears to derive from the problematic entanglement of community and national utopias with the practicalities of statehood we have been discussing.

This simple either-or assumption conflicts with another utopian vision that has also been influential in Zionist thought and politics from the beginning: the Jewish polity as "normal" (i.e., not exceptional; subject to the same rules as other polities), an enlightened society naturally at home in an enlightened world. In this utopia, the Jewish polity would be modern, open, advanced, cosmopolitan, and free. All citizens would be equal regardless of race, religion, or ethnicity. In their state, the Jews would somehow realize the ideal that ostensibly enlightened Europe had consistently failed to implement.

Theodor Herzl's *Altneuland*

Perhaps the best-known advocate for this kind of Zionist utopia was Theodor Herzl. Herzl's 1896 manifesto *The Jewish State* set forth his arguments that antisemitism in Europe was intractable, and the only rational responses were to define it as a national problem and to create a normal national situation for the Jews: a nation-state. He foresaw, correctly, that such a far-fetched plan would not be taken seriously:

> I must, in the first place, guard my scheme from being treated as Utopian by superficial critics who might commit this error of judgment if I did not warn them. I should obviously have done nothing to be ashamed of if I had described a Utopia on philanthropic lines; and I should also, in all probability, have obtained literary success more easily if I had set forth my plan in the irresponsible guise of a romantic tale. But this Utopia is far less attractive than any one of those portrayed by Sir Thomas More and his numerous forerunners and successors. And I believe that the situation of the Jews in many countries is grave enough to make such preliminary trifling superfluous.[1]

In 1897 Herzl laid the groundwork for carrying out his plan: he invited communal leaders from across the Jewish world to the First Zionist Congress in Basel, Switzerland. More than two hundred attendees, mostly European lay leaders, many of them *Chovevei Tzion* activists, gathered, and with great pomp and circumstance founded the Zionist Organization to galvanize political and material Jewish support worldwide for the polity envisioned in *The Jewish State*. Herzl believed that such a mass movement would have the power to convince European and Ottoman rulers to grant the Jews their place among the nations. Driven by his vision, Herzl sacrificed his inheritance and his health (he would die in 1904 at age 44). As frustrating as it was to be treated as a crackpot by world leaders, Herzl was particularly disappointed by the failure of the Jewish world to unite behind his efforts. While he had aimed to unite Jews of every origin and ideology behind his efforts, to Orthodox Jews he seemed a false messiah, to *Chovevei Tzion* he was a suspected assimilationist, and to Reform Jews he represented a threat to acculturation and integration. Furthermore, even those who supported his vision and joined the Zionist Organization were riven by religious, cultural, and strategic divisions over the nature of the projected polity as well as over how to achieve it.

Discouraged, in 1902 Hertzl published "a romantic tale" after all, the novel *Altneuland* (*Old New Land*), in which he imagined a visit to Palestine in 1922. The utopia described therein seems to have been intended to inspire the Jews to sign on to his vision and move them to action. *Altneuland* portrays the Jewish polity not merely as a technical response to eternal antisemitism, but as the opportunity to lead the way to a better future for the Jews and for all of humanity.[2] Among its key passages, *Altneuland* had this to say on national self-determination: "It was only at the end of the nineteenth century, when the other civilized nations had already attained to self-consciousness and given evidence thereof, that our own people — the pariah — realized that its salvation lay within itself, that nothing was to be expected from fantastic miracle workers. They realized then that the way of deliverance must be paved not by a single individual, but by a conscious and alert folk-personality. . . . And so the Jewish nation once more raised itself to nationhood."[3]

In the modern, enlightened world, passively awaiting the apocalypse — or praying for the messiah — would not bring change. If Greeks and Italians and Germans could achieve national self-determination by their own efforts, so could the Jews. And, Herzl envisioned, the result would be the defeat of antisemitism. Once the Jews became a normal nation like all the others, they would be pariahs no more: "And so the effects . . . made themselves felt on all sides . . . public opinion [of Jews] took a turn for the better. Jews were granted full citizenship rights not only on paper, but in everyday life. . . . Only after those Jews who were forced out of Europe had been settled in their own land, the well-meant measures of emancipation became effective everywhere. . . . Only when the Jews, forming the majority in Palestine, showed themselves tolerant, were they shown more toleration in all other countries."[4]

Troubled (like Yavetz, Lewinsky, and Jabotinsky) by the stereotype of the Old Jew, Herzl imagined that national normalization would lead to personal normalization. Living in a normal setting would "improve" the Jews morally, socially, and economically. Indeed, for Herzl, statehood as such was not the point; an enlightened society and proper education were the key aims: "We have no state, like the Europeans of your time. We are merely a society of citizens seeking to enjoy life through work and culture. We content ourselves with making our young people physically fit. We develop their bodies as well as their minds. . . . Jewish children used to be pale, weak, timid. Now look at them! . . . We took our children out of damp cellars and hovels and brought them into the sunlight. . . . Plants can be saved by transplantation into congenial soil. Human beings as well."[5]

This very focus on enlightenment and normalization naturally raised questions about how the Jewish polity could be particularly Jewish. Ahad Ha'am and the *Chovevei Tzion* were sharply critical of Herzl on this matter. For Herzl, however, "liberality [and] tolerance" were fundamentally Jewish values: "We stand and fall by the principle that whoever has given two years' service to the New Society as prescribed by our rules, and has conducted himself properly, is eligible to membership no matter what his race or creed. . . . Liberality, tolerance, love of mankind. Only then is Zion truly Zion!"[6]

Given this approach, the place of gentiles in the Jewish polity is a major concern of the novel. The non-Jewish "natives" in *Altneuland* are represented by a Haifa Arab, Reschid Bey (who speaks "German with a slight northern accent"):

[A guest inquires] Were not the older inhabitants of Palestine ruined by the Jewish immigration? And didn't they have to leave the country? . . .

[Reschid Bey responds] What a question! It was a great blessing for all of us. . . . Naturally, the land-owners gained most because they were able to sell to the Jewish society at high prices, or to wait for still higher ones. . . . Those who had nothing stood to lose nothing, and could only gain. And they did gain: Opportunities to work, means of livelihood, prosperity. Nothing could have been more wretched than an Arab village at the end of the nineteenth century. . . . Now everything is different. They benefitted from the progressive measures of the New Society whether they wanted to or not, whether they joined it or not. When the swamps were drained, the canals built, and the eucalyptus trees planted to drain and "cure" the marshy soil, the natives (who, naturally, were well acclimatized) were the first to be employed, and were paid well for their work.

The Jews have enriched us. Why should we be angry with them? They dwell among us like brothers. Why should we not love them? . . . He prays in a different house to the God Who is above us all. But our houses of worship stand side by side, and I always believe that our prayers, when they rise, mingle somewhere up above, and then continue on their way together until they appear before our Father. . . . I did not learn tolerance in the Occident. We Moslems have always had better relations with the Jews than you Christians.[7]

During the visitors' sojourn in Palestine, they witness an election campaign between the incumbent liberals and a nationalist party that seeks to disenfranchise the Arabs by excluding them from the New Society. In Herzl's utopia, the nationalists are trounced.

Nevertheless, for all its universalism, Herzl's vision does have a number of particularly Jewish elements. For example, he imagines the reestablishment of the jubilee year as a force for social equality; the currency is the shekel; his visitors encounter venerable yet liberal-minded rabbis, and participate in a moving Passover seder. In Haifa, they consider the options for an evening's entertainment:

At the national theater there is a biblical drama called "Moses." . . .
There's "Sabbetai Zevi" at the opera. And at some of the popular
theaters there are Yiddish farces. They are amusing, but not in
very good taste.[8]

Later, the visitors experience the Sabbath in Jerusalem:

Slowly and peacefully the Sabbath fell upon the bustling city.
Throngs of worshipers wended their way to the Temple and to
the many synagogues in the Old City and the New, there to pray
to the God Whose banner Israel had borne throughout the world
for thousands of years. . . .

They reached the Temple. The times had fulfilled themselves,
and it was rebuilt. Once more it had been erected with great quad-
rangular blocks of stone hewn from nearby quarries and hardened
by the action of the atmosphere. Once more the pillars of bronze
stood before the Holy Place of Israel. . . . In the forecourt was a
mighty bronze altar, with an enormous basin called the brazen
sea as in the olden days, when Solomon was king in Israel. . . .
The worshippers were crooning and murmuring the words of
the ritual, but [the Austrian Jewish visitor] Friedrich thought of
Heine's "Hebrew Melodies." . . . The choristers chanted a hymn
that had stirred yearnings for their own land in the hearts of a
homeless people for hundreds of years.[9]

The Jewishness of Herzl's vision seems in large part nostalgic and
religious. While he staked his whole plan on the assertion that the
Jews are a nation like other nations, and some ancient Jewish symbols
have been revived (the shekel, the jubilee year), Hebrew and Hebrew
culture are lacking. The performances of "Jewish" plays and operas
are in German, while crude popular entertainment is in Yiddish. In
a nod to Jewish messianism, "the times had fulfilled themselves and
[the Temple] was rebuilt"—but while the worshipers chant ancient

Hebrew prayers, the smitten visitor from Old Europe can only think of Heinrich Heine (1797–1856, a Jewish-born poet known both for German romanticism and for liberal political views). No sacrifices.

Comparing *Altneuland* to Lewinsky's cultural Zionist utopia, it is not hard to understand the cultural Zionists' rejection of Herzl's vision. While Lewinsky envisioned a modernized, biblical, Hebrew-speaking, agrarian Israel, Herzl described an enlightened, cosmopolitan, German-speaking polity that looked a lot like Vienna in Palestine.

Herzl's cosmopolitan utopia may have been a "romantic tale," but it gave concrete expression to an important strand in Jewish thought that originated a century earlier and still influences expectations of Israel. Indeed, it turns out that the values of equality, freedom, universal humanism, and education that permeate *Altneuland* had characterized pre-Zionist, Enlightenment utopian thinking long before Herzl.

The Empire of Reason

Thomas More's *Utopia* was an expression of the Renaissance spirit—a critical view of medieval institutions and beliefs, and a new faith in human potentiality and human freedom. The eighteenth-century Enlightenment built upon this critical humanist worldview, carrying it from the realm of intellectuals and artists to the world of social and political action. While utopias continued to be imagined and written in this period, they tended to take the form of manifestos and action plans rather than satires and fantasies. The ultimate implication of humanism was the realization that there was no reason to look at the ideal society through a lens of "if only." The lens should be: "If not now, when?" Israeli historian Amos Funkenstein (1937–1995) refers to the Enlightenment utopians as "'Realistic utopians' . . . [who] tried to show how the ideal social organization can and even must grow out of real or realizable starting conditions; humankind can and must change its own nature to the better if only given a realistic chance. . . . The belief in the human capacity to change nature, including human nature, with the aid of science, became, duly secularized, part of the ideology of many Enlighteners in the eighteenth century."[10]

The Enlightenment faith in the power of reason and the inevitability of progress, combined with a commitment to humanitarianism, led to important advances in the natural sciences and technology, to the development of the social sciences, to major social and political changes — most notably, the rise of democratic ideas, movements, and revolutions — and to Jewish emancipation.

After centuries of cruel discrimination and persecution, the Enlightenment seemed to offer the Jews an ideal future. A strong universalistic, cosmopolitan strand in Enlightenment thought rejected the old divisions and hierarchies based on class and faith. In a society guided by this ideal, Jews could expect to be equal in rights and responsibilities. They would be treated no differently from their fellow citizens — simply like human beings.

Meanwhile, however (as we have seen in the preceding chapters), throughout the premodern period, the Jews simultaneously held before their eyes two not necessarily compatible utopian visions, each of which would be refracted differently by this encounter with the Enlightenment: God's kingdom and David's kingdom.

In God's kingdom, modeled on the memory of the desert wandering and charismatic rule of the Judges, any sort of human government would be purely instrumental in enabling the nation to live in a perfect society governed by Torah law. This model seemingly melded the Enlightenment vision of the ideal rational society with the universalistic components of the theocracy. God's perfectly just rule over all humankind could be seen as being fulfilled in the Empire of Reason, which would realize, in the words of the leading Enlightenment thinker Nicolas de Condorcet (1743–94), "the abolition of inequality between nations, progress of equality within each nation, and the true perfection of mankind."[11] David's kingdom, in contrast, embodies a more nationalistic conception, modeled on the memory of Solomon's empire. A Davidic monarch would rule as the expression of God's will over a Jewish empire in the Land of Israel.

The two visions were not easily meshed. The messianic vision of the inevitable restoration of national sovereignty necessarily conflicted with the cosmopolitan ideal of a universal human identity. It was awkward to argue for emancipation, integration, and equality in Europe and then enter the synagogue and pray for the immediate establishment of David's kingdom and the ingathering of all the exiles in the ancestral homeland. From the latter vantage point, Enlightenment seemed to undermine and suppress both the Jewish religion and Jewish national identity.

And so, while some Jews (e.g., the "Reformers") sought to abandon a Jewish national identity and the belief in national restoration, others (who came to be called Orthodox) rejected Enlightenment as more of a threat than a promise.

Further complicating matters, the ongoing attempt to live by the light of the Torah's utopian vision—to live halakhically—had once been vital and authoritative in the context of the autonomous community that had characterized medieval Jewish life. Then, the synagogue had stood in for the Temple, prayer for sacrifice, rabbis for priests, lay leaders (oligarchs) for kings, and community for state. However, once Europe ushered in the Enlightenment, with its double demand of rational cosmopolitanism and a centralized state of all its citizens, the halakhic community became both intellectually unacceptable and politically untenable.

Here too the Jewish response was divided. Some Jews welcomed liberation from communal governance as well as from bonds of law and custom and social pressures they perceived as oppressive and backward. Others could not imagine a meaningful, sustainable Jewish existence that was not grounded in halakhic authority and community. All of the various movements and schools of thought in Jewish life in the past two centuries (Reform, Conservative, Orthodox, neo-Orthodox, and Reconstructionist among them) can be seen as attempts at finding a sustainable synthesis between these two extremes.

Ironically, it may be that the Enlightenment carried within it the seeds of its own undoing. By opening the gates of free inquiry, it invited self-criticism; by its commitment to progress and to rational government it provided support for the rise of the centralized nation-state. Late in the eighteenth century, philosophers Jean-Jacques Rousseau (1712–78) and Immanuel Kant (1724–1804) argued that reason may be a useful method for analyzing the natural world, but it is insufficient as grounds for understanding and guiding human morality. There must be something more, deeper, primal.

The Romantic movement that arose from this criticism valued individuality, spontaneity, and spirit over the dry syllogisms and generalizations of reason. It sought roots in the past. It valued individual and national identity over against the universalist Enlightenment vision. And this focus on particular identity dovetailed perfectly with the idea of the benevolent state that the Enlightenment had proposed. Thus, while democratic revolutions were fueled by Enlightenment ideas, so too was the rise of the absolutist states of the nineteenth century. Democracy is, after all, messy, often irrational, prone to unwise decisions; a philosopher-king, on the other hand, can be expected to rule ideally over an ideal state. And so, the Enlightenment led to two different utopian visions: the popular democracy and the absolutist monarchy.

Moses Mendelssohn and the Haskalah

Enlightenment's impact on Jewish discourse was first seen in the lives and works of the *maskilim*. Often translated as "enlightened Jews," the term is actually richer. It can mean enlightened ones, or enlighteners, or teachers, or wise ones. From the same root comes *Haskalah*, "Jewish Enlightenment."

It is impossible to talk about the Jewish response to Enlightenment without considering the towering figure of Moses Mendelssohn (1729–86), perhaps the outstanding exemplar of the *maskil*. Throughout his career as a scholar, thinker, activist, and leader Mendelssohn struggled to reconcile his religious faith, his concern for the welfare of the Jews, and his beliefs both in Enlightenment values and the value of the Enlightenment.

Mendelssohn's life and work can be seen as a microcosm of the challenges the Enlightenment posed for Jews. In 1783, after years of public and private efforts to advance the cause of Jewish emancipation and integration, Mendelssohn published *Jerusalem, or On Religious Power in Judaism*, a brief two-part work of political philosophy. The first part analyzes the purposes and powers of state and religion in general, and proposes an ideal relationship. It can be seen as a sketch for utopia—not as a fantastic journey, but, in the Platonic mode, as a systematic imagining of key characteristics of the ideal polity. The second part describes an ideal formulation of Judaism, in harmony with Enlightenment rationalism and openness.

According to Mendelssohn's version of Jewish history, the ideal past was the desert theocracy. Once the people demanded a king, this ideal past began to fall apart. All subsequent generations live in the shadow of that lost, perfect era. And history is not reversible. Today, religion and state are irrevocably separated:

> As the rabbis expressly state, *with the destruction of the Temple, all corporal and capital punishments and, indeed, even monetary fines, insofar as they are only national, have ceased to be legal.* . . . The civil bonds of the nation were dissolved; religious offenses were no longer crimes against the state, and the religion, as religion, knows of no punishment, no other penalty than the one the remorseful sinner *voluntarily* imposes upon himself. It knows of no coercion, uses only the staff [called] *gentleness*, and affects only the mind and heart.[12]

From his analysis, Mendelssohn suggests principles for an ideal Judaism and an ideal state. He does not see his words as a utopian description of unattainable perfection, but as a plea for immediate concrete action:

> Give to Caesar, and give to God too! To each his own, since the unity of interests is now destroyed!

And even today, no wiser advice than this can be given to the House of Jacob. Adapt yourselves to the morals and the constitution of the land to which you have been removed; but hold fast to the religion of your fathers too. Bear both burdens as well as you can! . . .

Rulers of the earth! . . . For the sake of your felicity and ours, do not use your powerful authority to transform some *eternal truth*, without which civil felicity can exist, into a *law*, some *religious opinion*, which is a matter of indifference to the state, into an *ordinance of the land*! Pay heed to the [right] *conduct* of men; upon this bring to bear the tribunal of wise laws, and leave us *thought and speech* which the Father of us all assigned to us as an inalienable heritage and granted to us as an immutable right.[13]

Interestingly, Mendelssohn titled this work "Jerusalem," even though it contains no references to Jerusalem, the Land of Israel, or the Jewish messianic hope. It seems that in his mind, Jerusalem symbolized utopia, the perfected society he envisioned. And that society was imagined not in Canaan and not on a mythical island, but in a contemporary European state, for it was not a satire or a dream, but a serious call for action by the enlightened rulers of Europe.

Isaac Satanow's Enlightened Kingdom

Isaac Satanow (1732–1804), another classic example of a *maskil*, would translate Mendelssohn's principles into a concrete plan.

A deeply knowledgeable and serious scholar of traditional Jewish texts educated in the Polish-Jewish milieu, Satanow settled in Berlin, where he devoted his efforts to building bridges between the tradition and modern European culture. He wrote commentaries, satires, dictionaries, and polemics. And one utopia. In 1793 he published *Matters of Dispute* (a phrase taken from Deuteronomy 17:8). Consciously modeled after one of the greatest works of medieval Jewish philosophy, Judah Halevi's twelfth-century dialogue the *Kuzari*, Satanow's work took the form of an imaginary conversation, in Hebrew, between a Jewish doctor and a gentile king.

He set the scene as follows: "Long, long ago, in one of the kingdoms of the western lands, there lived a Jew who served in the royal court, serving as the king's agent in every matter. This man was virtuous and God-fearing, wise of heart and loyal of spirit, a success at everything he did. And on top of all that, he learned the profession of medicine, and served as doctor to the king."[14]

In the course of a lengthy disputation on the relative merits of Judaism and Christianity, Satanow ascribed to the king a utopian vision:

The King: [W]hy should man be less than all living things on earth, in being free like them in everything except what does harm to their fellows? So now it is incumbent upon us to proclaim freedom to the inhabitants of our land in matters of the body and soul. Let every man walk in the name of his god without any restriction or control. We will walk in the name of our god according to the Christian religion, the Ishmaelites will behave according to the religion of the Quran, and the Jews will walk in the name of their god and behave according to the religion of Moses. Every man will do what is right in his own eyes — and may, accordingly, freely change religions. . . . And with respect to the welfare of the state, crafts and trade and government, let all the inhabitants of our land be equal; no man shall have preference on account of religion, but men shall advance according to their accomplishments, for we are all the children of one man and one god created us.

Having described the ideal state, the king goes on to discuss the popular Enlightenment question of how to improve the Jews to make them worthy of emancipation:

And so, doctor, with all my heart I wish to benefit your people and to straighten them out; but not in their beliefs and opinions, for that is not the king's authority; and besides, I see in you wisdom and knowledge in your Torah such that I, as king, have nothing to add or change. But rather, I wish to improve your civic and practical skills, so that you will live comfortably in the state, succeeding and contributing to the state's success. . . .

And so I intend to lighten your burden and remove any distinction between you and other peoples of the land regarding taxes and government service. . . . I have seen that there should be no distinctions based on religion, but only those between the righteous and the wicked, the wise and the ignorant, the industrious and the lazy.[15] . . .

So now we will treat [the Jews] like physicians do: before giving remedies, they first try to eliminate the causes of the disease. . . .

First: Christian and Jewish scholars will teach their people about love of mankind, which is necessary for the success of the state, so the people come to each other's aid. The Jews will view the Christians with love, and people will invite each other for meals, and will say: Our forefathers bequeathed to us falsehood, arousing hatred between us. And they will be careful not to speak deprecatingly of each other. Christian mothers will not teach their children to call out insults when a Jew passes by, and won't implant hatred in their hearts.

And then, we will attempt to remove the causes of the Jews' double poverty—material and intellectual. The reason for the material poverty is the interest that eats away at them: the law will now prohibit exacting an annual rate higher than 6% . . . ; loans will be for ten years with 10% of the principle to be repaid every year.[16]

Education in general knowledge as well as classical Jewish texts will be the key to "improving" the Jews and making them productive:

To eliminate the reasons for intellectual poverty . . . there will no longer be set over them leaders, teachers, and preachers who have no knowledge of books in German and Latin, and who have no understanding of astronomy, nature, etc. . . .

In every city they will appoint three educators, one responsible for each third of the [school] day. In the first third . . . the [Jewish] youth of the city will learn . . . Bible, Hebrew expression, penmanship, moral virtues and the laws of the religion; in the second, they will learn other languages; and in the third they will learn mathematics, surveying, geography, and astronomy, natural and experimental science, to instill wisdom in their souls and the love of God in their hearts.

And every day they will be granted an hour to stroll for refreshment. At the end of ten years, they will be examined by scholars, to determine each youth's aptitudes and achievements. Based on the results, the highest achievers will continue in higher academic study; next—those who will study the practical arts, all matter of works with wood, metal and stone; others will study commerce; and others agriculture; each according to his aptitude and inclination. And no man will be allowed to practice any trade or profession without a diploma certifying his training. This is to encourage the Jews to learn professions; and those who do will be exempt from the king's tax (the "Jew tax") and will even receive a medallion from the king.[17]

Satanow thus envisioned, in detail, a utopia based on the principles articulated in Mendelssohn's *Jerusalem*. In this utopia, a philosopher-king—an enlightened and humane absolute monarch situated in a Western European nation—sought to govern by the principles of rationalism and humanism. Satanow also expanded Mendelssohn's admonition to the Jews, "Adapt yourselves to the morals and the constitution of the land" into to a detailed program of education designed to "improve" the Jews. Overall, the *maskilim* shared a utopian vision that looked a lot like a contemporaneous European state, rebooted according to principles of rational government, civic equality, and freedom of conscience: a cosmopolitan society in the context of an absolutist national monarchy. Like other *maskilim*, Satanow held that recognition of the rule of reason would necessarily usher in an era of

Edenic happiness. His own "long, long ago" kingdom was neither a call for revolution nor a Cockaigne fantasy, but an ostensibly perfected version of the status quo, to be achieved not by radical upheaval but by spiritual awakening and education.

The Enlightenment utopia as envisioned by Satanow left to Zionism two important legacies: First, the cosmopolitan ideal of a state of all its citizens, as Herzl imagined it. (Ironically, while Herzl would later take up a number of ideas in *Matters of Dispute*—freedom of conscience, progressive education, mutual toleration, "improvement" of the Jews—he could not have read it. Satanow's Western European utopia was written in Hebrew and never translated, whereas Herzl's Palestinian utopia was written in German a century later.) Second, the idea that in order to achieve their aspiration—be it emancipation or national self-determination—the Jews needed to be improved. Herzl, Lewinsky, Jabotinsky, Lehmann, and Yavetz—like Satanow a century earlier—all held a negative stereotype of Old Jews as weak, narrow-minded, unproductive, alienated from nature, and rootless. All of them saw their utopian vision as dependent on an education that would eradicate this stereotype and make the Jews normal, whether by teaching them mathematics and languages or by training them to be farmers and soldiers. Zionist educational efforts as exemplified by Lehmann's youth village can thus be seen as natural descendants both of Satanow's educational vision and the various schools the *maskilim* established in nineteenth-century Europe to normalize the Jews by teaching them liberal arts and vocational skills along with traditional texts.

Like All the Nations

The eight years that Herzl was laying the groundwork for the Zionist movement, 1896–1904, fell right in the middle of the great wave of Jewish immigration to North America. While he was envisioning an enlightened, pluralistic, democratic, progressive Jewish state, my grandparents were en route—with hundreds of thousands of other Jews—to a place that claimed—and seemed—to embody all those qualities. Except, of course, it was not a Jewish state, but an ethnically and religiously pluralistic state that offered the Jews an otherwise utopian existence free of persecution, where their culture could flourish.

Within a few decades North America had become a major center of Jewish life, both numerically and culturally. And it was a commonplace that that flourishing was due to America's unique characteristics as an Enlightenment utopia—where (at least according to the mythology) individual talent and effort could overcome all the traditional barriers of race, religion, ethnicity, and class.

And so, when I chaperoned my eighth-grade Jewish day school students on the ritual annual trip to Washington, I was moved anew each year by the symbols of that utopia—the Capitol and the Supreme Court, the Lincoln Memorial and the National Archive, a meeting with our (Jewish) congressman. Like millions of other American Jews, I took for granted that Jewish well-being was supported by and congruent with the enlightened state—cosmopolitan, open, free, equal.

A century after Herzl, Jews around the world, including many Israelis, continue to hold that assumption of congruence. That is, there is a widespread belief that Jewish interests are indeed best served—and Jewish values implemented—in an open, democratic society; and so it follows that the Jewish state itself should be such a society. A state of all its citizens.

In such a state, of course, discrimination based on religion, ethnicity, gender, or other characteristics would be unacceptable. But this cosmopolitan utopian vision raises a number of difficult practical questions that do not have obvious answers. For example, must, and can, there be a full separation of religion and state in a Jewish state? Should minorities have group rights or only individual rights? What degree of minority cultural autonomy (if any) is acceptable? If Israel were to be modeled on Vienna—or the United States—what would remain Jewish about it? Would Israel still be a Jewish state if a Bedouin woman became prime minister? Is ethnic or religious segregation in housing or in education allowable? Can "separate but equal" be equal? What values should guide the immigration policy of the Jewish state?

Much of the political conflict in and around Israel appears to be rooted in the tension between particularistic (Torah, community, nation) utopias and this universalistic vision.

Further Reading

Avineri, Shlomo. *Theodor Herzl and the Foundation of the Jewish State*. Translated by Haim Watzman. London: Phoenix, 2014.

Feiner, Shmuel. *The Jewish Enlightenment*. Translated by Chaya Naor. Philadelphia: University of Pennsylvania Press, 2004.

Kymlicka, Will. *Multicultural Citizenship*. Oxford: Oxford University Press, 1995.

Litvak, Olga. *Haskalah: The Romantic Movement in Judaism*. New Brunswick NJ: Rutgers University Press, 2012.

Meyer, Michael. *The Origins of the Modern Jew: Jewish Identity and European Culture in Germany, 1749–1824*. Detroit MI: Wayne State University Press, 1967.

9

Promised Borders

When Abraham first encounters God, he is instructed to go "to the land that I will show you" (Gen. 12:1). That land—the land of promise, Canaan, the Land of Israel, the Holy Land—has been the constant focus of Jewish utopian dreams ever since. However, it is in the nature of utopia not to reveal its GPS coordinates. Thus, unsurprisingly, attempts to translate utopian maps into real borders have been fraught with controversy.

Locating the Land of Milk and Honey

When we made *aliyah* to a small, semirural community in the Galilee, I found myself surprised at my strong feelings of attachment to my new place. I had lived in culturally vibrant and naturally beautiful places in my life, and enjoyed them all. What was special here? Seeking to understand attachment to home and homeland, I encountered the writings of geographer Yi-Fu Tuan; for example: "This profound attachment to the homeland appears to be a worldwide phenomenon. It is not limited to any particular culture and economy. It is known to literate and nonliterate peoples, hunter-gatherers, and sedentary farmers, as well as city dwellers. The city or land is viewed as mother, and it nourishes; place is an archive of fond memories and splendid achievements that inspire the present; place is permanent and hence reassuring to man, who sees frailty in himself and chance and flux everywhere."[1]

And with respect to the Jews, in particular, Martin Buber links utopia with the land itself: "The prophet's spirit does not, like Plato's, believe that he possesses an abstract and general, a timeless concept of truth. . . . He does not confront man with a generally valid image of perfection, with . . . a utopia. Neither has he the choice between his native land and some other country which might be 'more suitable to him.' In his work of realization he is bound to the *topos*, to this place, to this people."[2]

It seems that from its earliest beginnings, Judaism's utopian dreams have been inseparably linked to a real place. In other words, the better place, for the Jews, has never been no-place; it has been some place particular. The Jews' vision of the perfected society was, from the very beginning, projected onto an identifiable piece of real estate—and this was so both before they entered the Promised Land and after they were exiled from it. Thus the question of the Zionist utopia's specific physical location has been fraught, from the bitter debate over Herzl's 1903 proposal to accept a "temporary refuge" in Uganda to the ongoing political divide over the wisdom and value of building Jewish settlements in territories conquered in 1967.

The preceding paragraph contains a glaring internal contradiction which, I believe, is the root of the strident polemic that characterizes much current discourse about Israel's borders: How can utopia be both no place and some place? Utopia is a vision meant to inspire action toward a better society. It is not a plot of land, with marked borders, to which one can purchase a ticket. So while the Jews always related their nostalgic and utopian dreams to the Land of Israel, and "Land of Israel" is ostensibly a geographical location, a close look at Jewish historical texts reveals a frustrating lack of clarity regarding exactly where the land begins and ends. In a sense, the *topos* itself turns out to be a utopian vision—not a map, but an expression of longing.

Perhaps this tension between some place and no place stems from the fact that while love of homeland is a universal phenomenon, the Jews' experience is unique. In general, nations are attached to the homelands in which they live, but the Jews have spent most of their history outside their homeland. Their love for it has been based on texts, on collective memory, not on lived experience. It has not been the day-to-day love of the peasant for his fields and woods, but a nostalgic longing for a distant landscape where life once was—and, yet again, someday, will be—good: "[A] good land, a land with streams and springs and fountains issuing from plain and hill; a land of wheat and barley, of vines, figs, and pomegranates, a land of olive trees and honey; a land where you may eat food without stint, where you will lack nothing; a land whose rocks are iron and from whose hills you can mine copper" (Deut. 8:7–9).

From the Psalmist to the medieval Hebrew poets to the modern romantic Zionists, the land itself stood for the longed-for utopia, a place of plenty, peace, and justice. Living in the land would restore and revitalize the Jewish people, as a nation and as a religion. But even though the Jews always knew where Israel was on the globe, it is telling that, other than specific place-references (mainly Jerusalem), the actual geography—and borders—were not part of their vision. The land was an abstract object of longing. A brief survey of historical geography can clarify this point.

Locating the Land with Maps

The discussion that follows is illustrated by a series of eight maps, consolidated for ease of comparison into three pages:

- Map 1, "Torah, Empire, and Rabbinic Borders," overlays maps that attempt to follow the Torah's border description in Numbers 34, the boundaries of Solomon's empire based on passages in Kings, and the Rabbis' description of the Holy Land, based on Midrash *Sifrei Devarim*.

- Map 2, "Zionist Proposal and Mandate Borders," compares the map of a Jewish National Home proposed by the Zionist delegation to the Versailles peace conference in 1919 with the border of Palestine according to the League of Nations Mandate to Great Britain (1923).

- Map 3, "Development of Borders 1947–67," compares the 1947 UN partition plan for Palestine, the 1949 armistice lines after Israel's war of independence, and the cease-fire lines after the 1967 war.

Torah Borders

The Torah contains many brief, general statements about the extent of the Promised Land, and one passage that seems to be a detailed description of its borders (Numbers 34).

General Statements about Borders

The general statements include the following:

Gen. 13:14–15: And the Lord said to Abram, after Lot had parted from him, "Raise your eyes and look out from where you are, to the north and south, to the east and west, for I give all the land that you see to you and your offspring forever."

Gen. 15:18–21: On that day the Lord made a covenant with Abram, saying, "To your offspring I assign this land, from the river of Egypt to the great river, the river Euphrates: the Kenites, the Kenizzites, the Kadmonites, the Hittites, the Perizzites, the Rephaim, the Amorites, the Canaanites, the Girgashites, and the Jebusites." (The "river of Egypt" is usually identified with Wadi el-Arish, in Sinai.)

Gen. 28:13–14: I am the Lord, the God of your father Abraham and the God of Isaac: the ground on which you are lying I will assign to you and to your offspring. Your descendants shall be as the dust of the earth; you shall spread out to the west and to the east, to the north and to the south.

Exod. 23:31: I will set your borders from the Sea of Reeds to the Sea of Philistia, and from the wilderness to the Euphrates.

Deut. 11:24: Every spot on which your foot treads shall be yours; your territory shall extend from the wilderness to the Lebanon and from the River—the Euphrates—to the Western Sea.

These promises strongly resemble texts found throughout the ancient Near East, in which emperors describe their domains as "stretching as far as you can see, from one end of the world to the other."[3] Indeed, a utopian understanding of such promises is reinforced by the fact that the Kadmonites and the Rephaim mentioned in Genesis 15:20 don't correspond to any known group, nation, or region. And, of course, there was never a time when the Israelites, as tribes or as an empire, achieved sovereignty over such a broad swath of the Middle East. The vagueness and expansiveness of these promissory statements, and their context of encouraging exhortations by God or Moses, suggest that they were not instructions for a cartographer, but rather a promise of space and sovereignty, a somewhat blurry image of an ideal future when the frontiers—and the enemies beyond them— would be safely far away.

Demarcation of Borders in Numbers 34

And what of the only detailed demarcation of the land in the Torah, in Numbers 34?

> Your southern sector shall extend from the wilderness of Zin alongside Edom. Your southern boundary shall start on the east from the tip of the Dead Sea. Your boundary shall then turn to pass south of the Ascent of Akrabbim and continue to Zin, and its limits shall be south of Kadesh-barnea, reaching Hazar-addar and continuing to Azmon. From Azmon the boundary shall turn toward the Wadi of Egypt and terminate at the Sea.
>
> For the western boundary you shall have the coast of the Great Sea; that shall serve as your western boundary.
>
> This shall be your northern boundary: draw a line from the Great Sea to Mount Hor; from Mount Hor draw a line to Lebo-hamath, and let the boundary reach Zedad. The boundary shall then run to Ziphron and terminate at Hazar-enan. This shall be your northern boundary.

For your eastern boundary you shall draw a line from Hazar-enan to Shepham. From Shepham the boundary shall descend to Riblah on the east side of Ain; from there the boundary shall continue downward and abut on the eastern slopes east of the Sea of Chinnereth. The boundary shall then descend along the Jordan and terminate at the Dead Sea. This shall be your land as defined by its boundaries on all sides. (Num. 34:3–12)

In this text, we seem to have a proper verbal map—actual instructions for a cartographer. Indeed, while many landmarks are uncertain, from the Middle Ages onward, a variety of maps based on this passage have been proposed. A modern consensus version appears in map 1.

It is important to keep in mind that of almost five hundred place names appearing in the Bible, nearly half remain without a confirmed modern geographic location, so all biblical maps are conjectural.[4] Regarding the Numbers 34 map, Nili Wazana, a leading scholar of biblical borders, offers this summary of the research: "Since the border delineations do not fully correspond with the Israelite settlement of any historical period, many scholars consider the description to represent an imagined territorial notion—a utopian ideal that was never realized. . . . Others think it reflects known borders, like David's kingdom, or . . . the Egyptian province of Canaan."[5]

In other words, even this detailed border description does not enable us to draw a clear map of a known geographical entity corresponding to the "Land of Canaan" or the "Land of Israel," defining the actual Israelite homeland in its entirety.

Two Prophetic Maps

Border descriptions of the Promised Land also appear in two prophetic books: Joshua and Ezekiel.

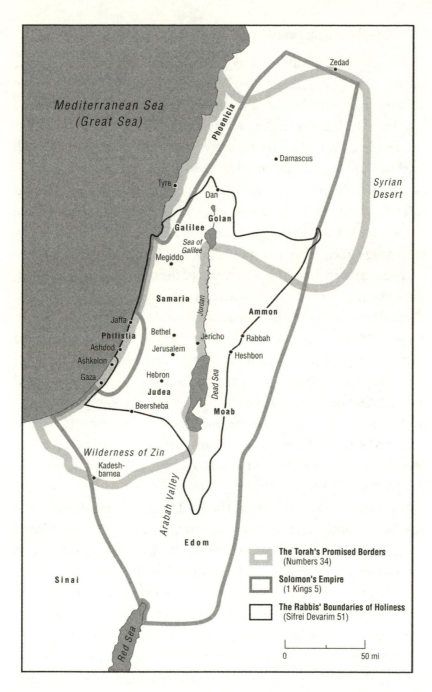

1. Torah, Empire, and Rabbinic Borders. Map by Erin Greb Cartography.

The book of Joshua summarizes Joshua's achievements in a series of battles with Canaanite nations: "Thus Joshua conquered the whole country, just as the Lord had promised Moses; and Joshua assigned it to Israel to share according to their tribal divisions. And the land had rest from war" (Josh. 11:23). However, a little further on we read: "Joshua was now old, advanced in years. The Lord said to him, 'You have grown old, you are advanced in years, and very much of the land still remains to be taken possession of. . . . I Myself will dispossess those nations for the Israelites; you have only to apportion their lands by lot among Israel, as I have commanded you'" (Josh. 13:1,6). Chapters 14–17 describe in detail the allotments of the tribes Judah, Manasseh, and Ephraim; however, in each case, the text points out that not all the allotted territory was actually conquered (15:63; 16:10; 17:12). Then, in chapter 18, Joshua chastises the remaining tribes, "How long will you be slack about going and taking possession of the land" (18:3), and sends out surveyors to divide the land into portions that are then distributed by lot. These descriptions are less detailed than those given for the first three tribes. And, apparently, they too were more ideal than real as, in his farewell address, Joshua states that the tribal allotments still contain unconquered territory—unfinished business that God will complete if they remain faithful (23:4–16).

We learn of the tribes' life in the land after Joshua's death in the next biblical book, Judges. After summarizing all the above-mentioned failures of conquest, the remainder of the book comprises a collection of narratives of skirmishes and battles, as the tribes attempt to take and hold their allotted territories. These conflicts continued later, even under the monarchy (e.g., 1 Sam. 31; 2 Sam. 12:15–22). Wazana summarizes the overall biblical picture of the conquest: "The picture arising from the Scriptures as a whole is that the kingdoms of Judah and Israel never fully controlled the territory known as 'the land of Canaan.' Philistia stretched along the southwestern coast, the Sidonians ruled over the northern coastal cities and the Lebanon, and even in the heart of the country, other peoples resided."[6]

Moreover, the Joshua description contains a number of confusing inconsistencies. For example, the description of the border between the northern tribe of Naphtali and the southern tribe of Judah (in 19:34) is quite a geographical contortion. In addition, one town, Aroer, is mentioned twice, in different tribes' allotments (13:15–16 and 13:24–25); and the story of the tribe of Dan's relocation to the north (in 19:40–45) does not specify its new location. Thus, with Joshua's "map," as with that in Numbers, we seem to have, in Wazana's words, "not . . . evidence of a real-life source but . . . instead a literary and ideological composition intended to identify the allotment promised by God to the Israelites as part of their covenant relationship."[7]

Borders in the Book of Ezekiel

The utopian character of Ezekiel's map is even more pronounced. The prophet makes no attempt to describe a realistic map, but rather sets forth a schematic future division of the land into equal horizontal strips, one for each tribe (Ezek. 48).

Ezekiel lived in Babylonia after the exile of 568 BCE. The conclusion of his collection of prophecies, chapters 40–48, comprises an elaborate vision of the future restored kingdom, its capital and cult:

> He brought me, in visions of God, to the Land of Israel, and He set me down on a very high mountain on which there seemed to be the outline of a city on the south. He brought me over to it, and there, standing at the gate, was a man who shone like copper. In his hand were a cord of linen and a measuring rod. The man spoke to me: "Mortal, look closely and listen attentively and note well everything I am going to show you—for you have been brought here in order to be shown—and report everything you see to the House of Israel." (Ezek. 40:2–4)

Chapters 40–46 narrate a comprehensive tour of the future Temple, complete with detailed measurements and instructions for the priests' service there. Then, in 47:13–15: "Thus said the Lord God: These shall be the boundaries of the land that you shall allot to the twelve tribes of Israel. Joseph shall receive two portions, and you shall share the rest equally. As I swore to give it to your fathers, so shall this land fall to you as your heritage. These are the boundaries of the land."

Following a brief survey of the perimeter of the land, following the lines of Numbers 34, chapter 48 continues: "These are the names of the tribes: At the northern end, along the Hethlon road [from] Lebo-hamath to Hazar-enan—which is the border of Damascus, with Hamath to the north—from the eastern border to the Sea: Dan—one [tribe]. Adjoining the territory of Dan, from the eastern border to the western border: Asher—one. Adjoining the territory of Asher, from the eastern border to the western border: Naphtali—one" (Ezek. 48:1–3). And the list continues, giving each tribe a strip from east to west, with the Temple compound and surrounding territory creating a break between the northern tribes (Dan, Asher, Naphtali, Manasseh, Ephraim, Reuben, and Judah) and the southern sector (Benjamin, Simeon, Issachar, Zebulun, and Gad). The description of the Temple compound and its surroundings, allotted to priests and Levites (48:8–22), is like the tribal territories: highly schematic, with different sectors laid out in rectangular blocks of ten thousand by twenty-five thousand cubits.

All in all, Ezekiel's "map" seems unrelated to any geographical reality. It is, rather, a vision of a utopian polity in which every tribe will receive an equal share of the land.

Biblical descriptions of the borders of the Land of Israel thus support the more general view of the Torah as a largely utopian document imagining an ideal future in the land. Inasmuch as the map in Numbers 34 differs from those set out in Joshua 13–19 and Ezekiel 47–48, and inasmuch as all three boundary descriptions do not purport to describe reality on the ground, we might view them rather as future maps, the limits of what the people can expect to attain once the present travails (desert wandering, wars of conquest, exile, respectively) are over.

Borders at the Height of Empire

The boundaries of the Israelite empire at its greatest extent, under King Solomon, are described in a typically vague and expansive passage in 1 Kings (5:4–5):

> For [Solomon] controlled the whole region west of the Euphrates—all the kings west of the Euphrates, from Tiphsah to Gaza—and he had peace on all his borders roundabout. All the days of Solomon, Judah and Israel from Dan to Beer-sheba dwelt in safety, everyone under his own vine and under his own fig tree.

Note that this description includes both Israel's territory ("from Dan to Beer-sheba") and that of other kingdoms that had become vassals to the Israelite ruler (Moab, Ammon, Edom, Aram) through conquest or diplomacy. The delineation of Solomon's empire in map 1 is based on the above text and other passages (e.g., 2 Sam. 8) mentioning kingdoms defeated by David and Solomon.

Beyond this, the Bible does not provide a verbal map of the empire's actual borders. Archaeologists continue to debate the extent of the Israelite empire—some arguing that the biblical account is largely accurate, while others insist it is an idealized picture with no basis in reality.[8] The evidence we have tends to be ambiguous. If we take the biblical description at its face value, as an accurate guide for drawing a real map, then it clearly includes territories not included in the borders described for Canaan in Numbers 34. Not all of this broad area would qualify as "the Land of Israel," as much of it comprised vassal kingdoms temporarily subject to rule by Israel but never assimilating politically or culturally. So the description in 1 Kings 5 might simply be a schematic vision, "a great empire, stretching from north to south and east to west." Or it might describe the actual territories under some form of control by David and Solomon at the peak of Israelite power: a multicultural empire. Alternatively, Wazana suggests that this description might depict the borders of the Persian province of Eber-hanahar, reflecting the reality known by the biblical author in the fifth century BCE.[9]

Nine centuries after Solomon, the Hasmonean king Alexander Yannai engaged in campaigns of conquest throughout his reign (104–78 BCE). By its conclusion, he had expanded his empire to include much of the territory ascribed by the Bible to David's rule (excluding the desert stretching from the Dead Sea to the Red Sea). Yet, like the earlier moment of empire, Yannai's conquests were unstable. Only fifteen years after his death his kingdom was wracked by civil war, which led in turn to a Roman takeover.

The Rabbis' Map

Through the first five centuries CE, in the absence of Jewish sovereignty, the Rabbis of the Mishnah and Talmud were concerned with implementing the laws of the Torah wherever the people lived. Many laws were interpreted as binding without reference to location; for example, the dietary, Sabbath, and tort laws, for which extensive interpretative legal structures were erected, were deemed applicable anywhere in the world. Other laws, such as those governing the priestly service and the Temple sacrifices, or criminal punishments such as flogging or execution, were relegated to the messianic future, when the nation would have sovereignty, with a king, a Temple cult, and an army. For these, the rabbinic discussions were more theoretical, since no actual practical questions or cases could be considered. A third category comprised laws that were land-based but not sovereignty-based: that is, agricultural laws, applicable only in the Land of Israel, without regard to the political status of Jewish life there. For this third category, which included the sabbatical laws , it was important to establish just where the borders were, so that people would know, for example, where they were obligated to refrain from farming in the seventh year, and from which areas they could purchase produce.

For this purpose, the Rabbis did not use the biblical map of Canaan or one based on Joshua's conquests or Solomon's empire, but the area settled by the returnees from Babylonian exile under the Persians (sixth to fifth centuries BCE). And yet the biblical books of Ezra and Nehemiah, the main sources for this period, only contain a list of towns where the returnees settled (Neh. 11:25–36)—no guidelines for a map. One rabbinic text (Midrash *Sifrei Devarim* 51 and parallels) does map borders for this region, likely based on the reality of Jewish settlement in the Rabbis' own time (although a basis in oral traditions is also possible). While this midrashic text includes many place names whose meaning has been lost, it has been used to draw a map, shown as "rabbinical borders" on map 1.

Note that the eastern and southern boundaries are vague, with few landmarks, while the northwestern border is extremely detailed. It seems the Rabbis were most concerned about specifying the border that passed between areas of denser Jewish population and a periphery where the population was sparse. Apparently they sought to exempt those who resided in the periphery from the economic burdens of the sabbatical observance by excluding them from the halakhic boundaries of the land.[10] Thus Jews living within the borders would be able to purchase sabbatical produce from their coreligionists living just on the other side—a boon to both.

Of course, the Rabbis were well aware of the biblical promises and descriptions. However, they were also concerned with defining boundaries in which the people could live and sustain themselves in real time. It seems that they made a distinction between ideal, divinely delineated, utopian borders and practical borders for their here and now.

Throughout the Middle Ages, Jews lived with these diverse and not congruent images of the Land of Israel:

- The boundaries of promise and of the empire—from Sinai to the Euphrates, from the desert to Lebanon

- The boundaries of Canaan, either promised or actually conquered
- The boundaries of holiness, according to *halakhah*

They recounted the boundaries of promise in the weekly Torah reading; they prayed three times daily for the restoration of David's monarchy; and when they studied the Talmud and its commentaries they pondered the halakhic map's details and implications. Thus, for medieval Jews, the Land of Israel was not a clearly defined geographical entity with coordinates that could be used to draw a map. Rather, it was—in any of its manifestations—an ideal, an object of desire, a holy place whose relevance in their lives was rooted either in the historical past or in the utopian future.

Defining Palestine

Perhaps the ancient Israelites' most tenacious enemies were the Philistines who occupied the southern coastal strip. Herodotus used the term Palestina (the Latin transcription of Philistia) in the fifth century BCE to refer to the entire region from the coast to Syria.[11] In the second century CE, at the time of the Jewish revolt against the Romans (the Bar Kokhba revolt), the Roman emperor, Hadrian, took steps to wipe out Jewish national identity, renaming Jerusalem Aelia Capitolina; Judea became Syria-Palestina.[12] By the Byzantine period, the province Palestina encompassed the coastal plain and central highlands, the Golan Heights and Galilee, much of today's Transjordan, the Negev desert, and part of Sinai. Under the Muslims, "Falastin" came to refer to the region west of the Jordan. Then, with the Crusades, the name fell into disuse. Under the Ottomans, from the sixteenth century, the area was divided into several districts, ruled from Beirut, Jerusalem, and Damascus. Only as a result of British activity in the region did a geographic entity called Palestine come to be demarcated, in a process that began during the British occupation of Egypt in the nineteenth century and ended with the designation of the British Mandate for Palestine after World War I.[13]

Significantly, when the British Balfour Declaration of 1917 supported "the establishment in Palestine of a national home for the Jewish people," it did so without specifying boundaries; indeed, there was no such entity as Palestine at that time.

At the Versailles peace conference in 1919, the Zionists were invited to submit a proposal for their desired national home. Their discussions of what to request centered not on biblical promises or memories, but on questions of economic viability: arable land and absorption of large numbers of immigrants. Sure enough, the map they ultimately presented, shown on map 2, was based not on biblical or traditional borders but on natural features and existing colonial-power agreements.

The Zionists viewed this proposal as maximalist but realistic. Negotiations regarding the disposition of former Ottoman territories continued through 1920–22. The British had the advantage of troops on the ground—and they were motivated by their historic support for the Zionist idea (which had given rise to the Balfour Declaration) as well as their strategic interests in protecting both the Suez Canal and a land bridge to India. However, the French and Arab rulers also put forward claims in the region. In the course of the process, the British set the border of the Mandate at the Jordan River, defining the territory eastward, to the Iraqi border, as an autonomous emirate, Transjordan. Thus ultimately the Mandate's borders were set mainly by Britain's needs, not by the Zionists' dreams.[14] The Mandate's borders, confirmed by the League of Nations in 1923, are also shown in map 2.

The Ongoing Debate over Partition, from 1937 to the Present

As the Jews took advantage of British rule—and of British assistance in developing and modernizing the land—their population grew and they established the institutions of a state-in-the-making. Meanwhile, even as the local Arab population benefited materially from this development, the Arabs saw it as a colonialist project that trampled upon their

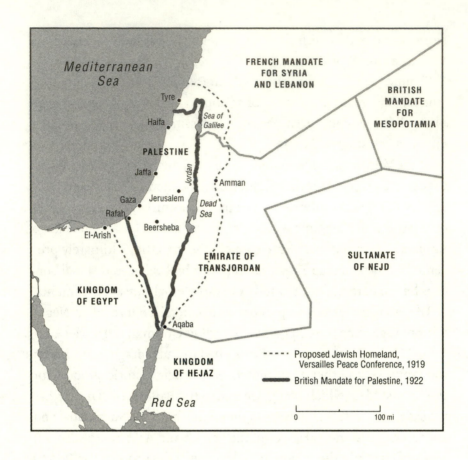

2. Zionist Proposal and Mandate Borders. Map by Erin Greb Cartography.

own nationalist aspirations. In response to an armed Arab uprising beginning in 1936, the British sent a commission of inquiry, the Peel Commission, which concluded in 1937 that the aspirations of these two nations could not possibly be fulfilled in one state. Partition into two separate polities was proposed.

The Arabs rejected partition as just another manifestation of colonialist intervention. The Jews were divided in their response, and the debate at the Twentieth Zionist Congress, in 1938, was long and anguished. The opposition's arguments included practical considerations (e.g., the land the Peel Commission had allocated for the Jewish state was only 20 percent of the Mandate territory—and this after the Jewish request for land east of the Jordan had been denied in 1923), but the most vocal and intransigent opponents argued from a religious perspective. For example, the leaders of the Orthodox Zionist party proclaimed: "The people of Israel did not surrender its right to the land of its fathers during thousands of years of exile, and will not now concede even one inch of the Land of Israel. We staunchly declare the eternal, complete and full right of the nation to its homeland within its historic boundaries, and absolutely reject any attempt to agree to the partition of Eretz Israel or to other proposals assaulting our rights."[15]

By contrast, proponents of Peel argued that what was essential was convincing the great powers to support Jewish sovereignty somewhere within the Land of Israel; once sovereignty was attained, borders could always be adjusted. In the end, the Zionist Congress voted (299–160) to accept partition in principle but to reject the proposed borders, opening the way to further negotiation. However, the British did not pursue partition, and tensions (and violence) continued until Britain handed the Mandate back to the United Nations, which voted in 1947 to partition Palestine into two states, with borders somewhat more favorable to the Jews than those offered in the Peel proposal (map 3).

The Arabs refused to accept the UN decision. From its passage in November 1947, local militias, reinforced by militias and state armies from Egypt, Lebanon, Syria, Jordan, and Iraq, fought the Jewish self-defense forces (and after Israel's 1948 declaration of statehood the

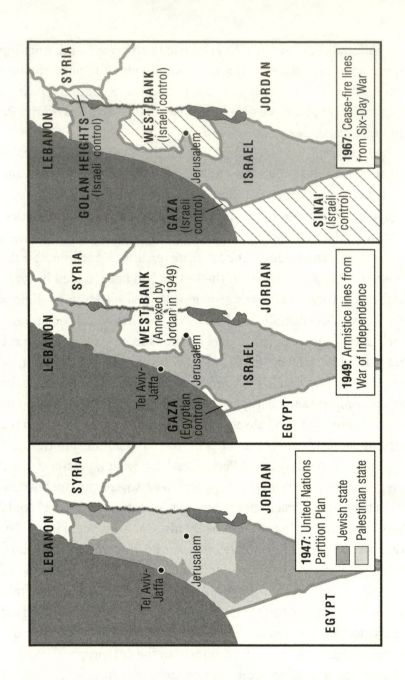

3. Development of Borders 1947–67. Map by Erin Greb Cartography.

army of Israel) for two years. When hostilities ceased with armistice agreements in mid-1949, Israel had pushed the borders out somewhat beyond the UN map; the armistice lines became the de facto borders of the new state (map 3). No Palestinian state was established; Jordan annexed the West Bank, and Egypt the Gaza strip. In signing these armistice agreements, the Jews formally accepted the concept of partition. However, religious, ideological, and practical opposition continued in Israeli political discourse—until the present.

In the 1960s, an ongoing dispute between Israel and Syria over water rights led Egypt to support Syria with belligerent acts of its own. When Egypt closed the Straits of Tiran (which gave access to Eilat) to Israeli shipping in 1967, Israel responded with a preemptive attack, and in short order wrested control of the Golan Heights from Syria, the West Bank from Jordan, and Sinai from Egypt (map 3).

Sinai was returned to Egypt in 1982, in the context of a peace treaty. Meanwhile, Israel's conquest of the West Bank brought back to life the religious, nationalistic, and practical opposition to partition—while providing a new focus for Palestinian nationalism. Over the years, Israel's long-term policy regarding the border has remained unclear. Antipartition activists have created facts on the ground with the establishment of Jewish communities in the West Bank, often initially in defiance of government policy, but then, ultimately, with government acquiescence and even support. The 2005 government decision to withdraw unilaterally from the Gaza strip and evacuate all Israeli settlements there led to a bitter and strident public controversy.

Mapping Utopia

Perhaps the most pervasive and divisive political conflict in Israel today is the question of the state's borders. While several areas are disputed, the key ideological conflict is over the status of the central highlands, referred to as the West Bank (of the Jordan) or, biblically, as Judea and Samaria.

Interestingly and ironically, the one area included in *all* ancient maps or descriptions of the Land of Israel is that of Judea and Samaria. By contrast, in ancient times the coastal plain and desert areas were most often outside the borders of the Israelite or Jewish polity. Yet from the 1937 Peel partition plan onward, the central highlands were considered the basis of a Palestinian state, while the coastal plain (ancient Philistia or Palestina) and the desert were assigned to the Jews.

Nowadays, debate rages in Israel. Should the central highlands region, ruled by Jordan from 1948 until Israel conquered it in 1967, become part of the state? Should it become all or part of a Palestinian state? Is there a third option?

This is not a new debate. It first arose in 1937 when the British proposed partitioning Palestine west of the Jordan, continued until the UN affirmed partition in 1947, simmered from independence until 1967, and since then has assumed a central and divisive role in Israeli political discourse, essentially redefining the political left and right. If these terms once referred to the spectrum between socialism and liberal nationalism, they have come to be identified with supporting or opposing, respectively, withdrawal from the West Bank. And these two poles have taken on a larger cultural meaning. Those who support holding the West Bank often cast their position as a reflection of strong Jewish national identity or religious faith, and depict the opposition as secular and cosmopolitan.[16] For their part, defenders of partition claim the virtues of rationalism, realism, and social justice, projecting a vision of Israel as a normal member (in the Enlightenment sense) of the family of nations.

The actual political and religious map is of course considerably more complex. The debate comprises claims and counterclaims in the areas of military strategy, demography, economics, culture, and history. However, what makes it particularly discordant and intractable is the entanglement of all these concerns with a spiritual dimension that straddles the line between religious faith and romantic nationalism. Put simply: many Jews believe that the Jewish people's connection to the Land of Israel is divinely ordained, mystical, undebatable—in which case all of the above considerations may be interesting, but they are trivial. While it is possible to engage in rational debate over whether the partition of Palestine is strategically advisable or demographically problematic, if the bottom line is a divine imperative the violation of which would be a sin, then pragmatic considerations are beside the point.

Moreover, as we've seen, there is no one image of the Promised Land's boundaries; there is a plethora. In ancient times there are those delineated in the Torah, Joshua, Kings, Ezekiel, and rabbinic midrash. In our own time, borders have been proposed based on these ancient sources as well as on absorptive capacity, natural features, defensibility, great power interests, international agreement, and conquest. And even if one of these images were to be agreed upon as utopian, and if that image could somehow be translated into reality "on the ground" in the form of state sovereignty over a clearly demarcated territory, that image still runs afoul of the utopian dilemma: It is impossible to convert, by force, an ideal no-place into a real someplace.

And furthermore, while a utopian or nostalgic geography may resonate with the utopia of a national home, it seems to be dissonant with other utopian visions, such as that of the normal state discussed in chapter 8 and the just society, our next topic.

Further Reading

Galnoor, Itzhak. *The Partition of Palestine: Decision Crossroads in the Zionist Movement*. Albany NY: SUNY Press, 1995.

Rainey, Anson R., and R. Steven Notley. *The Sacred Bridge: Carta's Atlas of the Biblical World*. Jerusalem: Carta, 2006.

Wazana, Nili. *All the Boundaries of the Land: The Promised Land in Biblical Thought in Light of the Ancient Near East*. Winona Lake IN: Eisenbrauns, 2013.

10

A Model of Social Justice

Both the biblical prophets and modern socialist Zionists envisioned the renewed Jewish state as a paragon among the nations, a model of social justice. However, socialist, religious, and national utopias turn out to be difficult, if not impossible, to harmonize.

Jews and Socialism

At a dinner with wealthy donors in an American suburb early in the second decade of this century, the conversation turned to the health care debate—and I launched into a paean for the Israeli system. In Israel, every citizen can choose among several national HMOs whose premiums are all paid out of a modest (4 percent) payroll tax. I went on about the feeling of security and peace of mind engendered by the ready availability of quality medical care with no limits, deductibles, or reimbursement claims. The response was a litany of horror stories about Israeli friends of cousins or cousins of friends who almost died while waiting in line for treatment in the Israeli health care system. And I realized that one person's utopia is another's dystopia. It turns out that there is no consensus regarding the utopian vision of the socioeconomic structure of the Jewish state—and even if there were, it is hard to live in the gap between utopian vision and practical reality.

Zionism and socialism can be seen to have been "joined from birth," but through the years they have had a fraught relationship. Some important Zionist leaders and movements saw the two as integrated and inseparable, while others adamantly viewed them as polar opposites. For much of the prestate period and the first three decades of statehood, socialist Zionist parties dominated political life in the *Yishuv* and the state, yet the social and economic implications of that domination were complicated (as we shall see). And even though today these parties have almost completely disappeared from the political map in Israel, their utopian vision of a Jewish state that would be a model of social justice—a vision with deep roots in the Jewish prophetic tradition—still influences perceptions and policies.

Socialism is not a single, clearly defined worldview or socioeconomic system. Rather, it developed along several different and often conflicting lines over the past two centuries. Beyond the general and vague common denominator of some degree of collective ownership and communal control of the means of production, socialist visions have differed along several axes delineated by the following polar pairs:

From...	To...
Collective entities (e.g., cooperatives, communes) in a free market economy	Total abolition of private property
Anarchy, or local control (community)	Centralized state control
Evolution	Revolution
Utopia	Apocalypse
Nationalism	Cosmopolitanism

The cluster of positions on the right side of this table is generally associated with the socialism advocated by Karl Marx and his disciples. Inexorable material processes are carrying us forward toward a revolutionary, cataclysmic restructuring of society and the economy; national and religious distinctions will fall away along with social class; all persons shall be equal; all property shall belong to all; and rational, scientific planning and management will assure plenty and happiness. Efforts to imagine the details of the end result, to build small-scale models, or to progress incrementally are counterproductive, distracting from and delaying the revolutionary process. Marx, like the biblical Daniel, was not interested in the vision of the ideal, but in deciphering and facilitating the process leading to the overthrow of history.

The other side of this spectrum has encompassed a variety of different thinkers and movements, including Lewinsky and Herzl, with their visions of free-market economies ameliorated by cooperative associations, nationalized major resources, and a social safety-net; various Western European social democratic parties; the labor union movement in the West; the utopian communitarians, from Fourier to the Russian Narodniks who idealized and idolized the traditional village commune; and the kibbutzniks.[1]

Since socialism in all its expressions, like the Enlightenment, challenged the old order of social class, hereditary, and clerical hierarchies, it tended to attract Jews, for the Jews had learned that their interests seemed never to be served by that order. This was true in western Europe, where Jews were disproportionately involved in the revolutions of 1848, and it was true on a massive scale in Russia late in the century, where the oppression of the Jews by the old regime was such that it was hard to imagine a livable future except through emigration or revolution.

And as we saw with the Enlightenment, so too with socialism did cosmopolitanism pose a central challenge to the Jews hoping to benefit from the promise of liberation. Could one be a loyal Jew and a Marxist? If religion and nationality were vestiges of the old order, must the Jews relinquish theirs in the interest of class solidarity? In Russia in the 1880s and 1890s these were not academic questions, but matters of agonizing personal struggle that tore apart friendships and families, stimulated endless hours of discussion, and gave rise to a number of different courses of action. Some Jews rejected socialism and any revolutionary activism, assuming that the Jews, with God's help, would survive this persecution, like all those that came before, by maintaining their communities and commitments. Others turned their backs on those communities and commitments, seeking to shed their Jewish identity and become at one with the Russian (or the universal) proletariat. And in between were those who insisted on somehow maintaining loyalty to both masters: their Jewish roots and their commitment to a different, better future. In this last category, two directions dominated: the Yiddishist socialist Bund and the attempt to synthesize socialism with Zionism.[2]

The Bund, founded in Vilna in 1897 to agitate among the Jewish workers for action contributing to a general revolution, grew rapidly, reaching thirty thousand members by 1905 (when Lenin's Bolshevik party had only eight thousand).[3] The Bund rejected religion, and opposed the idea of a Jewish national state. It saw its specific focus on the education—and welfare—of the Jewish worker, in Yiddish, as instrumental and temporary: a localized part of the larger struggle for a new Russia and a new world. As the Russian socialist parties repeatedly humiliated the Bund, rejecting its attempts to forge a relationship of autonomy or federation even as other nationalities (e.g., Ukrainian, Polish, Georgian) were granted such privileges, cosmopolitanism receded ever further into the ideal future, and the Bund functioned as a proud force for Jewish welfare, self-defense, and culture. However, even though the Bund found itself defending the preservation of Jewish national culture, parallel to other national cultures, it never accepted the idea of a Jewish state.

Romantic Socialist Zionism: Moses Hess

Moses Hess (1812–75) is generally described as a proto-Zionist, one of a few European Jewish thinkers who proposed Jewish national restoration in the Land of Israel before *Chovevei Tzion* and before Herzl. However, he was more than that. It was Hess who articulated the idea that the restored Jewish state must be a "light unto the nations," a model of an ideal society—a socialist utopia.

Hess grew up in an Orthodox environment in Germany. Attending Bonn University, he was exposed to the romanticism then popular among his generation—and discovered socialism. He was a studious,

and by all accounts saintly, type who lived his life in poverty, supporting himself with various part-time and temporary writing and edit-
ing jobs. He wandered about Europe, finally settling in Paris in 1854.
At first, his conversion to socialism led him to distance himself from
his Jewishness; he came to see Judaism as obsolete. However, as he
observed midcentury developments around him in Europe (antisemitism, failed revolutions, the Italian national awakening) and developments in socialist thought (he worked for a time with Ferdinand
Lasalle, a socialist leader who advocated progressive change, not apocalyptic upheaval), he reconsidered, and sought to articulate a position
synthesizing socialism and Judaism. For a time a member of Marx's
inner circle, apparently helping him write the *Communist Manifesto*
(he would later be labeled the first German communist), ultimately
by midcentury he broke with Marx, espousing a very different view
of socialism — combined with Jewish national identity.[4]

In his magnum opus, *Rome and Jerusalem* (1862), Hess weaves
together (not always coherently) several key concepts.

One is a utopian faith in the possibility of a just, socialist society
achieved by human efforts toward self-perfection:

> But when the perfected organism of the historical races reaches
> its final stage of development, the various strivings of history will
> also reach their ultimate harmony in a perfected human soci-
> ety. Just as only after the completion of the organic life-sphere,
> namely, after the creation of man, the Sabbath of Nature began,
> so will the historical Sabbath begin only after the completion of
> the development of social life, after the creation of a harmonious
> social organization in which production and consumption will be
> in a state of equilibrium. We stand at present on the eve of the
> historical Sabbath.[5]

Just as the biblical utopia — the Sabbath — could only come into being
once the world was completed through the creation of humanity (on
the sixth day), so too the "historical Sabbath" — the redemption of

humankind—can only come into being once the economic order has been completed and perfected, through socialism.

Hess also espouses a romantic belief in the sanctity and eternity of nations: "In theoretical anti-national humanitarianism I can only see, mildly speaking, an idealistic dream, but not a semblance of reality. . . . Just as Nature does not produce flowers and fruits of a general character, nor general plants and animals, but produces particular plant and animal types, so does the creative power in history produce only folk types."[6] In these words Hess rejects Marx's cosmopolitanism, arguing that just as there is no such thing as an absolute, undifferentiated flower—every flower is of a particular genus and species—so too with persons: there can be no "general human," as every person must belong to a particular folk (nation). As such, nations are not just a by-product—or tool—of capitalist oppression, but a healthy, natural phenomenon.

Furthermore, Hess proclaims that Judaism represents a unique synthesis of nationality with religion—a religion with a moral mission: "Fortified by its racial instinct and by its cultural and historical mission to unite all humanity in the name of the Eternal Creator, this people has conserved its nationality, in the form of its religion, and united both inseparably with the memories of its ancestral land."[7] This sentence represents a remarkable synthesis of romantic nationalism, the Jewish concept of covenant, and messianism. Hess is saying that the Jews constitute a nation ("race") that is bound to a set of moral values, a physical homeland, and a vision of a perfect world.

Alas, in his view, the Jews' historical experience of dispersal and oppression has torn this synthesis apart, and given rise to partial, distorted, and unsustainable expressions of Judaism. In particular, he rejects Reform Judaism for its distancing itself from Jewish nationalism, and Orthodoxy for its rigidity and fanaticism. He calls for the rejuvenation of the Jewish nationality and religion by colonizing Palestine. Creating a natural Jewish nation-state will then restore the Jews to their original status as not only equals among the nations, but as leaders in the struggle for a perfect society. Thus the establishment of the Jewish state will be a vital step in bringing the whole world closer to (socialist) perfection:

> The day on which the Jewish tribes return to their fatherland will be epoch-making in the history of humanity. Oh, how will the East tremble at your coming! How quickly, under the influence of labor and industry, will the enervation of the people vanish, in the land where voluptuousness, idleness and robbery have held sway for thousands of years. You will become the moral stay of the East. . . . You are the triumphal arch of the future histori-cal epoch, under which the great covenant of humanity will be written and sealed in your presence as the witnesses of the past and future. The Biblical traditions which you will revive will also sanctify anew our Occidental society and destroy the weed of materialism together with its roots.[8]

Hess envisions an ideal future in which the socialist Jewish polity will serve as a beacon, a model, a teacher for all humankind. Together, he affirms, utopian socialism, romantic nationalism, and Jewish messianism will usher in the redemption.

Not Utopia, but Apocalypse

Remembering the Russian revolution, David Ben-Gurion said in 1928: "Many among us trembled for the fate of the daring experiment being undertaken in Russia, out of inner sympathy for that apocalyptic impatience which characterized the Communist Party. [We understood why] they refused to wait for stychic processes to take their due course and wished in one massive surge of willpower to storm ahead, to bring redemption closer, for we, too, are redemption-seekers who refuse to wait."[9] Ben Gurion's "apocalyptic impatience" expressed a Marxist version of socialist Zionism best articulated by Ber Borochov (1881–1917), a *Chovev Tzion* who spent much of his short life developing a theory synthesizing Zionism and socialism. Borochov argued that on account of antisemitism and the Jews' anomalous economic position (paupers, not proletarians), ultimately both the Jewish bourgeois and the masses would have no choice but to emigrate to Palestine. There, the capitalists would build factories, the masses would become an industrial proletariat, and the inevitable class struggle would ensue, leading to revolution. In other words, the Zionist component of his vision was not an ideal of return, or a restoration of Jewish independence and pride, but rather just a particular subset—driven by Jewish suffering—of the general processes churning toward revolution. He termed these processes "stychic" (from the Greek root *styche*, meaning fate). But if the revolution is an apocalyptic process—fated to occur—then what role do human choices play? "What role can our will, our consciousness, play in the historical processes of Jewish life? Organization, planning. . . . To regulate historical processes . . . to facilitate and accelerate their progress, to conserve social energy, and to obtain the optimum results from the labor put forth."[10]

In a classic apocalyptic approach, Borochov argues that the emigration to Palestine and the socialist revolution there are coming, willy-nilly, but nonetheless the Jews are obligated to "facilitate and accelerate" the process. Just what the "optimum results" will be, however, he doesn't say.

Borochov's "inevitable" outcomes did not occur. Most Russian Jews emigrated to America, not Palestine, and those who did go to Palestine did not rise to fulfill his prediction of a Marxist class struggle. For the most part, socialism found expression in utopian agricultural communities. In the cities and in the society of Palestine as a whole, the nationalist agenda anesthetized the class struggle.[11]

Nonetheless, Borochov's analysis found an echo in Zionist political life. Among his most noteworthy disciples was David Ben-Gurion, who saw the Russian revolution as a harbinger of things to come, admired Lenin, and sought to model institutions in the Jewish state-in-the-making after the Soviet example.

However, as committed as Borochov and his followers were to Marxism, their "delayed cosmopolitanism" seems disingenuous in retrospect. They did not *really mean* that they dreamt of the disappearance of Jewish identity in the future; they were too warmly attached to their own identity to believably make such an argument. They took from Marx his apocalyptic view of revolutionary change, but related to his cosmopolitan vision as a utopian ideal: "some day, if only."

Hess's Legacy: Nachman Syrkin's Socialist Zionist State

At the turn of the century, Nachman Syrkin (1867–1924) would translate Hess's vague vision of a socialist Jewish state into a detailed utopian plan. Like Borochov, Syrkin came from an Orthodox family in Russia. He rebelled already in high school, attending a secular school from which he was soon expelled. Making his way to the Belarusian city of Minsk (a pluralistic hotbed of Jewish culture and political activism), he became involved both in *Chovevei Tzion* and underground socialist activities. He exhibited intense, ascetic studiousness and great erudition. From 1888 to 1903 he studied at the University of Berlin, writing two doctorates: in the philosophy of history and in epistemology. In those same years he formulated his synthesis of Zionism and socialism.

Syrkin described that synthesis in *The Socialist Zionist State* (1898). As he explained, Jewish nationalism was an organic, natural phenomenon, a healthy expression of the overall structure of human society. And socialism was not an apocalyptic inevitability, but a utopian ideal. The socialist Jewish state would be the fulfillment of the Jews' ancient prophetic mission to bring justice to the world.

Yet Syrkin's book is not merely an exhortation to build a just society. It is a utopian vision, in which he translates the just society into detailed institutions:

> The land will be the common property of the group, which will work it and build on it using communally owned machinery. The houses, factories, and the means of production will also be common property. . . . The time allotted for a task—and hence its value—will be determined empirically, given the machines

available. . . . However, all work is not equivalent. Not only time, but the degree of unpleasantness of a task must be taken into account. Qualitative differences between types of work will be compensated for quantitatively. For example, an hour and a half of factory work or two hours of menial labor will be accounted as equivalent to one hour of happy agricultural work. . . . If we take an hour of agricultural work as a standard unit, we may estimate that four hours of labor daily will be enough to insure a wholesome and comfortable life, as well as to repay the initial investment — with interest — to the national bank.[12]

Note his reflection of the widespread Zionist idealization and idolization (as we saw in Lewinsky) of "happy" (!) agricultural labor. Note too that the vision is not of a rigid egalitarianism; rather, it specifies a degree of economic and cultural freedom:

No one . . . will be forced to work but everyone will be guaranteed the right to work. Members will receive from the labor administration scrip according to the number of standard work-hours to their credit. . . . This scrip will be used to purchase all the necessities of life, to pay rent, to pay taxes to cover administration, roads, and schools, and to pay back capital and interest to the national bank. . . . Any surplus may be used freely according to personal choice. Individuals' standard of living will be based on the quantity of work they perform. Regarding the content filling their lives — they will have the greatest degree of freedom.[13]

As we saw in chapters 7 and 8, Herzl (in 1902) envisioned not a state but a "cooperative society," and in 1925, Jabotinsky imagined an anarchic utopia with no state structures. Syrkin, writing before them both, also explicitly envisioned a utopia in which a society-wide commitment to justice would make state mechanisms of social control unnecessary and obsolete:

The government of the land will be severely limited in scope, concerned only with regulating the economy. There will be no other governing structures, such as a state.... The members have come together to only control the ownership of goods, not to rule over each other; thus, the state becomes superfluous, replaced by the union of free workers. Competition and conflict among individuals will be very rare under conditions of social equality, clear relationships, and free self-determination. Trivial conflicts will be settled through open discussion. More serious acts will have to be treated medically as unfortunate deviations from the healthy and the good.[14]

Syrkin's argument may be seen as echoing the biblical antimonarchists: if everyone were to live justly (according to God's law—or according to socialist principles), then there would be no need for the apparatus of a state with its coercive powers. By the same token, in the perfected society crime will be seen as a disease, not to be punished by force but cured by education.

Unlike Marx, Syrkin does not envision the elimination of social classes via a "dictatorship of the proletariat." Rather, he imagines the social classes coexisting in harmony. Barriers between industry and agriculture, and between urban and rural identities, will also diminish:

The middle class will live happily in the new society. These immigrants may invest the capital they bring in foreign enterprises and thus afford a higher standard of living in the Jewish state, but this wealth will not buy them any social or political advantage.... Only the very rich bourgeoisie may not find it worthwhile to go to the Jewish state, but they have always followed the principle, "the homeland is wherever life is good."...

The various settlement groups will ultimately merge . . . into a social and economic unit. They will establish a center to regulate the country's economy.... There will be no industrial cities and agricultural villages, but rather, the country will be one huge industrial village in which industry and agriculture are interspersed. The opposition between urban and country life will no longer exist. However, there will be a few centers, serving as the seats of the economic administration, and containing the large theaters, institutions of higher learning, museums, etc. The population of these centers will be transient. People will live in them for limited periods, for a particular purpose, and then move back home.[15]

To Syrkin, the Jews' peaceful relations with their neighbors is a worthy goal toward which the Jewish polity ought to strive. Yet, the outside world is unlikely to be a "perfect," peaceable place: "In regard to the outside world the Jewish land will be neutral. It will strive for world peace and social justice in all countries. It will maintain warm and mutually supportive relationships with the progressive elements in all civilized countries. However, for defense in case of attack, there will be a people's militia. In case of war every man will be called to arms."[16]

Unabashedly and proudly utopian, Syrkin rejects apocalyptic determinism. He insists that redemption is to be found in human striving and building toward an ideal:

The Jewish state, if it is destined to come into being, can only be socialist. Zionism must fuse with socialism if it is to become the ideal of the whole Jewish people—of the Jewish proletariat in all its forms, the middle class, the intelligentsia, and the ideologists. . . . All Jews will be invested in the success of Zionism, and none will stand aside. The messianic hope, which was always the greatest longing of exiled Jewry, will be transformed into political action. Judaism's present miserable existence will give way to a glorious renewal.[17]

Both Syrkin and Hess saw their socialist utopian vision as a kind of return to and fulfillment of the social agenda of the biblical prophets. Syrkin refers to the Jews' history of suffering as a result of their "monotheistic faith, . . . the quest for the absolute, and . . . the moral life." And he describes the Jews as "a people faithful to the Torah and the prophets, whose entire history was nothing else than the unending struggle of the prophetic ideal for realization."[18] He calls on the Jews to adopt socialism not only for their own liberation from oppression, but as a return to their glorious past and "true identity."[19] Hess too draws a parallel between the biblical past and the socialist future when he exhorts: "The Biblical traditions which you will revive will also sanctify anew our Occidental society and destroy the weed of materialism together with its roots."[20]

Neither Hess nor Syrkin delve into details, trying to actually identify specific socialist principles or mechanisms in biblical texts. Both of them take for granted that the Torah and prophets instilled in the Jewish nation a general commitment to justice, a concern for the weak, and a skeptical stance regarding wealth and power. This general assumption of a biblically rooted Jewish commitment to a just and humane society would become a common theme in Zionist education and political rhetoric. Here, for example, are the thoughts of Ben-Zion Mossinson (1878–1942), a pioneering educator in the *Yishuv*, on Bible curriculum, from 1911: "The Bible needs to portray in the eyes of the students the full life of our people in its land, to awaken in the hearts of the young Hebrews a powerful love of this life and a strong urge to renew the days of our people as of old. To this end all Bible education must be directed. . . . The prophets were national activists, activists among the people in the truest sense of the word. Political and social questions stand at the center of their ideas."[21]

And David Ben-Gurion was famous for his fascination with the biblical prophets and his belief that the Jewish state must be inspired and guided by the values they taught with regard to both social justice and national liberation.[22]

It seems that the socialist Zionists saw their ideal as a secularization of the messianic tradition: the Jews' return to sovereignty complete with restoration of the utopian Torah society—but without the Torah. Indeed, both Hess and Syrkin make this explicit connection between

Jewish messianism and socialism in the texts quoted above. In their view, socialism would enable the Jews to arrive, by their own efforts, at the utopia of social justice the Torah had envisioned, redeeming themselves and ultimately all of humankind.

But is the socialist vision's linkage to the biblical prophets a legitimate interpretation—or is it merely a rhetorical gimmick? Are the socialists really channeling the prophets, or are they exploiting them, taking their words out of their proper cultural context? We will now explore this question by examining one of the best-known prophetic utopian visions.

"In That Day": Isaiah's Utopian Vision

The Prophets section of the Hebrew Bible comprises two parts: a continuation of the Torah's historical narrative (Joshua, Samuel, Kings), and the writings (mostly in poetry) of fifteen prophets (Isaiah through Malachi) who lived from the eighth through the fifth centuries BCE.

While scholars and believers have argued for a variety of definitions of "prophet," here a simple one ought to suffice: individuals who saw themselves and were perceived by at least some listeners as qualified to speak in God's name. Whether the claim to prophecy was supported by personal qualities, by a perceived authenticity, by poetic or rhetorical skills, by piercing social and political analysis, or even by political organizing skills, the prophet characteristically "spoke truth to power," generally conveying an unpopular message. Jeremiah, for example, did prison time for his utterances (see Jer. 38). Oftentimes the prophets seem to have been political outsiders; their relationship to the established leadership of priests and kings was fraught and complicated. While the monarchy and the Temple were holy and indispensable in their view, their dominant message was a call to restore the centrality of the Sinai covenant. They taught that the nation's history, past and future, had been and would be determined by its loyalty to God and the Torah—by its acceptance or rejection of idolatry and injustice.

While some of the prophecies describe an ideal future in purely monarchic terms (e.g., Micah 5:1–5; Zechariah 9:9–10)—or purely priestly terms (e.g., Ezekiel 44)—an important recurring image is a utopian synthesis between two ideals: the desert theocracy and the dynastic king. Justice will prevail in a kingdom ruled by a king who is the agent of divine justice. An oft-quoted and much-loved passage from Isaiah (11:1–10) beautifully expresses this synthesis:

> But a shoot shall grow out of the stump of Jesse,
> A twig shall sprout from his stock.
> The spirit of the Lord shall alight upon him:
> A spirit of wisdom and insight,
> A spirit of counsel and valor,
> A spirit of devotion and reverence for the Lord.
> He shall sense the truth by his reverence for the Lord:
> He shall not judge by what his eyes behold,
> Nor decide by what his ears perceive.
> Thus he shall judge the poor with equity
> And decide with justice for the lowly of the land.
> He shall strike down a land with the rod of his mouth
> And slay the wicked with the breath of his lips.
> Justice shall be the girdle of his loins,
> And faithfulness the girdle of his waist.
> The wolf shall dwell with the lamb,
> The leopard lie down with the kid;
> The calf and the beast of prey shall feed together,
> With a little boy to herd them.
> The cow and the bear shall graze,
> Their young shall lie down together;
> And the lion, like the ox, shall eat straw.
> A babe shall play
> Over a viper's hole,
> And an infant pass his hand
> Over an adder's den.

In all of My sacred mount
Nothing evil or vile shall be done;
For the land shall be filled with devotion to the Lord
As the water covers the sea.
In that day,
The stock of Jesse that has remained standing
Shall become a standard to peoples—
Nations shall seek his counsel
And his abode shall be honored.[23]

This passage is rich in allusions and hints—and has left commentators and scholars arguing for centuries over what Isaiah really meant.[24] Many traditional commentators ascribed to the prophet knowledge of the future, and thus associated this prophecy with the Jewish experience after 586 BCE, when the nation was in exile, with no Davidic king and no state. However, it is of interest to try to read the passage as it would have been read by Isaiah's contemporaries. It is likely that Isaiah wrote this poem during the reign of King Ahaz in Judah (ca. 744–28 BCE). Ahaz was a descendant of David. His reign is summarized in 2 Kings (16:2–4): "He did not do what was pleasing to the Lord his God, as his ancestor David had done, but followed the ways of the kings of Israel. He even consigned his son to the fire, in the abhorrent fashion of the nations which the Lord had dispossessed before the Israelites. He sacrificed and made offerings at the shrines, on the hills, and under every leafy tree."

Note that this evaluation is not significantly worse than those of most of Ahaz's predecessors. Thus, Isaiah's experience of Davidic rule was not exactly ideal. Indeed, while both David and Solomon's days of empire may have appeared glorious in retrospect, neither the father nor the son was a paragon of virtue (see 2 Sam. 11, David and Bathsheba; and 1 Kings 11, Solomon's idolatry). Neither seems to have fulfilled the Torah's instruction: "When he is seated on his royal throne, he shall have a copy of this Teaching written for him on a scroll by the levitical priests. Let it remain with him and let him read in it all his life, so that he may learn to revere the Lord his God, to observe faithfully every word of this Teaching as well as these laws" (Deut. 17:18–19). Taken in Isaiah's own historical context, his prophecy can be read as an expression of disappointment and exasperation with the current reality of Davidic rule. Isaiah seems to be envisioning a restart: let's skip David and all that has brought us to our present disgrace; return to the original rootstock, David's father Jesse; and hope for a fresh sprout from it.

Isaiah's arboreal imagery contains a number of allusions his readers would have caught, among them the tree of knowledge of good and evil in Eden (Gen. 2–3), the staff of Judahite sovereignty (Gen. 49:10), and Aaron's flowering staff of divine election (Num. 17:16–26).[25]

Isaiah imagines a king who, unlike Ahaz and his predecessors, will be wise, devout, God-fearing, and just. This king will look out for the interests of the poor and weak. Upon this king will "rest God's spirit." This language echoes Numbers 11:24–25, where God's spirit "rested upon" Moses and the seventy elders, and recalls how, in 1 Samuel 16:13–14, God's spirit trumped dynastic succession, departing from Saul and resting then on the young shepherd David. The prophet's emphasis on justice, insight, care in judgment, and concern for the lowly also seems to echo Moses' charge to the judges he appoints in the desert: "Hear out your fellow men, and decide justly between any man and a fellow Israelite or a stranger. You shall not be partial in judgment: hear out low and high alike. Fear no man, for judgment is God's" (Deut. 1:16–18).

Isaiah seems to be saying that despite God's establishing the Davidic dynasty, the monarchy as we have experienced it, devoid of God's spirit, is a dead stump. He imagines a future when the hereditary root of Jesse will be revitalized by God's spirit, restoring a prior, purer time when justice prevailed. Indeed, the text goes on to suggest, such an ideal kingdom will be nothing less than a return not only to the desert, but to Eden, when all the animals were herbivores, before the offspring of humans and of snakes were sentenced to eternal enmity (Gen. 3:14–15).

We saw in chapter 7 that the monarchists depict the chaos of the Judges' theocracy as equivalent to Sodom. Here, Isaiah hints that the current monarchic reality is reminiscent of the world just before the waters of the Flood covered the earth:

For the land shall be filled with devotion to the Lord
As the water covers the sea. (Isa. 11: 9)

This language echoes Genesis 6:11, which recounts: "The earth became corrupt before God; the earth was filled with lawlessness."

Trying to read Isaiah as his contemporaries might have, this prophecy can be understood as a utopian vision, criticizing current reality and longing for a better one. If only there were a king who fulfilled not only genetic, but spiritual requirements, we could be living in Paradise. A miracle is not necessary, just royal leadership worthy of its position. Not in a future world, but in this one. Isaiah brings forward the tension between theocracy and monarchy and suggests that it is not a zero-sum game. Rather, a king upon whom rests God's spirit can merge these two ideals, so that

The stock of Jesse that has remained standing
Shall become a standard to peoples —
Nations shall seek his counsel
And his abode shall be honored.

Though Plato lived three centuries after Isaiah, he was probably not familiar with the prophet's writings. So, after reading Isaiah, it is striking to read his words on the philosopher-king in *The Republic*: "I said: Until philosophers are kings, or the kings and princes of this world have the spirit and power of philosophy, and political greatness and wisdom meet in one, and those commoner natures who pursue either to the exclusion of the other are compelled to stand aside, cities will never have rest from their evils—nor the human race, as I believe—

and then only will this our State have a possibility of life and behold the light of day."[26]

For both Plato and Isaiah, the key requisite for achieving utopia is the leadership of a just and wise king. It is interesting to consider: Is this conclusion an admission that utopia is eternally beyond our reach? Is it a passive cop-out, suggesting that achieving the ideal is dependent on our leaders, and not on us? Or, perhaps, might it be a call for patient optimism: Utopia will come, but not today and not tomorrow? Just and wise rulers are rare but not impossible, all we can do is hope, educate, and act in society so as to place them in power.

Isaiah saw himself as calling for a return to the covenant, envisioning, finally, the realization of the Torah's utopia. For him, standing between the present reality and that vision was social injustice—in particular, oppression of the poor and weak by the rich and the strong. Hess and Syrkin saw themselves as standing on Isaiah's shoulders, updating his (and his fellow prophets') visions to a modern context: a Jewish state demonstrating a radical commitment to social justice, to eliminating inequality, class conflict, and oppression. They saw themselves not as cosmopolitan socialist rebels against Jewish identity, but rather as the true heirs of the tradition. They were extracting what they upheld as a key "Jewish value"—economic justice—from the tradition and setting it as a foundation stone of the renewed Jewish polity.

Yet it appears that the Author (or authors) of the Bible were not socialists. The predominant economic model seems to be free-market with corrections, such as the jubilee year, and mechanisms for supporting the weak and the poor, in view of the reality that "there will never cease to be needy ones in your land" (Deut. 15:11). Isaiah is typical of the prophets in envisioning a polity whose rulers exemplify and enforce norms of just dealings, fair treatment of all, and mercy for the weak. So even though the Bible did not seem to endorse socialism, the socialist Zionists linked the Bible's utopian vision with their own. Both visions, after all, were critiques of a reality characterized by injustice, and both were expressions of a desire for a better, more just, place.

Aren't We There Yet?

Syrkin's and Hess's utopian visions hovered in the popular imagination throughout the period that the socialist parties dominated political life, in the *Yishuv* and then in the state, until the "upheaval" of 1977, when the Revisionist leader Menachem Begin became prime minister. During that time of socialist supremacy, the kibbutz was seen as emblematic of Israel's utopian vision, and a hothouse for the production of elite leadership—New Jews—in the army and in civilian life. The *Histadrut* (national labor federation) was an omnipresent force in industry and public services. Israel was expected to be a light unto the nations, with an egalitarian society (everyone on a first-name basis, no neckties, a simple and folksy culture, a plain and proletarian cuisine) and a true citizens' army—the great leveler. Israel's National Insurance Institute, its progressive income tax, maternity leave, child care—all elements of a welfare state—seemed to be signs of progress toward a just and merciful society. One could get the impression—and many did—that Hess's and Syrkin's utopia was well on the way toward realization.

Beyond Israel, too, Jews—and gentiles—around the world were moved by the idea that the Jewish polity represented a messianic, perfected, society in the making. Israel would not be just any Jewish state, but a Jewish state modeling social justice.

However, a closer look reveals that the utopia a great many Israelis (and others) thought they saw approaching was more a reflection of what they wanted than of what Israel was. As it turned out, the socialist parties were significantly less interested in socialist economic arrangements than in national solidarity (which in and of itself helped defuse the class struggle).[27] Despite the various policies and symbols described above, even during the rule of the socialist parties, the *Yishuv* and the state were mostly urban, and mostly capitalistic. The kibbutz never comprised more than three percent of the population, and over time underwent a painful process of privatization and retreat from egalitarianism. Israel needed investment for development; it needed national symbols and institutions to build a cohesive society out of disparate immigrant and religious groups; it needed a strong army with public support to exist in a precarious environment. Therefore, socialist leaders needed tycoons, a permanent urban population, and Orthodox coalition votes—all of which were conspicuously absent from Syrkin's vision.

It seems fair to say that if Nachman Syrkin were to come to visit Israel today, he would be thrilled to see a thriving Jewish polity with some impressive social achievements—first and foremost universal health care. And yet, he would surely be disappointed by the yawning chasm between his vision and reality. Israel has been spared none of the ills of modern Western societies, from the existence of both tycoons and slums to the phenomena of ethnic tensions, drug addiction, organized crime, human trafficking, femicide, homelessness, and environmental degradation. He would surely admonish Israel's leaders for failing to implement his economic plan, which was intended to eliminate all of these problems.

But, of course, the failure to fully achieve utopia is inherent in the concept. Moreover, in Israel's case, this process is made all the more difficult by the need somehow to reconcile, synthesize, or prioritize the competing visions of all the utopias we have encountered in the preceding chapters. In the following chapter, we will examine some specific case studies of how conflicting utopias are manifest in current political discourse.

Further Reading

Frankel, Jonathan. *Prophecy and Politics: Socialism, Nationalism, and the Russian Jews, 1862–1917.* Cambridge: Cambridge University Press, 1981.

Kugel, James. *How to Read the Bible: A Guide to the Scripture, Then and Now.* New York: Free Press, 2007, 538–68.

Rubenstein, Sondra Miller. *The Communist Movement in Palestine and Israel, 1919–1984.* Boulder: Westview Press, 1985.

Sternhell, Zeev. *The Founding Myths of Israel: Nationalism, Socialism, and the Making of the Jewish State.* Translated by David Maisel. Princeton NJ: Princeton University Press, 1998.

Part 3

The Modern State of Israel

Reality Meets Utopia

11

Visions in Collision

A Jewish state—we want it all: an ethnic nation-state that is a paragon of social justice; a warm community that is a powerful state; a normal modern state that is ruled by Jewish law; an equal member of the family of nations living within divinely ordained boundaries. But alas, if it is impossible fully to translate even one utopia into reality, how much the more so to implement six in the same place!

Just consider the divergent visions examined in the preceding chapters:

- The Torah ideal (ca. 1000 BCE): Future life in the land, according to Torah law (chapter 2)
- The prophets' vision (Isaiah, ca. 700 BCE): Restoration of the ideal monarchy (chapter 10)
- The Promised Land (Genesis 15:18–21, ca. 1000 BCE): Restored ideal borders (chapter 9)
- Apocalypse (Book of Daniel, ca. 200 BCE): Not utopia, but expectation of the imminent, inevitable end of history (chapter 3)
- Anarchy (Zev Jabotinsky, 1925): A nonstate—some form of anarchy, theocracy, confederation (chapter 7)
- Community (Mark Zborowsky and Elizabeth Herzog, 1952): The medieval community as an ideal (chapter 5)
- A Torah state (Zev Yavetz, 1903): Modernized version of life in the land according to Torah law (chapter 4)
- A national home (Elchanan Lewinsky, 1892): Return to organic cultural roots (chapter 6)

- A normal state (Theodor Herzl, 1902): An enlightened, modern, cosmopolitan polity (chapter 8)
- A socialist society (Nachman Syrkin, 1898): A Jewish polity based on socialist economic principles (chapter 10)

Much of Israeli political discourse—and world Jewry's discourse about Israel—can be seen to reflect the dissonance among these competing utopian visions and the frustration inherent in the attempt to implement any utopia in a real place here and now.

This chapter examines the conflicts of utopian visions with each other and with reality through two different perspectives: (a) a sociological view, showing how Israeli society is divided along ethnic and religious lines into competing groups who envision very different ideal futures and (b) a topical view, looking at how utopian visions collide in several major areas of policy and practice.

A Sociological Perspective: The "Four Tribes"

In a 2015 lecture that has become a classic of Israeli political and cultural commentary, President Reuven Rivlin set forth a view of Israeli society as divided among four "tribes," each committed to a different set of utopian dreams. He asked, "Will this be a secular, liberal state, Jewish and democratic? Will it be a state based on Jewish religious law? Or a religious democratic state? Will it be a state of all its citizens, of all its national ethnic groups?"

Rivlin elaborated:

The "new Israeli order" is not an apocalyptic prophecy. It is the reality. A reality that can already be seen in the composition of the first-grade classes in the Israeli education system. Today, the first-grade classes are composed of about 38% secular Jews, about 15% national-religious, about one-quarter Arabs, and close to one-quarter *charedim* [ultra-Orthodox]. . . . A child from Beit El [an Orthodox Zionist settlement in the West Bank], a child from Rahat [a Bedouin town], a child from Herzliya [a mostly secular city] and a child from Beitar Illit [a *charedi* town] — not only do they not meet each other, but they are educated toward a totally different outlook regarding the basic values and desired character of the State of Israel....

From an economic standpoint, the current reality is unviable. The mathematics is simple, any child can see it.... The severe and painful epidemic of poverty, which is already having a major effect in Israel, will only expand and worsen. From a political standpoint, Israeli politics is built to a great extent as an inter-tribal zero-sum game. One tribe, the Arabs, whether or not by its own choice, is not really a partner in the game. The other three, it seems, are absorbed by a struggle for survival, a struggle over budgets and resources for education, housing, or infrastructure, each on behalf of their own sector.

In the "new Israeli order," in which each sector experiences itself as a minority, this dynamic will be infinitely more destructive....

In the past, the Israel Defense Forces served as a central tool for fashioning the Israeli character. In the military, Israeli society would confront itself, would consolidate, and shape itself morally, socially and in many ways economically. However, in the emerging Israeli order, more than half of the population does not serve in the military. Israelis will meet, for the first time, if at all, only in the work place. In any case, the mutual ignorance and lack of a common language between these four populations, which are becoming ever more similar in size, merely increase the tension, fear, hostility and the competitiveness between them.[1]

Let's look more closely at President Rivlin's "tribes" — their utopias and their impact.

The Palestinian Arab Citizens

Approximately twenty percent of Israel's citizens are Palestinian Arabs — Muslim, Christian, and Druze. Some live in integrated cities, but most reside in ethnically homogeneous rural villages. These villages, whose economy and lifestyle were agrarian before 1948 and whose social structure was premodern and patriarchal, have not kept up with Israel's rate of economic development, and are mostly in the lower deciles of any socioeconomic ranking.

The relationship among development, cultural autonomy, conflicting national aspirations, and majority-minority discrimination is complex and daunting. Most Arabs wish to preserve their culture, and choose to send their children to Arabic-language public schools (although it is not a simple, free choice, as most Arabs and Jews still live in separate, homogeneous communities, with their own local schools). While officially these schools are equivalent in standards, resources, and curriculum to the Hebrew-language public schools, "separate but equal" rarely is. Since local municipalities are partially responsible for funding public schools, wealthier communities can provide educational advantages. Moreover, since in Arab schools Hebrew is a second language, Arabs are at a disadvantage in higher education and the labor market. Meanwhile, many Jews perceive Arab citizens as unwelcome and at least potentially disloyal, given that they share a culture with surrounding countries that have long been enemies of the State of Israel and that many Arab Israelis identify with Palestinian national aspirations. This leads to formal and informal discrimination in housing, employment, and access to various public resources such as parks, pools, and academic programs.

If Israel is "the nation-state of the Jewish people," fulfillment of the utopian dream of Jewish self-determination, including sovereignty, Arab citizens might well ask, "So, are we full citizens? Is this our state too? Is discrimination built in? Are we economically disadvantaged because we refuse to assimilate — or because the Jews refuse to allow us to integrate?"

In a Jewish nationalist utopia and in a Torah state, the status of non-Jews is indeed a question. In a utopia of social justice and equality—and in a Herzlian normal state—it is not. Of all the conflicts between utopian visions of Israel, the question of the status of the Palestinian Arabs is perhaps the most vexing and the most consequential. It stands at the very heart of a century-old dilemma—what to do about national minorities in ethnic nation-states. We saw in chapter 4 how the first Ashkenazic chief rabbi of the state, Isaac Herzog, wrestled with this very dilemma, concluding that in messianic times, the halakhic question of the status of the *ger toshav* (resident alien) will be relevant—but in our times, the ideal of a liberal democratic state appropriate for a member of the family of enlightened nations will have to suffice.

The attempt to realize a utopia of a national home that is a sovereign state—a place where one particular ethnic group fulfills its dream of being alone, pure, totally "self-determined"—has, to date, never led to a happy ending. Until around 1942, a number of Zionist leaders proposed solutions based on some kind of federated polity with the Palestinians. The flood of history washed these off the table, but arguably they may still hold some promise (see chapter 12).

The Ultra-Orthodox

While the correlation between ethnic identity and economic class is most glaring in the case of the Palestinian Arabs in Israel, a similar correlation within the Jewish population gives expression to a different utopian conflict. Jews who identify as *charedi* (usually translated as ultra-Orthodox) comprise about twelve percent of the total population. The political and spiritual heirs of the anti-Zionist Orthodoxy of Agudat Israel, they tend to live in homogeneous urban neighborhoods, to maximize their segregation from the secular society and preserve what they see as the halakhic community. Their schools, while publicly funded, are curricularly independent, and tend to teach almost only traditional Jewish texts. Approximately half of the men are not employed, studying full-time in yeshivot (traditional talmudic academies) funded by modest government stipends and private philanthropy. Nonparticipation in the work force—and the associated poverty—is encouraged by a government policy that grants exemptions from military service only to those who study full-time (i.e., who don't work). As a whole, this population, too, is in the lowest socioeconomic deciles.

In an ideal normal state—or in one driven by a vision of social justice—it would be unthinkable for a large minority to withdraw from the economy, consume welfare services, and perpetuate and expand its numbers through publicly supported sectarian education. Even in Yavetz's Torah utopia, yeshiva education included a general studies curriculum, and international commerce and involvement in global affairs were points of national pride.

Ironically, the *charedim* don't envision a Jewish state at all; their utopia is the premodern halakhic community, existing within a secular state. The concessions and institutions they use their political bargaining power to attain are similar to the ones the *charedi* parties sought in the Polish parliament in the 1930s. They solely want the autonomy—and resources—needed to maintain their communal way of life. While many argue that their impact stems from Israel's parliamentary system, which grants minority parties disproportionate power in coalition bargaining, I would suggest that there is an additional factor at work: a general acceptance of the parable we've already encountered of the two camels meeting at a narrow passage, interpreted to imply that the less observant must give way to the more. If the *charedim* care a lot about matters about which everyone else doesn't have a passionate or even a clear opinion, then they should have the right of way. For example, it is taken for granted that all army base kitchens must be kosher, even though most soldiers do not observe the dietary laws outside the base, and would prefer a more varied menu; because that preference is not a religious commitment, as kashrut is for the observant minority, it is set aside. For these reasons, the state enforces rabbinical authority in matters of public Sabbath observance, dietary laws, and marriage and divorce.

Perhaps a solution lies in a renegotiation of the 1947 understanding. An ideal normal state would worry about the well-being and economic development of all its citizens. Thus, while on the one hand it is hard to imagine a Jewish state in which a halakhic community could not exist in security and dignity, it is also hard to imagine a normal state in which a halakhic community would be able to employ state power to enforce its particular norms on the larger society of unbelievers and exclude itself from consensus obligations such as military service and basic education. A larger degree of disengagement of rabbinical from state authority—thus pushing the ultra-Orthodox to compete as equals in the identity marketplace—might actually open up new directions in halakhic development and help advance the utopian vision of a revitalized *halakhah*.

Orthodox Zionists

President Rivlin's designation of the national-religious public as a separate tribe can be seen as recognition of a development that originated in 1967. Before the Six-Day War, the Orthodox Zionist public and their politicians formed part of the mainstream, even as they fought against the majority (mainly through coalition wrangling) to preserve certain markers of "Jewishness" in the state and its culture. As opposed to the *charedim*, they served in the army, sought higher education, and were fully integrated into the economic, political, and cultural life of the country, despite its domination by a secular majority. For them, the necessity of the state and the vision of the national home outweighed the challenges to *halakhah* posed by the realities of Israeli life. Creative solutions were sought and found (see, for example, the case of the sabbatical year in chapter 4).

However, this ostensibly harmonious integration contained a hidden theological trap. Orthodox Zionism was able to overcome the traditional opposition to "forcing the [messianic] end" only by recognizing the Zionist endeavor as "the first blossoming of our redemption." The Jewish state, despite its imperfections, was interpreted as part of an apocalyptic process leading to the full restoration of kingdom and Temple; prophecy was seen as unfolding in real history. While this was a very preliminary blossoming, it nonetheless allowed—required— Orthodox Zionists to participate in (rather than oppose) the process.

The euphoria that followed the seemingly miraculous 1967 victory helped shift "the first blossoming of our redemption" from a liturgical formula to an expression of apocalyptic activism. Feeling swept up in an apocalyptic historical moment—the extensions of Jewish state sovereignty over Jerusalem's Old City and the biblical "heartland" of Judea and Samaria serving as evidence of an accelerated redemptive process—many Orthodox Zionists came to believe utopia was already within reach. Biblical promises of expansive borders were being fulfilled. Jews were sovereign in Jerusalem and on the Temple Mount. The point was rapidly approaching when over half the world's Jews would be living in Israel (45 percent as of 2018).[2]

Many Orthodox Zionists interpreted all of this as a call to action to facilitate the advance of utopia. If current events were the fulfillment of a biblical vision, then the restrictions of liberal democracy—of a normal state—were no longer relevant. The land needed to be cleansed of gentiles and their symbols. For example, in 1984, a gentle, scholarly classmate of mine at the Hebrew University was arrested—and later convicted—of plotting to dynamite the Mosque of Omar on the Temple Mount.

Post-1967, Orthodox Zionism largely shifted from aligning with the liberal mainstream to a focus on settling and retaining the areas conquered in 1967—even, in some cases, to the point of civil disobedience and violent rebellion. Prime Minister Yitzchak Rabin was assassinated in 1995 by a member of this "tribe" who believed he was fulfilling a halakhic obligation. For this group, the vision of a national home came to mean the realization of the biblical utopia: Jewish national hegemony in a state ruled by Torah. Now.

Translated into a political program, this apocalyptic view, resonating with populist romantic nationalism (if only we could be "just us" here), has created a political force that openly questions democratic norms such as free expression, judicial independence, and minority rights. This is far from what Herzl or Lewinsky or Jabotinsky or even Yavetz had in mind. The political problem is not the competition among utopian visions, which is arguably healthy in a democracy. The problem is the apocalyptic mindset, which denies such competition, convinced that one particular vision is divinely sanctioned, inevitable—and imminent.

The Fourth Tribe

In my view, President Rivlin's characterization of the fourth tribe— "secular Jews"—is an oversimplification. This population would better be depicted as "Jews other than Orthodox," comprising many subgroups, which can be sorted into three categories:

1. The heirs of Israel's Ashkenazic founding elite, the New Jews: strong, brave, productive, suntanned, worldly, rooted in the land, and moral. The question this ideal has posed for Israeli educators and cultural leaders for over a century is this: The New Jews' newness is obvious; but wherein lies their Jewishness? According to the Orthodox tribes, secular Israelis have disconnected from their historical and national roots to the point of having assimilated into global culture. Strength, productivity, and a suntan have become their whole identity; even Hebrew culture is increasingly pushed aside by English, the global lingua franca. While some Jews in this tribe do indeed feel alienated from all aspects of Jewish tradition (there was even a small movement, in the 1950s, the "Canaanites," who advocated trying to reconnect with prebiblical roots), most see this disparaging description as a distortion. They believe in Ahad Ha'am's view: that Israeli secular national culture is just as authentically Jewish as the culture of the *charedim*. For them, living in Israel, speaking Hebrew, building and defending the Jewish nation-state, living by the Jewish calendar are valid and sufficient expressions of Jewish identity.

2. Jews descended from North African and Middle Eastern immigrants who identify as *Masorti* (traditional). While considered members of the "secular" tribe, this subgroup does not share the New Jews' antipathy to rabbis and to rabbinical tradition. They see the tradition as part of their identity, even if they don't feel obligated to observe every commandment. Hence the familiar popular description of a *Masorti* Jew: one who consistently attends an Orthodox synagogue on Sabbath morning and then roots for the home team at a professional soccer game in the afternoon. *Masorti* Jews neither fully live by *halakhah* nor rebel against it; they respect it but keep a certain distance and independence.[3]

3. Jews who identify with the liberal movements (Reform, Conservative, Reconstructionist) and reject the all-or-nothing approach to tradition that characterizes the classic Old Jew–New Jew conflict. These movements, representing a small minority (5–10 percent) of the population, reject the title "secular," as they define themselves as religious. Their culture and interests, however, are more consonant with those of the secular tribe than with the two Orthodox groups. And by defining themselves as religious, they compete with (meaning, threaten the authority of) Orthodoxy. Since Orthodoxy is backed by state power and resources, the liberal movements suffer discrimination. For example, the Ministry of Interior does not recognize marriages and conversions performed by liberal rabbis; with a few exceptions due to recent court rulings, the Ministry of Religion only pays for Orthodox rabbis' salaries; and the government funds Orthodox rabbinical seminaries but not liberal ones.

The difficulties faced by the liberal movements raise a vexing question regarding their utopian vision: Should they fight for the separation of religion from state, for a cosmopolitan, enlightened society on the American model, which has well served their values and their interests there—or should they fight to be included as equals in a Torah state or Jewish national home, where Jewish religious life is supported (and controlled) by the state? Which is the ideal: that Reform rabbis be paid by the state like their Orthodox colleagues—or that no rabbis be paid by the state?

For better or for worse, it seems that Israel has fulfilled the vision of normalcy: Israel has been spared few, if any, of the ills of modern society. As such, some members of the fourth tribe—especially those who judge the morality of state policies purely by standards of national and personal self-interest (*realpolitik*) may see utopia as having been achieved: Israel is like any other state. However, these Jews are not the mainstream. For the most part, secular, *masorti*, and liberal Jews in Israeli society have never given up on the belief that the Jewish state must be a "better place," and never stopped struggling to define their utopian visions.

In essence, all three subgroups of the fourth tribe can be seen to share Ahad Ha'am's belief that Jewish culture (with or without belief in a divine power) has moral content. A Jewish national home must be characterized by a high level of personal morality, humaneness, and social justice. Thus the familiar expectation that the Israeli army be the "most moral army in the world." Thus Israelis' (and world Jewry's) fascination with Israeli medical aid missions to natural disaster sites worldwide; their pride in Israeli scientific achievements; and their denial, or embarrassment, or activism, when Israel is criticized for its policies regarding human trafficking, refugee absorption, and women's rights.

Like Herzl, Lewinsky, and Syrkin, non-Orthodox Israelis expect the Jewish state to be more than "just Jewish." They expect it to aspire to humanistic ideals—fairness, concern for the weak, sanctity of human life, concern for the environment. A powerful expression of this expectation can be seen in a 1988 essay by the prominent secular novelist, academic, and Member of Knesset Yizhar Smilansky (1916–2006): "To exist, to survive, not to be destroyed, yes, of course, there is no question. But . . . even in the struggle to exist, there are things that are forbidden to the Jew by virtue of his being a Jew. For example, to take what is not his. For example, to ignore the tears of the oppressed. For example, to drive out his neighbors. For example, to oppress in his fellow humans what he hates when they oppress in him."[4]

For the fourth tribe, the key challenge is formulating a clear vision out of the blurry intersection of four competing utopias: (a) the enlightened, cosmopolitan, free society; (b) the Jewish national home, where Jewish culture is dominant; (c) the Torah state, where "Jewish values" set the moral tone; and (d) a society where the individual is supreme and the fittest survive and thrive.

A Topical Perspective: Five Arenas Where Utopias Collide

While President Rivlin's characterization of Israeli society is helpful in understanding key issues that roil the body politic of Israel, it can be argued that his mapping of utopian visions onto identity groups also oversimplifies the reality of divergent thought across allied groups as well as shared thought among divergent groups. Thus it is helpful to examine the conflict of visions by policy area in addition to social groupings. Furthermore, it is arguably simplistic to assign to political actors one particular utopia over against competing visions. Rather, it seems, many Israelis—as well as outside observers—are carrying around more than one vision in their heads, and dealing with the dissonance by ignoring it, fudging it, or compartmentalizing—and ultimately just assuming that somehow, at some point, it will all work out.

Let us now consider five examples emblematic of the main areas of tension:

- The Sabbath: As a key marker of Jewish identity through the generations, the Sabbath is a tradition where *halakhah*, communal solidarity, culture, and social justice meet. In and of itself it is utopian. It is also an apt example of the fraught interface between traditional observance and state policies.

- The Welfare State: Economic justice and mercy (concern for society's weakest members) are important concerns of the Torah, of states worldwide, and certainly of every utopia. However, the ideal division of responsibility among the state, the community, and the individual remains the focus of an ongoing controversy in many modern democracies. What course should a Jewish state chart?

- Immigration: A nation-state is concerned primarily with its citizens' welfare; a Jewish state is expected to worry about Jews throughout the world; and a state embodying universalistic humane values is supposed to help alleviate human suffering everywhere. The tension among these three concerns finds its sharpest expression in immigration policy.

- Living on the Land: A common feature of Jewish utopian dreams is their rootedness in geography. While the borders may be uncertain and even controversial, the Jewish state was never imagined as being nowhere. From the Torah onward, "the Land of Israel" was the ideal. But now that there is a Jewish state in that land, the question of how to treat the land demands answering. Ownership and sovereignty imply responsibility: How should the Jewish state develop, exploit, and conserve the Promised Land? (Discussion of the intersection of utopian visions and where to draw the borders of Israel appears in chapter 9.)

- Israel and the Diaspora: It seems that until the messianic ingathering, large numbers of Jews will live both in Israel and in communities around the world. Is this a compromise or an ideal? For Herzl and Lewinsky, vibrant Jewish life in the Diaspora, alongside the Jewish national home, was part of their vision, made possible by the Jewish polity; Yavetz, on the other hand, envisioned a total ingathering. As we shall see, these visions have consequences. Should Israel be seen as one Jewish community among many equals? As *primus inter pares*? As a beacon? As a refuge of last resort? As the only authentic expression of

Jewish nationhood? Should the Diaspora be seen as a passing phase? What should be diaspora Jews' obligations to Israel? What should be Israel's obligations to diaspora Jewry?

The Sabbath

In 1947, in order to gain Orthodox support for the UN partition plan calling for a Jewish state, the Zionist leadership promised that the Sabbath would be the official day of rest in the projected state.

In 1976, Prime Minister Yitzchak Rabin dissolved the government and called new elections when the National Religious Party withdrew from the coalition over a delivery to Israel of jet fighters on the Sabbath. Such crises recur periodically around issues like highway or railway maintenance projects on the Sabbath.

Our family made *aliyah* in 1990. We left an active and close-knit urban Conservative community where our children attended Jewish day schools and settled in a semirural area in the Galilee served by a county public school. Before we made *aliyah*, our kids typically joined us for services. Suddenly, parties on Friday night and athletic competitions on Saturday, which we had never confronted, became part of our children's lives. It took us years to get used to our teenagers telling us of plans to go to a pop concert on Friday night. "No, in Israel? Can't be!," we'd say, and they'd laugh.

In Israel in 2020 the Jewish Sabbath (from sundown Friday to nightfall on Saturday) remains the official day of rest. Government offices and most businesses are required to close (special dispensation is given to hospitals, utilities, and the like). With some local exceptions, public transportation does not run, though Ben Gurion International Airport is open and busy. Jewish schools are closed, but public schools serving the Palestinian Arab population are open. Friday night is a preferred time for popular music performances. Suburban shopping malls are packed on Saturday, as are zoos, museums, beaches, amusement parks, national parks, and restaurants. Only patrons who have access to cars can get to these places (gas stations are open).

In Yavetz's Torah-state utopia—as in Lewinsky's national home and even Herzl's cosmopolitan old new land—the Sabbath was an idyll, a time of peace and spiritual elevation, "a taste of the world to come." When, finally, the Jews were living in a place where Jewish culture was dominant, the Sabbath would emerge from all the challenges it faced in the modernizing Western world and regain its role as distinguisher and sustainer of the Jewish people. State power would not be needed to enforce Sabbath *halakhah*; rather, it would arise organically, as part of a renewed and upgraded encounter between the utopian spirit of the Sabbath and the new reality of life in the Land of Israel. A revitalized *halakhah*—a revitalized Sabbath. A glimpse of this vision can be seen in the idyllic description of life on an Orthodox kibbutz we met in chapter 4.

And yet, the Sabbath, traditionally seen as a taste of utopia, turns out to be a fraught meeting-place for modern utopian visions. If Israel were a homogeneous traditional community, all of whose members were committed to a halakhic life, there would be consensual adherence to the rabbis' rulings as to how to observe the day. If Israel were an enlightened, cosmopolitan society, characterized by freedom of—and freedom from—religion, Sabbath observance would be a matter of personal choice. In Lewinsky's national home, the Sabbath would be a national institution, a particularly joyous expression of the shared general culture. And using Moses Hess's imagery, we might imagine a socialist Jewish state sanctifying the Sabbath (in some form) as symbolizing the rejection of capitalist materialism. But since Israel is "all of the above" in vision—and "none of the above" in reality—the day of rest is a day of conflict.

While the interface of these visions regarding the Sabbath is complex and multidimensional, it can be reduced, for clarity, to two major dichotomies.

A State or a Community

The *halakhah* evolved over the past two millennia in the context of a semiautonomous community existing as an island in a larger, gentile polity. While the Jewish community had some enforcement powers in certain areas, it was essentially a voluntary assemblage comprising members who shared a belief that the *halakhah* represented God's commandments, as interpreted by the rabbis. This arrangement, especially in the example of the Sabbath, made observance easier and defused potential conflicts. The existence of an outside world beyond the Sabbath-observing community eliminated significant difficulties in living with the *halakhah*. When the Jewish community was not responsible for defense, public safety, electricity generation, and so on, it was able to take advantage of these services provided on the Sabbath by the non-Jewish state. Halakhic solutions were not needed. With modernization, however, the barrier between inside and outside the community broke down. Indeed, the Sabbath came under attack as Jews became increasingly involved in outside society—in business, education, the army, and social and cultural activities.

Utopians like Yavetz and Lewinsky had dreamed that if the "outside" were to be Jewish too, then this tension would disappear. They had envisioned the Jewish state as an encompassing Jewish community where everyone would share the commitment to the Sabbath. However, states exist to bring together disparate groups and communities in order to provide defense, economic order, and other vital services. Their mandate does not include dictating religious beliefs and private behaviors, which are left to individuals or to voluntary associations (communities). Even Satanow's ideal state, an absolute monarchy, just like Syrkin's socialist society, conscientiously avoided meddling in its citizens' beliefs. So one major source of Sabbath conflict is the confusion between visions: Should Israel be a community or a state?

A National Home or an Enlightened State

Another dimension of the Sabbath conflict stems from the idea contained in Ahad Ha'am's famous dictum, "More than Israel has kept the Sabbath, the Sabbath has kept Israel." In the secular, cultural Zionist vision, it was unthinkable that the Sabbath, with all its powerful historical resonance, would not be an important institution in the renewed Jewish polity. Without halakhic rules, the assumption seems to have been that through education, through identification with the Jewish historical experience, through a commitment to "Jewish values," the Sabbath would become an organic part of Jewish national life. The new national cultural consensus would happen naturally, by virtue of the Jews coming back together in their ancestral land and renewing their relationship with their past. No enforcement.

Meanwhile, the dream of an enlightened, pluralistic, open polity, as in *Altneuland*, did not include such homogeneity. In Herzl's and Satanow's utopias, Jews, Christians, and Muslims would live side by side; the general culture—and the state—would be neutral regarding religious beliefs and cultural traditions. So the question that arises is: Leaving aside the whole matter of *halakhah* and its enforcement, what should be the place of the Sabbath in a *culturally* Jewish state? Just as it is hard to imagine a Jewish national home where Hebrew would not be the dominant language, it is hard to imagine an ethnically Jewish polity where the Sabbath would disappear from the cultural milieu. But then, what happens to the freedom of religion of those who don't believe in the Sabbath—or in Judaism at all—when, for example, maintaining a Jewish cultural milieu is seen to require halting all public transportation on the Sabbath?

This dichotomy is more vexing than the previous one, as while the *halakhah* is relatively clear, "culture" is not. The state could decide to relinquish all halakhic decision-making—and enforcement—leaving these to individuals and communities. But for a nation-state to abdicate any authority with respect to culture seems impossible. Decisions about official languages, symbols, the calendar (e.g., legal holidays) cannot be left to the individual, or to the voluntary sector. So willy-nilly, a Jewish state must address the place of the Sabbath in national culture. It seems that some kind of compromise between the vision of a national home and the utopia of a modern, enlightened, open state—however uneasy—cannot be avoided. Perhaps it will always be a work in progress.

And, of course, the Sabbath is just one—highly symbolic—example of a range of conflicts among the utopias of national home, halakhic community, and enlightened state; others include the authority to perform marriages, divorces, and conversions; gender equality; and religious pluralism.

Certainly, Israel cannot avoid a long-term, ongoing conversation about how best to engineer syntheses or at least compromises among the competing visions. In my view, the challenge for the Jewish state is to restore the Sabbath as a foretaste of utopia for the broadest section of the population, without infringing on the right of individuals and communities to adhere to differing definitions. For this, I would suggest the following possible directions:

1. Recognition that the Sabbath should be governed by community norms rather than by the state. According to this view, the individual and the community would decide norms and practices pertaining to the Sabbath—allowing for an infinite variety of individual practices and local norms without state interference.

2. Acceptance of certain minimal national norms in relation to the formal weekly day of rest, established through a secular, democratic process weighing costs and benefits, with input from religious authorities and all other stakeholders. For example, the state might decide that on balance, it is best that trains not run on the Sabbath; but authorities would reach this decision after input from all parties and not because the state is obligated, by virtue of Israel's being a Jewish state, to conform to a particular interpretation of *halakhah*.

3. Exploration and experimentation with alternative means of Sabbath rest and *oneg* (pleasure) in the modern era. One alternative drawing a lot of interest in recent years is to distinguish between culture and commerce on the Sabbath, by creating a Sabbath that in both theory and practice would offer a respite from rampant materialism and consumption. Such a Sabbath

could be meaningful even for the majority of the population who do not feel bound by *halakhah*.

The Welfare State

On a pleasant summer evening in 2011, among a few thousand marching and strolling down the main thoroughfare of the Galilean city of Karmiel, I found myself between the mayor with his retinue and a delegation of young men from the nearby Arab village of Majd-el-Krum waving red hammer-and-sickle flags. The atmosphere was festive, and of course I ran into old friends. Rhythmically chanting "The People! Demand! Social Justice!," we all ended up at a large park, where various speakers railed against the tycoons whose greed, facilitated by government policies, makes life miserable for all of us.

This was the local manifestation of the Great Tel Aviv Cottage Cheese Protest of that summer. The high cost of that Israeli dairy staple became a symbol and a rallying cry for a widespread sense of frustration over high food prices, a shortage of affordable housing, and the increasingly glaring income inequality in Israeli society. There was a lot of talk about the mobilization of youth and of social media as a force for change; several young activists launched political careers; a government commission was established. But neither Yavetz's nor Syrkin's socialist utopias came any closer to realization, any more than the more modest social-democratic visions of Lewinsky and Herzl. Nor did the price of cottage cheese come down.

When examining the interplay of competing visions of socialist utopia, national home, traditional community, and normal state in Israel's socioeconomic development, the Israeli experience may be seen to prove the Marxist argument that there is a conflict between nationalism and socialism: if the nation is composed of different socioeconomic classes whose interests conflict, it has an interest in suppressing that conflict for the sake of national unity. Although nominally socialist parties dominated Israeli politics from the prestate period until 1977, and although the national labor federation (*Histadrut*) was a major center of political and economic power, nevertheless Israel lagged behind European states in developing social welfare programs, and made no attempt to attack—or even moderate—ever-widening income inequality.[5]

The kibbutzim, seen by all the world as the symbol of the Israeli socialist utopia, never comprised more than 3 percent of the population. And as Buber pointed out, the ability of the kibbutz to survive and thrive stemmed less from its socialist commitment than from the harnessing and adapting of its socialist structure to serve personal and national goals. The small, pioneering, egalitarian community was well suited to serve the national needs of claiming and reclaiming agricultural land, rebuilding a nationalist connection to the land, and defending borders. The kibbutz saw itself and was seen by many as a step on the way to a socialist utopia both locally and nationally. However, its commitment to an ideal of social justice was overshadowed by its commitment to the ideal of building the Jewish nation-state and creating the New Jew.

Over the years, as socialist islands in a capitalist sea, the kibbutzim endured a number of financial crises, bailed out each time by the government, which saw their survival as a national—or at least political—priority. In 1977, for the first time, the labor party and its allies lost control of the government coalition. And in 1985, a government reform to combat massive inflation saddled many kibbutzim with unsustainable debts. Meanwhile, however, these kibbutzim had seen themselves as perpetual communities, providing "to each according to his [lifelong] needs" out of current operating funds—with no vested pensions. And so it happened that in 1987 Kibbutz Bet Oren (on Mt. Carmel, near Haifa) voted to disband in the face of its economic collapse—leaving its elderly, veteran members without income and without assets. This watershed moment caused a great public outcry and much soul-searching in the kibbutz movement.

The "Bet Oren Affair" came at a time when the development of welfare state institutions created in the 1950s and 1960s (for example the

National Insurance Institute, which provides not only disability, unemployment, and retirement benefits, but also, since 1954, paid maternity leave) had slowed in the face of scarce resources, rising individualism, and security pressures. It cast a glaring spotlight on the gap between the vision of a Jewish socialist community and the aspiration to be a normal state. Still, the welfare state has continued to develop. For example, among its achievements:

1976: Guaranteed paid sick leave for all employees

1980: Guaranteed minimum income law (income subsidy to those needing it to reach a certain minimum income, updated periodically)

1995: Universal health care

2007: Universal pension fund requirement (in addition to social security, all employers and employees are required to make at least a set minimum monthly contribution into a recognized private pension fund)

2012: Free day-care from age three

Meanwhile, despite these measures, a powerful and constant theme in Israeli public discourse is the assertion of victimhood by different populations feeling left out of the state's impressive technological and economic achievements: single-parent families, persons with special needs, members of Ethiopian or Middle Eastern ethnic groups, Holocaust survivors, senior citizens, residents of the periphery or of big city slums, residents of border communities, farmers, young couples, Palestinian citizens, and more. In some cases, such claims are expressed through public campaigns and demonstrations; in others, there is sufficient support to organize a political party and even attain representation in the Knesset (for example, the Pensioners' Party, which sat in the Knesset 2006–9).

Sometimes it feels as though this discourse of competitive victimhood drowns out or distorts what might be a more important conversation about competing visions. But when resources are scarce and distractions (e.g., matters of war and peace) are many, it can be hard to stay focused on utopia. In any case, despite the competition for resources and the ongoing tension between national solidarity and individual responsibility, perhaps Israel's development as a welfare state can be seen not as a conflict but as a confluence of visions. Programs and policies like those mentioned above can be viewed as small steps toward a socialist utopia; but at the same time they seem clearly to be tools for building national solidarity. And as such, they are rational actions by a normal state concerned for stability and economic development. Of the utopians we have met, all would probably have been pleased with Israel's efforts in this sphere, but disappointed with the rate of progress — after all, they were utopians. Only Jabotinsky, perhaps, with his anarchic, survival-of-the-fittest vision, would have found fault with the direction of development of the Israeli welfare state.

Immigration

I was leading an in-service seminar on teaching the holiday of Purim for teachers at a Jewish middle school in the Galilee when one participant asked, "How are we supposed to explain this to the gentile students in our classes?" I felt a bit blindsided by the question. Gentiles? Who knew? Isn't the point of a Jewish state that we don't have to explain ourselves to anyone anymore? Jewish state — Jewish culture — Jewish schools — Jewish content — Jewish kids. Lewinsky's utopia. So, who were these gentiles? From 1982 to 2000 Israel controlled a "security zone" along the border in southern Lebanon. Taking advantage of the bitter ethnic and religious fragmentation of Lebanese society, Israel cultivated a relationship with a local ally, a Christian militia known as the South Lebanese Army. Israel withdrew in 2000. Without their Israeli protectors, these locals and their families suddenly faced the threat of violent revenge. Israel granted asylum to about 750 families. Unwelcome in Arab villages, they settled in Jewish towns in the Galilee, and their children attend Jewish schools.

In 1977, an Israeli freighter encountered a leaking boat in the Pacific and rescued its passengers: sixty-six Vietnamese refugees fleeing the Communist takeover of their country. Brought back to Israel and granted citizenship, they were the vanguard of more than three hundred Vietnamese immigrants over the next two years. Later, in 1993, several dozen Muslim refugees from the violence in Bosnia were admitted to Israel and granted permanent residency.

Among the waves of immigration from the former Soviet Union and Ethiopia in the 1990s were a small percentage of individuals who qualified for citizenship under the Law of Return (one Jewish grandparent) but who were in fact Christian believers. Once settled in Israel, they gave public expression to their beliefs.

After 1967, the economic disparity between Israel and the occupied territories led to Palestinians from those territories serving Israel as a major source of cheap labor in building, manufacturing, and services. As Palestinian violent resistance to the status quo arose, from the late 1980s, this relationship soured, and Israel began to import temporary workers, via labor contractors, from the Far East, Africa, and Latin America. About sixteen thousand of these workers opted to remain in the country beyond their visas, hoping for some kind of permanent status.

In the wake of war and oppression in Eritrea and Sudan in the early twenty-first century, about forty-six thousand refugees managed to cross Sinai and enter Israel illegally. So far, only about a third have submitted formal requests for amnesty. Of those processed so far, the acceptance rate is under 0.2 percent.

The above five paragraphs contain a brief but basically complete history of non-Jewish immigration to Israel since 1948: a few almost negligible episodes. The drama of Jewish immigration, on the other hand, represents a central theme in Israeli collective memory: the Allies' refusal to accept Jews fleeing Nazi terror; the ongoing struggle with the British over Palestine immigration quotas; the swashbuckling and heroic efforts to break or circumvent the British blockade; the post-1948 waves of mass immigration, first from Europe, then from North

Africa and the Middle East, and later from the former Soviet Union and Ethiopia. The dream of ingathering, with its biblical prophetic echoes; the necessity of a sovereign state to serve as safe haven in the face of unimaginable persecution; and the ongoing, daunting challenge of building a shared identity and shared citizenship in a society of immigrants—these are defining concepts in Israel's self-perception.

In the reality of the second half of the twentieth century, the statement in the Israeli declaration of independence—"The State of Israel will be open for Jewish immigration and for the ingathering of the exiles"—seemed intuitively obvious to the most casual observer. The trauma of the Holocaust and the struggle for independence cast a long shadow. Wasn't the point of this whole exercise the sense of redemption and liberation that came from finally having a place whose borders we, and only we, controlled? The utopias of the prophets, of Yavetz, Lewinsky, and Herzl, converged in the glorious vision of return from exile.

But now the twentieth century has given way to the twenty-first, and the Jewish state finds itself in a different world. The rescue of sixty-six "boat people" in 1977 was a cause for great pride and self-congratulation—Israel would not go down the path of the hard-hearted Allies during the Holocaust. But today the seas are congested with leaky boats, and the desert borderlands crowded with human smugglers' caravans. Colonialism, global capitalism, global warming, cell phones, and the Internet—all have contributed to unleashing a flood of refugees whose economic and political impact on wealthy destination nations is a subject of bitter debate. Israel may see itself as small and embattled, but to outsiders it looks like a wealthy and secure democracy.

In a world of ethnic nation-states, refugees from other nations are a problem, a reason to build border walls. In the nation-state of the Jewish people, absorbing Jewish refugees, no matter how high the social and economic cost, is an unquestioned obligation; but absorbing gentile refugees is not. On the other hand, a state committed to universal social justice, to serving as a light unto the nations, would feel obligated to do its part in addressing this crisis. A Torah state, crafting its policy, might consider the biblical injunction, "You shall not oppress a stranger, for you know the feelings of the stranger, having yourselves been strangers in the land of Egypt" (Exod. 23:9). And a normal state would seek to strike a rational balance among its obligations to its own economic development, to its citizens' welfare, to its role as a member of the family of nations, and to its commitment to universal humanitarian values.

Morally and practically, there appears to be no perfect solution to the immigration crisis. Open borders are not practical; totally impassable borders are cruel. Israeli political discourse about this issue, when it can be separated from demagoguery, gives clear and painful expression to the conflict among utopian visions of the Jewish state. In the past decade, this conflict has been the stuff of daily headlines. Typically, the government, based on a commitment to the rule of law—and concern for the "Jewishness" of the state—announces a plan to deport a number of asylum-seekers, or prepares to deport an illegal foreign worker who has lived in Israel for a decade and started a family. Philanthropic and civic organizations respond with petitions, lawsuits, fund drives, and protests, based on "knowing the feelings of the stranger" and Jewish historical experience. Then the government either quietly backs down on its own or is forced to do so by the courts. It is an interesting irony that a leading organization in these struggles on behalf of refugees is HIAS—the Hebrew Immigrant Aid Society—founded in New York in 1881 to help Jewish refugees fleeing Russian persecution.

This struggle is, of course, similar to that occurring in other Western states, with the same players: lower socioeconomic classes fearful of competition for scarce resources; more established classes fearful of disorder and crime brought by "others"; humanitarians who believe that these costs are either imaginary or worth paying; and the silent majority who are ambivalent or indifferent. The question is, should Israel be different from other Western states? The utopian conflict is acute: Should a Jewish national home, nation-state of the Jewish people, be closed to gentile immigration in order to preserve its character and resources? Or, in view of Jewish historical experience, commitment to enlightenment, and the Torah's exhortations, should the Jewish state seek to maximize its role as a haven for refugees? What makes a better place better?

Living on the Land

Israelis growing up in the 1970s still sang Nathan Alterman's "Morning Song" (1934) in school, addressing the "motherland":

> We'll dress you in a gown of concrete and cement,
> And we'll spread for you carpets of gardens.[6]

And popular author Meir Shalev has written about his own school experience in the 1950s:

> In the years in which I studied the Anopheles mosquito at school, Zionism decided to renew its youth by draining the Hula [swamp]. You may be interested to note that a Dutch engineer, an expert in swamp drainage, was brought in. The man warned that the peaty ground, that same ground for which the project leaders were so hopeful, may behave in unknown, perhaps even harmful ways. Then the Jewish National Fund's hydrologist stood, banged the table with his fist and announced: "Our peat is Zionist peat, our peat will not harm a thing."[7]

The draining of the Hula swamp in the 1950s led to a number of serious unintended consequences, including underground peat fires, soil deterioration, land subsidence, pollution of the Sea of Galilee, and habitat destruction, leading to several species extinctions. Indeed, in the 1990s a section of the valley was deliberately reflooded to restore the ecological equilibrium.

The story of the Hula epitomizes the ongoing tension between development and preserving the environment. The first Zionist settlers, arriving in 1882, set out to "redeem" the swamp and desert, restoring through hard work their imagined memory of the "land of milk and honey." In their historical context they never could have imagined that a "gown of concrete" and "carpets of gardens" might some day be anything other than beautiful and healthy. And yet anyone traveling through the country today cannot miss that Israel has indeed "dressed [the land] in a gown of concrete and cement"—and a purple veil of pollution.

From the first stirrings of Zionist thought (see Yavetz and Lewinsky, for example), the biblical idyll of the prosperous peasant working his ancestral soil, living a peaceful life, enjoying the fruits of his labors, was central to the Zionist vision. The longing for a return to Jewish national normalcy—rootedness in the national soil; productive, dignified labor; a "natural" economy without the distortions of capitalism or persecution; a healthy closeness to nature—was a recurrent theme in all Zionist utopias. New Jews were not envisioned as tycoons or high-tech entrepreneurs, but as farmers. Whether socialist kibbutzniks or independent smallholders, they would be restored and normalized by getting their hands dirty with the soil of the Land of Israel. And just as the Jew had been corrupted and denatured by exile from the land, so the land itself had suffered by its abandonment by the Jews, deteriorating into swamp and desert. Reclaiming the Jews and reclaiming the land went together.

Key as well throughout the prestate and early state period was the Zionist concept of "economic carrying capacity": the land had to absorb mass immigration and provide a reasonable quality of life for the returning exiles. Thus there was a utopian and practical consensus that development—planting forests, draining swamps, irrigating deserts, building roads and neighborhoods, laying water pipelines, establishing new towns and farming settlements—was for the good. The New Jews would convert an empty (!) wasteland—a poor backwater of the Ottoman Empire—into a productive, populous, prosperous state. Agriculture would be the backbone of the new economy and culture.

The Agricultural Ideal

The romantic nationalist ideal never resulted in a real return to the land: since the earliest days of Zionist settlement, at least 80 percent of the population always lived in cities. However, the utopian dream of "a land of milk and honey," reflecting biblical images of the Promised Land, led to a number of policies and activities that turned out to be unwise. Draining the swamps generated unforeseen environmental problems. Pursuing the agrarian dream—and making the desert bloom—led to the diversion of scarce water resources to water-intensive agriculture: crops such as citrus fruit and cotton benefited from water subsidies. As a result, key aquifers have been depleted; streams have gone dry as the spring water feeding them has been captured; and the Sea of Galilee and the Dead Sea have been greatly diminished in size, leading to further unintended consequences. A classic, ironic case study: the shrinkage of the Dead Sea has led to the phenomenon of massive sinkholes along the shore, disrupting travel and tourism, hurting the communities in the area; meanwhile, an important business (in addition to tourism) for one of those kibbutzim has long been the capture and bottling of the water from a local spring feeding the Dead Sea. Today, Israel is a leader in desalination technology, which has somewhat ameliorated this ongoing water crisis; but desalination is energy-intensive. There is no free lunch. There appears to be a conflict between Lewinsky's and Syrkin's utopias: the fulfillment of a romantic agrarian dream is not necessarily consonant with the vision of a society in which rational planning governs the distribution of resources for the good of all.

Growth

Another utopian dissonance can be found in the area of population growth. Mass immigration and natural increase have made Israel into a very crowded country in which the ability to provide for basic needs has not kept pace with the population. Not only water, but hospital beds, classrooms, railroad cars, and green space are all in short supply. For example, compared to other developed countries in the OECD (Organization for Economic Cooperation and Development, with thirty-six member countries), Israel is at or near top ranking in population density, private car use and traffic congestion, and school class size (26.5); and in the bottom third in hospital beds, at three for every thousand people.

Future projections are daunting. Population growth—both by immigration and by natural increase—has always been seen as a national priority. This focus on growth has several roots:

- The model of the homogeneous nation-state—implying that all the Jews should live in Israel—reinforced by biblical images of the exiles' return
- A post-Holocaust urge to replace the Jewish people's demographic losses
- A drive of political necessity—the existence of a specifically Jewish state being dependent on maintaining a Jewish majority in the land

And so Israel provides child subsidies and immigrant subsidies, and invests in efforts to attract and support Jewish immigration. As such, it seems that the vision of the national home—and the fear of demographic threats—conflict with the dream of a normal state or a socialist utopia, in which the force driving policymaking would be the maximum good of all citizens, including those of future generations as well.

Public vs. Private Interests

Dressing the land in a "gown of concrete" can be seen, of course, as the consequence of population growth: all these people need houses and stores, factories and highways. But another utopian conflict is at work here. While both Lewinsky and Herzl imagined a welfare state, they explicitly rejected socialism, envisioning a capitalist economy. While for his part Syrkin did not think social classes would disappear, he did envision a collective economic organization. The real Israel, meanwhile, like other modern states, is caught in perpetual tension between private and public interests: between real estate developers and hotel chains on the one hand and the public's access to beaches and other natural resources on the other; between the strangling impact of the private car and the public development of mass transit and bicycle infrastructure; between the middle-class dream of a single-family home and the public interest in preventing suburban sprawl. In many cases, if not most, it seems that private interests trump public ones.

The above example of the kibbutz selling bottled water diverted from a stream flowing through a nature reserve is emblematic of this conflict, seen also in the familiar examples of chemical factories dumping waste into rivers, entrepreneurs fencing off public shoreline and charging admission to the beach, and developers building luxury homes or hotels in the midst of environmentally sensitive landscapes. As in any other mass democracy, in Israel money is power, and the government often appears powerless to intervene.

Israel is of course influenced by world trends, and many environmental activists and organizations are at work to save the land, the water, and the air from human depredations. Sometimes these efforts even yield impressive successes, as in a recent campaign to enforce the law requiring that all Sea of Galilee beaches be free and open to the public; or the successful conclusion of a years-long legal struggle to have a huge storage tank of toxic ammonia removed from densely populated Haifa. But as in the rest of the world, local political interests, corporate profiteering, and individual ignorance and selfishness can make it difficult to act in the public interest.

Yavetz, Lewinsky, Herzl, and Syrkin all imagined that in the Jewish utopia, a synthesis of Jewish tradition and modern rational governance would yield a society where the public interest was always served and class harmony would prevail. Jabotinsky, on the other hand, believed that the eternal struggle for power would result in an equilibrium of mutual deterrence, leading to a stable and healthy society. In Israel today, neither the harmony nor the equilibrium have been achieved, and so Israel is indeed "like all the nations," struggling to navigate the tension between social ideals and the reality of raw power. While this tension is manifest in different areas of life (e.g., labor relations, media control), perhaps the central arena is the control of and care for the land itself.

Israel and the Diaspora

As a high school exchange student in Israel I lived with an adopted family with whom I remained in touch for many years. They were immigrants from the 1920s, "old fashioned" socialist Zionists. Once Senya and Rachel came to visit us in the United States, and I excitedly related that the secretary at the synagogue I now served had once been Senya's student in elementary school in Haifa! I suggested inviting her family over for a reunion, but Senya and Rachel demurred: "We're not interested in meeting Israelis who have left Israel!"

Many years later, I helped facilitate a youth exchange between a nearby community in the Galilee and their partner Jewish community in the United States. In the debriefing after the ten-day trip, I asked the Israeli kids to reflect on what they had learned. Several said that before the trip they had looked down on American Jews as materialistic—as enjoying the fleshpots of the United States while Israelis sacrifice material well-being and cope with the threat of terror and the obligation of military service for the sake of the Jewish people. But they came away with the feeling that it is actually harder to be a Jew in the Diaspora than in Israel. Israelis simply *are* Jewish—all they have to do is breathe. The Americans have to make choices, pay dues, make an effort not to lose their identity, make compromises, decide to make a commitment—every day of their lives.

While it seems that in Yavetz's Torah state, all the Jews will have returned to the land, neither Lewinsky nor Herzl imagined a total ingathering. Lewinsky saw the future Jewish polity as a cultural center, helping to sustain active Jewish life around the world. Herzl thought that the Jews' normalization and entry into the family of nations would change their status in the Diaspora: Jews could demand their rights as equals, and with the end of Jewish rootlessness would come the end of antisemitism. Regardless, the idea that all Jews have a moral, or at least national, obligation to immigrate became a widely shared view. This assumption stands behind my adoptive parents'—and many others'—disparagement of *yordim* (those who have "gone down" from Israel). It stands behind many Israelis' denigration of diaspora Jews as persisting in their addiction to the fleshpots of exile. And it stands behind philanthropic and governmental efforts to identify and cultivate potential *olim* ("those who ascend"—Jewish immigrants) around the world, and subsidize their immigration and absorption.

Where does this assumption of moral asymmetry between Israeli and diaspora Jews come from? I suggest four roots:

1. In interpreting and applying the laws of the Torah, the Rabbis of the Mishnah and Talmud distinguish between laws that are universally applicable (e.g., the Sabbath) and those only in effect for Jews living in the Land of Israel (e.g., the sabbatical year). This means that one who lives in the land has more opportunities to fulfill divine commandments than one living abroad—which in turn means that life in the land is preferable. As the Rambam (Moses Maimonides, 1135–1204) summarized the matter in his great halakhic code:

   It is always forbidden to move abroad from the land of Israel, except to study Torah, or to get married, or to save others from the pagans; but these on the assumption that he will return; also, one may go abroad for business, but not dwell there unless there is severe famine in the land of Israel. . . . A person must always live in the land of Israel, even in a city that is mostly pagans— and not abroad, even in a city that is mostly Jews; for everyone who leaves the land is as if he worshipped idols.[8]

The Rambam, it should be mentioned, was born in Spain and lived most of his life in Egypt.

2. The Torah, of course, assumed that the entire nation would enter and live in the land (except for the tribes of Reuben, Gad, and half of Manasseh; see Numbers 32). Indeed, the harshest future punishment the Torah could imagine was exile, and once the nation would repent, they would be restored — presumably *in toto*. "Then the Lord your God will restore your fortunes and take you back in love. He will bring you together again from all the peoples where the Lord your God has scattered you. Even if your outcasts are at the ends of the world, from there the Lord your God will gather you, from there He will fetch you" (Deut. 30:3–4). Even secular Zionists, modern nationalists, couldn't resist framing their endeavor in the terms of this and similar traditional texts. At least at the rhetorical level, the Jewish national movement became conflated with the messianic vision of ingathering — the end of exile. And so, those who don't get on board are missing — or even delaying — the apocalyptic train.

3. Ahad Ha'am attacked Herzl's call for mass immigration, arguing that, aside from being unrealistic, a cultural groundwork must be put in place first. However, early on during the British Mandate, it became clear that Jews and Palestinian Arabs were locked in a demographic struggle and Jewish population growth through immigration to Palestine was a national necessity. So *aliyah* became a Zionist *mitzvah* (commandment). And its acquisition of an aura of heroic national dedication cast those who stayed in the Diaspora as sinners by omission.

4. Among diaspora Jews in open societies, the past half century has seen a growing concern about the precariousness of Jewish continuity. To remain Jewish in an open society requires commitment and effort, and some observers note a decreasing willingness to make that commitment and expend that effort. To many Jews in Israel and in the Diaspora too, Israel looks like the

reincarnation of the ideal community, where Jewish belonging—Jewish identity—is organic, unshakeable, and the only hope for Jewish survival.

The Israel-Diaspora asymmetry can be seen an as expression of a utopian conflict. Should the Jewish nation—in Israel and elsewhere—educate, plan, and build toward a Torah utopia in which all the Jews in the world live in the Land of Israel? Or, in the spirit of Herzl and Lewinsky, should the ideal be more of an equal and synergetic relationship among Jews living in a variety of communities worldwide? The tension between these two utopian visions of Jewish life trickles down into the ongoing conversation between Israelis and diaspora Jews, influencing education, philanthropy, communal politics, and allocation of resources.

For example, consider the Birthright program that brings young diaspora Jews on a free educational tour of Israel to bolster their Jewish identity. An argument can also be made that visiting diaspora Jewish communities can correspondingly have impact on young Israelis' Jewish identity. Perhaps there should be a symmetrical Birthright program, sponsoring tours in the other direction—but not if the consensus message is that only Israel has something to teach. Another example: Jews around the world, since pre-Zionist times, have seen their fellow Jews living in Palestine and then Israel as objects of philanthropy, special recipients of *tzedakah* (charity) contributions. Originally, such philanthropy supported those pious immigrants who came to pray and study in the Holy Land—vicariously performing mitzvot for the donors. Later Zionist philanthropy built on this model, collecting funds to buy land, to build institutions, to support economic development, education, defense, and so on. Zionist donors couldn't or wouldn't perform the Zionist mitzvah of immigration themselves, but they felt obligated to support those who did. However, in a symmetrical vision, Israeli tycoons (and ordinary donors) would also be solicited—to fund struggling Jewish schools and charitable institutions in the Diaspora.

And, of course, a long-standing question that has taken center stage in recent decades is what voice diaspora Jews should have in determining Israeli policies. If they are not directly affected (e.g., they won't experience bombardments, their children won't be drafted, their air won't be polluted) by Israeli policies, what right should they have to influence them? But on the other hand, if Israel demands their support, morally, politically, and financially, shouldn't diaspora Jewry have a say? This becomes more complicated when diaspora Jews perceive that Israel's behavior as a state *does* affect them directly, as disputes over Israeli government policies become matters of partisan politics in the countries of the Diaspora. If Israel is to be a normal, modern, enlightened state, then, clearly, only its citizens should get the vote—and be expected to pay the bills. If Israel is one Jewish community among many, then relationships of mutual assistance with the others would be expected—but so would the political autonomy of each community. And if Israel is the nation-state of the Jewish people, a national home, then all Jews everywhere are indeed important to and obligated by the state, and can be expected to support it and have a voice in its deliberations.

To see how such utopian visions collide, imagine two small Jewish communities in the Diaspora, one liberal, one *charedi*. In the *charedi* synagogue, strict gender separation is maintained, and only men may take on liturgical and communal leadership roles. The liberal community, on the other hand, implements gender equality in every sphere. The two communities may each disapprove of the other's beliefs and practices, but they recognize communal autonomy, leave each other alone, and will help each other in an emergency (such as offering temporary space if the other's building is flooded). Conflict will only arise when they try to combine for a service or the like. Meanwhile, in Jerusalem, the plaza in front of the Western Wall of the Temple compound is administered by a *charedi* body that enforces strict gender separation and forbids women from reading the Torah, even in their separate area. Israel has used state power to convert the Western Wall plaza—a historical site that has become a national symbol—into a *charedi* synagogue.

Responses to this conflict will differ depending on how we understand the relationship between Israel and the Diaspora:

- If Israel is a modern, enlightened democracy, then rabbis must not use state power to infringe upon the rights of citizens to pray—or not pray—as they see fit, where they see fit. In any case, this is a matter for the state's institutions to work out. Citizens who feel that the status quo is unfair to liberal Jews and to women should use the means of democratic struggle—speaking out, lobbying, voting, demonstrating—to move toward change.

- If Israel is one Jewish community among many, the same conclusion stands: that community's religious practices and the treatment of religious symbols are matters for internal decision-making.

- If Israel aspires to be the national home of the entire Jewish nation, including diaspora Jewry, then Jews throughout the world have a right—and, perhaps, even an obligation—to join the conversation on how to administer such a central national site. If this is the case, of course, difficult problems arise: diaspora Jews are themselves deeply divided on this question, and have no representative political structure to present a unified opinion. And even if they did, how should they express their view and how much weight should it have? Is it acceptable for them to support Israeli organizations struggling for change? Directly lobby the Israeli government? Visit Israel and join demonstrations? Threaten to withhold support from Israel unless their view is accepted? Lobby their own governments to put pressure on Israel?

The example of the Western Wall plaza, vexing as it is, is "easy" compared to other issues that roil Israel-Diaspora relations in our time, as for example policies regarding the current treatment and long-term plan for the territories ruled by Israel since 1967 or the status of the Palestinian Arab minority in Israel. If the Western Wall controversy can be seen as an internal Jewish matter, these questions are "matters of state," with global geopolitical consequences. In these questions of Israel-Diaspora relations, the dilemma finds its clear expression: to pursue a vision of Israel as a state like any other—or as a state *not* like any other.

To conclude, a midrash:

The Torah states, "Will one man sin and You will punish the whole congregation?" (Num. 16:22). Rabbi Shimon bar Yochai taught, "This can be explained by the parable of people sitting in a boat: One of them took a drill and started to drill a hole under his seat. They said to him, 'What are you doing?' He answered, 'What does it matter to you? I am only drilling under my own seat!' They said to him, 'But all of us will drown!'"[9]

Further Reading

Ben Porat, Guy. *Between State and Synagogue: The Secularization of Contemporary Israel*. Cambridge: Cambridge University Press, 2012.

Brenner, Michael. *In Search of Israel: The History of an Idea*. Princeton NJ: Princeton University Press, 2018.

Shapira, Anita. *Israel: A History*. Translated by Anthony Berris. Waltham MA: Brandeis University Press, 2012.

Tal, Alon. *The Land Is Full: Addressing Overpopulation in Israel*. New Haven CT: Yale University Press, 2016.

Troy, Gil, ed. *The Zionist Ideas: Visions for the Jewish Homeland, Then, Now, Tomorrow*. Philadelphia: The Jewish Publication Society, 2018.

Yakobson, Alexander, and Amnon Rubinstein. *Israel and the Family of Nations: The Jewish Nation-State and Human Rights*. Translated by Ruth Morris and Ruchie Avital. London: Routledge, 2009.

12

A Utopian Travel Blog

The following is a sketch of my proposed utopia — eutopia — outopia — for the Jewish state. It is a personal vision, admittedly fragmentary, informed by what I have learned in writing the preceding eleven chapters and by my experiences living in both the Diaspora and Israel. The fictitious traveler is not me, but his or her observations nevertheless reflect my value priorities. Readers who find that this utopia does not articulate what they hope for are encouraged to envision their own utopias, to enrich the discussion we need to have.

First Impressions

We arrived late afternoon (Wednesday). Our guide, Reuven, shepherded us out of Ben Gurion Airport, onto our bus, and through check-in at our Tel Aviv hotel, a small, cute place a few blocks from the beach. We were all pretty out of it, but after some time to shower and relax, I was eager to get out. Reuven led us on a stroll to get to know our neighborhood, and we congregated on some benches along the beach promenade to watch the sunset and get an overview and introduction to the trip. Reuven appears to be extremely knowledgeable, and presents information in a very interesting way; he seems not to feel the need to flood us with details (thank God). As an American immigrant who has lived here for over thirty years, he is good at imagining how we see things. He loves living here — at times, in his introduction, he sounds as though he thinks he has found utopia. Too good to be true? We'll wait and see.

Day 1, Thursday: Tel Aviv

Morning

We spent some of the morning on a bike tour of the city, with free time to explore a bit on our own. Hot and humid! But having such a magnificent beach right in town certainly compensates! Reuven showed us some photographs of the beach from years ago, pointing out that it was almost twice as wide then; the shrinkage—and thus crowding—resulting from the rising sea level have given rise to a plan to create an artificial island a mile out to sea, to serve as a municipal park with beaches, green space, and cultural venues, to be reached via a causeway. He pointed out the first stages—construction vessels visible toward the horizon.

I was surprised to discover that, for a large, dense metropolis, Tel Aviv is remarkably clean and quiet. Reuven explained that this is the result of a long struggle to implement what seemed at the time a radical vision. Its main elements are these:

A massive retrofitting of the transportation infrastructure to make bicycle travel a preferred option. Tel Aviv is flat and the weather is usually warm and clear. By reducing and limiting motorized traffic, walkers and bikers have been able to take over the city. There is also a subway and an efficient network of electric bus and minibus routes, especially to connect the city center with suburbs and intercity trains and buses. Within all metropolitan areas in Israel, all of these routes are free. There are, of course, taxis and delivery trucks (all electric) as well as private cars (also electric), but the latter are by no means dominant. Thus traffic jams and the eternal parking shortage—those plagues of early twenty-first-century urban life—have largely been eliminated. Evidently other flat cities, like Beersheba, have successfully adopted the same model. In Haifa and Jerusalem, both built on mountains, the mix is different: less reliance on bicycles.

Reuven noted, with pride, that this shift to electric transportation was largely facilitated by an Israeli invention: an extraordinary three-layer paint that, when applied, creates solar-electric panels on any surface. Thus vehicles—and building roofs and walls—can be cheaply converted into sources of electric power.

The fostering of decentralized commercial and cultural activity, with covered markets (often in buildings that used to house supermarkets) and small shops, as well as community centers and parks, spread throughout the city, in every neighborhood. This strengthens community, spreads around (deconcentrates) economic activity, and encourages walking and biking.

The markets, by the way, feel very "retro." It's rare to see items packaged in single-use plastic. People come with their own baskets, bags, and carts—and even glass, metal, and plastic containers for bulk items. Reuven noted that this norm is the result of an intensive, decade-long campaign involving educational efforts as well as carrot-and-stick policies to change behaviors. Though I gather that most produce comes from rural farms outside the metropolis, I noticed as we walked and biked the many herb and vegetable beds and fruit trees in pocket parks throughout the city—and on roofs. The city government subsidizes and guides these neighborhood projects.

Afternoon

After lunch, we visited a center for immigrant absorption, a large campus northeast of the city center. First the director gave us an overview of immigration policies and described the center's work; then we met in small groups with a number of the residents and staff.

New immigrants have the option of living in a center like this (there are several around the country) for up to a year, while they learn the language and culture, get vocational training if necessary, and "find their place" in terms of jobs and housing. There are intensive language courses, vocational counseling, and social and cultural activities for different age groups (students, young adults, families with kids, the middle-aged, senior citizens). Most of the center's residents are Jews, immigrating under the "Law of Return," which grants automatic citizenship to any immigrant with at least one Jewish grandparent. Of these, we met some who chose to move to Israel seeking a more "fully Jewish" life, others who seemed to be seeking personal escape or adventure, and some fleeing difficult conditions in their countries of origin. The accommodations and other services provided in the center are free; once the immigrants move out, the government provides no further economic support.

We also met Christian, Muslim, and Hindu immigrants who arrived in Israel as refugees from war, famine, and persecution in their home countries. They comprise about 20 percent of the center's residents. Israel has an interministerial committee on immigration, whose professional staff reviews economic data and projections and sets an annual quota for immigrants not covered by the Law of Return. They also study the world refugee situation and its driving factors, and set priorities and criteria to guide the processing of applications. Preliminary determinations are made through advance applications at Israeli embassies and consulates abroad, or in some cases at the border crossing. However, there are always some prospective immigrants who get as far as the absorption center but whose applications are ultimately denied, usually based on concerns about their prospective economic and social absorption. In these cases, Israeli diplomats find them another destination country, and the Absorption Ministry gives them a ticket and a grant to help in the transition. While Jewish immigrants may choose to bypass the absorption center and move directly to housing and jobs they arrange on their own or through family or friends, immigrants arriving outside the Law of Return framework are required to live in a center for at least their first four months in the country. Ultimately, if they wish to apply for citizenship, they will have to pass a test in language, geography, and civics, and convince an interview committee of their good character and ability to support themselves.

We learned that a dozen of the center's staff members are working under the terms of their Israeli national service. Every Israeli citizen between ages eighteen and twenty, regardless of religion or ethnicity, is required to devote two years to national service. The wide range of service options include the military, the medical system, formal and informal education, immigrant absorption, and national parks and nature reserves. For some Israelis, these two years are a chance to pursue ideals; for others, an opportunity to explore a professional direction; for others, an adventure; and for some, a frustrating obstacle in their life plans. Members of the group we met live at the center and help in Hebrew instruction and organizing cultural and social events. They seem to be a cohesive group having a great time. Interestingly, a few of them are not Israelis, but diaspora Jews who had signed up for a two-year "gap" program of service-learning in Israel. In parallel, every year a few thousand Israelis are selected to do their national service abroad, working in educational and cultural programming in Jewish communities or in a humanitarian capacity in developing countries.

Evening

To taste Israeli culture, a few of the national service staffers from the immigrant absorption center invited us to join them at a concert at a large club — small tables, drinks served. At first it felt a bit weird: On stage, four vocalists, accompanied by four instrumentalists (proficient in both Middle Eastern and Western instruments) — garbed in a variety of robes and turbans and dreadlocks — performed something of a fusion of North African Jewish liturgical poetry, rock, and jazz. The leader encouraged everyone in attendance to sing along and clap with the music — but not to applaud, since the songs were all prayers — so there was silence after each piece. Two hours later, the place was alive, with people dancing in the aisles.

After my first day, it occurs to me to say how satisfying I am finding it to be able to understand my environment (signs, ads, etc.) and communicate with people easily in Hebrew. I was fortunate to have been born in the decades after the policy shift among Jewish educators in North America towards investing major resources (including time) into

Hebrew language instruction. Thanks to the burgeoning of immersion programs and immersion schools, Hebrew has been reclaimed in the largest diaspora communities as a cornerstone of Jewish identity. Not always, in the American environment, was that commitment easy to swallow for people like me, growing up with it. But once we walked out of the hotel door last night onto the streets of Tel Aviv, I was moved to take back all my complaints. Not at all a stranger in a strange land.

Day 2, Friday: Tel Aviv

Morning

We were all amused and a bit concerned when we saw that today's itinerary was to include a visit to a garbage dump. But it turned out to be a truly eye-opening morning. Just outside the city is Hiriya, formerly the municipal landfill, visible from afar as a flat-topped mountain whose core is twentieth-century garbage. The site, and hundreds of acres around it, have been converted to a huge multiuse park: community vegetable gardens, fields of wildflowers, walking paths, water features, shady groves—and a center for recycling, upcycling, and waste reduction. After a walk around the tree-shaded summit to an observation platform with a panoramic view of the Tel Aviv metropolis, we drove back down to the base. We weren't dressed for kayaking, so we made do with paddle-boating on the artificial lake. Then we visited a waste-reduction education center for schools and individual visitors (staffed mostly by Israelis doing their national service); an arts and crafts village of studios and small businesses, all producing art and consumer goods out of reclaimed materials; a huge state-of-the-art garbage separation plant, producing tons of compost as well as various raw material streams for construction, manufacturing, and energy generation; and a research lab. This was all impressive, but not particularly unique in today's world.

What really stood out was our visit to the Institute for Consumption Reduction (ICR), a think tank, research institute, and incubator that over the past two decades has quietly led a revolution in the Israeli economy. The incubator has supported startups and local efforts countrywide to convert sales into service through a practice of rent-return-reuse for everything from furniture to clothing, from toys to tools: tool and toy libraries, furniture and clothing exchanges. It has managed to make the second-hand economy mainstream. Of course it wasn't easy, confronting ingrained cultural attitudes and corporate interests. The institute engaged in public relations campaigns, developed school curricula, trained educators and community organizers, and lobbied for local and national legislation to support reuse and the institutions fostering it. Amazingly, today, despite a rising standard of living, per capita consumption of new durable goods in Israel has been dropping by a few percentage points every year for over a decade—in parallel with a reduction in the volume of garbage arriving for sorting at Hiriya.

The ICR also played a major role in the shift in transportation culture I mentioned before. Through investing in infrastructure—and ongoing subsidies—for bikes, electric buses, and trains, the country finally reached a tipping point when the number of private cars began to drop, rather than grow, each year—and the plague of ubiquitous traffic congestion began to subside. Part of this effort was focused on reducing the process of suburban sprawl: changing zoning laws to stop new developments of single family housing, creating incentives for denser (and higher) construction. Inspired, we all bought recycled and upcycled gifts in the artists' village for friends and family back home.

For lunch, we drove back toward the coast, to the old Reading power plant at the north end of the city. Since Israel derives all of its electric power from wind turbines, hydroelectric, geothermal, and solar energy, the old fossil-fuel plants have been phased out. Reading Station's smokestack, now a solar collector, has an observation deck near the top with a panoramic view of the city and the coastline. What stood out from on high was the greenness—most buildings in the city have rooftop gardens. The city gives tax breaks for green roofs on older buildings, and approval of new construction requires a green roof plan. In many residential buildings the roof gardens are communal, while commercial structures generally engage a gardening contractor. At the base of the smokestack is a tourism complex including several restaurants that make a point of serving vegetables that are "roof-to-table."

Afternoon

At lunch, Reuven warned us that the afternoon would be less hands-on and more "heavy." We were scheduled for a program on Israel's constitution at Independence Hall.

Once the home of Tel Aviv's first mayor, then an art museum, "Independence Hall" was the venue for the formal ceremony of Israel's declaration of independence, as the British were about to pull out in 1948. We saw a well-done multimedia presentation describing the historical context, and in the restored hall we listened to a scratchy recording of Ben-Gurion reading the declaration. Goose bumps.

That declaration had promised that a constitution for the new state would be enacted no later than October 1, 1948. The promise was not kept — it took almost a century to finally agree upon a constitution. Led by a very charismatic professor from Tel Aviv University, we studied the text in small groups. Given the historical background (which she presented succinctly), it was not hard to understand why it took so long. Reconciling different visions of "Jewish state" into a binding document with wide public support proved to be a huge challenge.

Here (sans the historical background) are some of the highlights I took away from that "heavy" — but fascinating — session.

The preamble states that Israel is the "nation-state of the Jewish people," which is also the "state of all its citizens." That double declaration led the framers to a series of careful compromises:

- **Religion and state:** Israel chose the British model. Judaism is the established religion, but there is full freedom of — and freedom from — religion. Saturday is the official day of rest and the Jewish holidays are state holidays. Citizens are free to turn to any clergy person or religious court or council, of any religion, in matters of conversion, marriage, divorce, and burial; civil marriage and burial are options, and there are secular state family courts. There is no chief rabbi; each community or network of communities has established its own leadership hierarchy. There is, however, a rabbinical advisory committee, comprising rabbis from different denominations, which prepares background papers to advise the government and parliament in decisions with clear religious implications (e.g., medical ethics, interpretations of "day of rest" policies, limits of communal autonomy).

- **Guaranteed freedoms:** Discrimination in employment, housing, trade, public services, and education on the basis of race, religion, ethnicity, gender, and sexual orientation is forbidden, as is hate speech. Freedom of assembly, worship, movement, residency, and expression are guaranteed.

- **Government structure:** The Knesset comprises two houses of Parliament:

  - An upper house of seventy-one members chosen in nationwide elections through proportional representation (voters vote for a party, not a candidate; and parties must choose their list of candidates in primary elections). The number of members reflects the seventy-one members in the Sanhedrin, the high court and legislative body described in the Talmud. Upper house Knesset members are salaried state employees, full time for their four-year term.

  - A lower house of 120 members divided among five regional assemblies (proportional to population): the Negev, Tel Aviv Metro, Jerusalem Metro, Haifa Metro and the coastal strip, and the Galilee. Here again the numeric choice is significant: rabbinic literature refers to *Hakenesset Hagedolah* ("The Great Assembly") of 120 leaders and teachers, believed to have ruled the Jewish autonomy in the Land of Israel during the Second Temple period (538 BCE–70 CE). Notably, lower house representatives are not elected, but chosen at random (like jurors in other Western countries) for a two-year term. Each regional assembly meets biweekly for a full day, and the entire house meets together once a year for three weeks. Assembly members are reimbursed for their time (lost wages) and expenses.

- The lower house may recommend legislation, but only the upper house may actually initiate and formulate it. The lower house holds veto power over any legislation passed by the upper house.

- All legislation is subject to judicial review by the Supreme Court.

- The prime minister, leader of the parliamentary majority (or a majority coalition) in the upper house, is the chief executive, charged with carrying out parliament's decisions. In order to facilitate this, the prime minister selects twelve ministers who comprise the cabinet, and a majority in the upper house must approve their appointments. Significantly, these ministers are not Knesset members; rather, they have professional expertise and experience in their ministry's area of activity (e.g., education, trade, environment, defense). Of course, the legislative-executive relationship is dynamic: the prime minister and other ministers not only execute laws, but initiate laws and lobby for their passage.

- **Language:** While Hebrew is of course the majority language, both Hebrew and Arabic are the official languages. All government documents, publications, and forms, as well as all street signs, must appear in both languages.

- **Minority group rights:** The interests of the large Palestinian Arab minority are represented by the neighboring state of Palestine, which is defined as the nation-state of the Palestinian people — and a state of all its citizens. Symmetrically, the interests of the Jewish minority who are citizens of Palestine are represented by the Israeli government vis-à-vis the Palestine government. A provision calls for the establishment of bina-tional advisory committees—e.g., on education, holy places, communal autonomy—as the need arises.

- **Amendments to the constitution:** These require a 75 percent majority of both houses of parliament, and must pass on three readings, with a minimum of two years between the first and the third.

I still had a million questions, but by the end of the afternoon my mind was numb. Reuven promised, though, that in the days ahead we would explore in depth some of the specific issues that arose.

Evening

We had a relaxed Sabbath dinner in a private room in a Tunisian restau-rant. Then we sat around the table for a long time, as Reuven—who, it turns out, is an accomplished guitarist and song leader—led us on a musical survey of Israeli history, through folk and popular songs.

Afterwards, some people crashed, but a few of us went for a long stroll through different neighborhoods. We were curious to see what the Sabbath eve felt like in the "first Hebrew city" (as Tel Aviv was proudly acclaimed, with its 1909 founding in the dunes north of ancient Yafo). Music seemed to be emanating from everywhere: open windows as families gathered around their dinner tables; public sing-alongs of traditional Sabbath hymns (*zemirot*) and folk and popular songs in parks and community centers; concerts of classical, pop, and avant-garde music at venues large and small. We stood for a while outside a Hasidic synagogue, humming and swaying to the exuberant, rhythmic chanting of *zemirot*.

Cafés and restaurants were crowded, as were the sidewalks and parks. The stores all seemed to be closed. Reuven later confirmed that this is the law on the Sabbath. Public transport does operate, but on a reduced schedule. Some routes, running from suburban areas through town to the beach, use autonomous vehicles that stop automatically at every station.

Day 3, Saturday: Tel Aviv

Morning

Reuven suggested optional destinations for Saturday morning: synagogues of every possible denomination and ethnic tradition, as well as lectures, study groups, and musical events. I took an autonomous bus out to an eastern suburb. The large and beautiful sanctuary of the egalitarian Reform synagogue there was packed with Israelis of all ages. The liturgy, accompanied by a small band, was almost entirely sung, and the intense, contagious spirit reminded me of the Hasidic synagogue last night.

Afternoon

A nap, the beach, iced coffee along the promenade. Hung out at a coffee bar with a small group of university students, bored and happy to practice their English. I learned a lot. They were (I am not making this up) an Orthodox kibbutznik, a Sudanian refugee, a Palestinian from a Galilee village, and a "secular" Jew from Haifa. They are all classmates in a dual MA program in materials science and economics. Unlike students in general (in my experience), they seemed uninterested in complaining about "the system." Education in Israel is free through university (first degree), and they said scholarships are usually available for graduate work. Also, all four of them work as teaching assistants.

They all grew up in the period after the Great Reform in Israeli education, when popular protests drove the government to a major reorganization of the system and, indeed, of national priorities. Teacher training requirements were tightened, salaries were increased, and maximum class size in elementary and secondary schools was dropped from forty to twenty five. But, most significantly, the entire system through twelfth grade was unified. Whereas previously there had been four separate, parallel systems—Arab, Jewish secular, public Orthodox, and private Orthodox—all schools are now mandated to follow a national core curriculum that includes bilingual education in Hebrew and Arabic. That said, thirty percent of a school's curriculum is under the control of local school boards, so communities can mold schools to meet their needs—up to a point. And while generally children attend their neighborhood school, there are procedures for enrolling in a different school based on religious or ideological commitments or special interest or needs. There are still some private schools, generally serving religious communities (Orthodox, Catholic, etc.) and funded by tuition and philanthropy, but even these must teach the core curriculum.

As participant-observers, the economics students agreed that this reform—which had necessitated moving political mountains—had done a lot to integrate Israeli society and to reduce socioeconomic, ethnic, and religious stratification.

The four students are all hoping to catch the wave in materials science since the huge success of Israeli electricity-generating paint. When I wondered if my fresh MA in comparative literature would be marketable here, they were surprisingly enthusiastic. It turns out that the Great Reform also reorganized high school education to help prioritize the humanities, and there are still shortages of teachers and curriculum developers in these fields.

Evening

Just as I was feeling smug about my Hebrew, I discovered there is a small—but growing—movement to displace it! We went to a theater in Jaffa, the ancient seaport that is at once quaint and kitschy, old and new, but certainly an interesting center of cultural creativity—and hopping on Saturday night. The play we saw was in Aramaic—the vernacular language in these parts in talmudic times. (Indeed, the Talmud is mostly written in Aramaic, so the language has remained familiar to the Jews over the centuries.) Written in Hebrew characters, Aramaic shares much of its vocabulary and grammar with Hebrew, but also shares a fair amount of grammar and vocabulary with Arabic, so it can be seen as a "bridge" language. (For my part, I delightedly discovered I could understand some of the Aramaic dialogue on my own, though I did have to refer a lot to the projected subtitles.) What if, the Aramaic activists say, Jews and Arabs could all speak to each other here in an official neutral language that is a "cousin" of both their respective national languages? Then no one would have to relinquish anything in terms of identity or national pride.

Already, there is an Aramaic newspaper, high schools offering Aramaic electives, a university department, a publishing house, and a network of Aramaic clubs serving as meeting places for Jews and Palestinians. There have even been a few hit popular songs in Aramaic.

I wonder if this will develop. Esperanto never succeeded in overcoming the link between nationalism and language, and in the meantime, English has become a global lingua franca.

Day 4, Sunday: Jerusalem

Morning

Our first stop in Jerusalem was the Temple Mount, and all of us were excited by the prospect. I knew that for centuries this holy site had been a focus of interreligious and nationalistic strife and violence. Yet I couldn't remember any incidents in recent years, so I was curious.

The entire site is now a free national park under joint Israeli and Palestinian administration. The mosques are open for tourists (by guided tour only—free every half-hour) except for prayer times, when only worshipers are admitted. A large section of the plaza has been turned into a meditation garden. Aesthetic benches, ringed by trees and bushes in planters, and insulated by stone and wood partitions, serve as spaces for individual prayer and meditation, as well as semi-enclosed areas suitable for organized prayer by small groups (up to about fifty people). We assembled in one of these areas, and Reuven led us in a medley of songs about the Temple, based on passages from Psalms. Then we had some time to wander about on our own. It gave me a chance to ponder the problematic relationship between holiness and ownership. Others of these assembly spaces, I noticed, were occupied by groups of Orthodox men, Orthodox women, egalitarian prayer groups, secular groups like ours, and also Muslims and Christians.

We walked down to the Western Wall plaza, which, apparently, had lost much of its significance with the opening up of the Temple Mount itself. Nevertheless, holiness, it seems, lingers. The entire area adjacent to the Western Wall and on around to the south, like the meditation garden on the mount, contains a number of semienclosed terraces and plazas, allowing a variety of religious expression to go on simultaneously.

We spent the rest of the morning touring the Old City, visiting archaeological and historical sites and learning about the history of the city and its various communities. Falafel from a street vendor for lunch.

Afternoon

We walked out of the Old City and through an ultra-Orthodox neighborhood, fascinated by how this community persists in its distinctive dress and culture even as they partake of modern technology. We ended up at a community center downtown, where a panel of rabbis serving various segments of the local population (ultra-Orthodox, Zionist Orthodox, liberal, secular) had gathered to address "the Jewishness of the Jewish state."

We were surprised by the collegiality among the speakers. Surprisingly, even though they all hold very different ideas regarding how Jews should live their Judaism—and clearly view their colleagues' positions as inauthentic, morally problematic, or just plain wrong—they pretty much agreed on how the Jewish state should be Jewish:

- In general, the state should be secular, not intervening in the religious lives of its citizens. Its Jewishness as a state resides in its location in the Land of Israel, and in its dominant culture (Hebrew, calendar).

- Marriage, divorce, and conversion are communal matters, not state functions. If one community does not accept the conversions, marriages, or divorces performed by another, that is not a matter for state intervention.

- Kosher food must be available in public institutions like the army, universities, museum cafeterias, etc., but nonkosher food may also be available, as long as a clear distinction is maintained. There is no restriction on the sale of nonkosher food in shops and restaurants, though labeling must be clear. Of course, certain establishments choose to sell or serve only kosher products. But as in Jewish communities all over the world, there are different kashrut standards and supervisory networks, and consumers are free to patronize the stores, restaurants, and brands that fit their needs and beliefs.

- An important function of the state is to strike a careful balance between individual rights, community prerogative, and state authority. Religious life should primarily be a community matter rather than a state function: hence, the adoption of a national school curriculum that allows local communities to exert some autonomy. People can choose to live together in neighborhoods or rural communities according to a common religious or cultural denominator, but this choice may not infringe on freedom of residency. No admissions committees are allowed.

- A group of 250 or more adults may organize themselves into a community (generally involving geographic proximity, a statement of principles, and a financial commitment), and request partial funding from the government for a religious leader, whose authority extends only to this community. Communities are free to organize into networks or movements, with a hierarchy of leadership and nationwide institutions such as training programs for clergy or teachers — but without government funding.

Having agreed that *halakhah*, and religious traditions in general, are matters for the individual and community, the rabbis surprised us by then pointing proudly to a number of government policies that certainly looked to me like applications of halakhic concepts in the governance of the state:

The liberal rabbi spoke eloquently about the challenges — and successes — in trying to extract an economic doctrine from the Torah. She quoted Deuteronomy 15:11: "There will never cease to be needy ones in your land, which is why I command you to open your hand to the poor" as evidence that the Torah did not envision socialism. Rather, the law of the jubilee year can be seen as permission for individuals to compete, to accumulate resources — but with the caveat that this accumulation is not unlimited, and will be subject to a periodic "reset." Israeli policymakers had taken the jubilee principle to mean that the personal freedom to accumulate wealth had to be limited. Society has no use for billionaires — or for extreme poverty. Thus, all taxation except income tax and estate tax has been eliminated, and the income tax is highly progressive, with a negative tax for the lowest earners, and an extremely high tax rate for the highest ones. So far, the disparity between the richest and the poorest, measured by the Gini Index of income inequality (on a scale of 0–1), has fallen from among the highest in the OECD early in the twenty-first century (0.43 in 2010) to among the lowest today (0.20). (Reuven later explained how this jubilee mindset had made it into law: since the lower house of the Knesset was not elected but randomly selected, the power of "big money" in the political process had been partially neutralized.)

The Zionist Orthodox rabbi was eager to tell us about the way the sabbatical year has been reinterpreted. The actual agricultural *shemitah*, letting the land rest every seventh year, has been left as a private or communal matter. Some farmers observe it; others avail themselves of halakhic methods to circumvent it. Some ignore it. Produce is labeled accordingly, and consumers are free to choose. In recent sabbatical years, a kind of traditionalist nostalgia among the secular public has created market pressure on farmers to find halakhic solutions.

Meanwhile, policymakers' efforts to extract and apply a general principle from the *shemitah* concept have resulted in a universal sabbatical option. All employers and employees make a required monthly contribution, parallel to the required pension contribution, to a sabbatical fund, which finances, every seventh year, a sabbatical year at full salary. The ministry of education, as well as public and private institutions, offer a rich menu of courses, workshops, and degree programs geared to this market, providing enrichment, professional advancement, and career change support.

The secular rabbi (ordained by a Humanistic seminary) talked about his involvement in a project grounded in a new interpretation of kashrut. This old idea has achieved new popularity in Israel today. The point is that what we eat should be an expression of our moral values, and hence consumers should know about, care about, and seek to influence the labor conditions and environmental impact surrounding the growth and preparation of food. A national organization publishes standards, and its professional staff advises food growers and processors, as well as inspects their operations in order to grant a seal of approval. When a less ambitious prototype of this was first proposed late in the twentieth century, it didn't get off the ground. However, in the past decade, in the wake of some high-profile scandals (dangerous work environments at food processors, agricultural pollution of ground water), the project gained new traction, and the "ethical kashrut" seal has become almost a marketing necessity.

Evening

At dinner at our hotel we noticed a poster in the lobby for a performance, down the street, of the old musical comedy *Camelot* by a local English-speaking theater group (there's lots of English in Jerusalem!).

A group of us strolled over. Great fun. Afterwards, in a bar, we got into a deep (possibly alcohol-enhanced) discussion about whether the good old days ("one brief and shining moment") are ever as good as we remember them—and whether it is not perhaps a bad idea to let them color our hopes for the future.

Day 5, Monday: Jerusalem

Morning

We joined about ten other groups like ours for a session at the Knesset, to be conducted by the speaker (chair) of the upper house.

The speaker, wearing a stylish hijab, ascended the platform in a wheelchair (Reuven later filled us in: she suffered a childhood spinal injury). She spoke a clear, easy-to-understand Hebrew with a faint accent. Her relaxed, informal manner and warm smile belied her powerful position. Starting out as a social worker, she was bitten by the politics bug when she was selected (randomly) to serve for a year in the lower house of Knesset. She became a community activist in her hometown, the mixed city of Lod, and gradually worked her way up the ranks in a centrist party. Now she is serving her third term in the upper house of the Knesset.

Her topic was (once again) how the nation-state of the Jewish people can be a state of all its citizens. She explained that the sword that had finally cut the Gordian knot of Israeli-Palestinian conflict was the resurrection of the old idea of two symmetrical ethnic nation-states living side-by-side. Each nation has a national home and self-determination; each has a potential place of refuge and a cultural center for members of the nation who live elsewhere. The two are independent democratic states, but their constitutions, which were developed in tandem, contain a number of distinctive features:

- **Open borders:** Any holder of an Israeli or Palestinian passport may cross the border without restriction, and stay as a tourist for up to three months; longer stays require a temporary or permanent visa. Israel and Palestine constitute a free-trade zone: no customs restrictions between them.

· **Bilingual communications:** Hebrew and Arabic must be taught in all education systems and appear on all road signs and government publications and forms.

· **Minority representation:** Each state represents the interests of its national minority living in the other state.

· **Joint governmental administration of select areas and resources:** These include the city of Jerusalem; water, pollution and waste management; customs duties; holy sites; intercity highways; and rail lines.

According to her analysis, the turning point came when grassroots movements in both nations arose with the explicit agenda of shifting the discourse from one of competitive victimhood to one of competing visions. Out of this ferment, political parties, or factions within existing parties, formed, demanding a leadership prepared to accept the principle of symmetry—that is, that both the Jews and the Palestinians are nations, equal in their authenticity, equal in their right to national self-determination, and equal in their claims of attachment to the Land of Israel. In time, and admittedly it was far from a smooth process, this led to a public and formal acceptance of the division of the land into two states—and also, to acceptance of shared responsibility for the suffering caused by the conflict over the decades. Thus, the way to the tandem constitution was opened.

The speaker spoke movingly of her own experience as a full and equal Palestinian citizen of Israel, able to accept and live with the Jewishness of her state because her identity as a Palestinian draws support and enrichment from the Palestinian national home just a short drive away. The harmony—and open border—and bilingual culture—eliminate, in her opinion, any sense of dual loyalty, or resentment of the Jewish majority culture. Symmetrically, many Jews have chosen to live in mixed cities or in homogeneous communities in Palestine, where they are full and equal citizens.

An unintended positive consequence of this resolution of the Israel-Palestine conflict has been the amelioration of the tension that had existed for decades surrounding the identity of Jewish immigrants from North African and Middle Eastern countries. As the speaker pointed out, the process of cultural equalization and harmonization has largely removed the stigma that had attached to them or that they had attached to themselves as "Jewish Arabs." Israel has also become more Middle Eastern and less European since the new order was instituted. She believes that opening Israel to the world just beyond its borders has enriched its culture.

Captivated by her, we gave her a standing ovation as if all of this had somehow been her doing.

From the Knesset we walked to the National Library, a magnificent structure housing the world's most complete collection of Jewish literature from biblical times to the present, including many ancient manuscripts, personal archives, and rare early modern periodicals. After a tour, we heard a short presentation on the Jewish Text Digitization Project, a multidecade undertaking recently completed. The library has been completely digitized and organized into a searchable database, meaning that any scholar — or layperson — anywhere in the world will now have access to the entire body of Jewish literature. Taken together with the rise of Hebrew language learning in the Diaspora in recent decades, this opens up opportunities not just for scholarship, but for Jews everywhere to connect, through text, with their religious tradition, secular culture, and national history.

Afternoon

After lunch at the library cafeteria, we rode the light rail out to Yad Vashem, the national museum, archive, and memorial devoted to the Holocaust. As the Holocaust recedes into the past, the task of preserving and interpreting its memory becomes more difficult and more important. We toured the main historical exhibit and visited temporary exhibits, among them a disturbing one on "genocides in the world in the past century."

Then we assembled for a fascinating presentation on the evolution of Yad Vashem itself. As we learned, Holocaust interpretation has changed significantly over the years in response to changing cultural attitudes. Whereas when Yad Vashem was founded in 1953, the message of the main exhibit hall was that the "answer" to the Holocaust was the State of Israel, over time there has been a shift toward an awareness that no nation—not even the Jewish one—is immune to the destructive virus of xenophobic hypernationalism. Now that the Holocaust can be viewed in historical context, from a distance, the tendency is no longer to see it as revelatory, but rather as an event in human history— important, pivotal, but subject to rational understanding as an event in the flow of history. We cannot learn from it God's ways—or God's absence. Nor does it prove the validity of nationalism—or the failure of Enlightenment. It was a Jewish disaster—but also a universal one. It was complex, and demonstrated every kind of human behavior, good and evil. It is to be studied, and its victims and heroes memorialized, but it conveys no clear message—in particular, no clear national one.

From Yad Vashem we walked over to Israel's central military cemetery on Mt. Herzl. Reuven led us to the graves of various founding fathers and mothers and spoke about their contributions. In the Herzl Museum I was fascinated by a film about Herzl's utopian novel *Altneuland* and other Zionist utopias from the turn of the twentieth century, such as those of Elchanan Lewinsky, Nachman Syrkin, and Zev Yavetz (none of whom I had heard of before today). It is interesting how different elements from each of them have found their way into the reality of Israel today. It is rather remarkable, when I think about it, how the Jewish state has managed to be, simultaneously, a Jewish cultural and religious center and refuge (a national home); a liberal, cosmopolitan democracy; and a state whose economy emits a whiff of socialism. And all of this in a sovereign, independent state that is fully integrated into the region and the world.

I know Herzl's historical image has gone through its ups and downs. His motivation, his personality, his contributions, his talents have all been evaluated and re-evaluated—differently according to the nation's current mood and priorities. But bottom line—he burned himself out lighting a flame; and while I know you can't play "what might have been," still, I find it hard to believe that all this would have ever come to be without him.

Evening

Back at the hotel, we divided up into two- and threesomes, and were picked up for home-hospitality dinners with families of what they call here Anglo-Saxon immigrants. Our gracious and culinarily talented (!) host family, Hannah and Michael, a couple in their mid-sixties, have three adult children. The oldest child is a farmer in the Galilee, the middle child is a biomedical engineer living around the corner, and the youngest is doing her national service teaching Hebrew in Omaha.

A doctor and a textile artist, Hannah and Michael had previously been involved in a liberal congregation in the United States. Neither spoke Hebrew, and they had always considered themselves "armchair (philanthropic) Zionists." However, what most people saw as a passing political aberration in the United States years ago turned out to be the beginning of a cultural shift, and within a few years, the long-held assumption that the United States was the real Promised Land for the Jews began to unravel. Many Jews, especially in middle-class suburbs, began to feel unwelcome and even unsafe. Suddenly, my hosts found themselves looking into *aliyah*—and then, actually moving to Jerusalem.

Linguistically and culturally—and especially professionally, for the doctor—it was a hard adjustment, but it was also an exciting time, as those were the pioneering years of movement towards the new constitution. Michael and Hannah have clearly built a satisfying life for themselves here, and are proud to have been part of the drama of the past few decades.

Meanwhile, many other American Jews threw themselves into politics, refusing to accept the long-term failure of the American dream. And in the end, the "good guys" triumphed. However, the experiences of those years realigned U.S. Jewry's perspective on the promises and risks of the American dream and its relationship to Jewish identity. That's why, for example, all of my tour-mates and I had been taught to speak Hebrew.

It was an eye-opening evening, and I even got to buy a beautiful shawl, hand-woven by Michael, at a serious discount, for my mother.

Day 6, Tuesday: Palestine

Morning

While the Palestine capitol, a graceful, airy building, is located in east Jerusalem, the center of the country's cultural and political life is a dozen miles to the north, the bustling, growing city of Ramallah, today's first stop. Driving through the business district, it is obvious that Arabic is the dominant language, but it is also striking that street signs, and most advertising signs, are bilingual. Hebrew is everywhere. And from the license plates, the presence of Israelis is also apparent.

In a conference room in a government office building, we met with a forty-fivish member of the Palestinian parliament. Originally a history teacher, he served as a high school principal while earning an MA in political science. He was then elected mayor of his town, and after two terms was elected as his area's representative in parliament. Now he is completing his first two-year term. Palestine has a unicameral legislature; the MPs represent geographical districts.

Our speaker had come of age politically during the years when Palestine and Israel were moving toward a resolution and the State of Palestine was being envisioned, crafted, and implemented. He described a difficult process, a transition from patriarchal, premodern norms of leadership and governance to liberal democracy. There were other hurdles, too, especially the economic disparity between Israel and Palestine at the start of the process. That, in fact, is still an issue—a source of popular discontent and political tensions. And yet the Palestinian economy has been developing at record-breaking rates, so (from his perspective) the society's main concerns today are less economic and more cultural. Essentially, the Palestinians are struggling with the difficult transition that the Jews experienced over a century earlier. The younger generation is drawn to everything new, to material success, to the open society; thus traditional family authority, gender roles, and village community relationships are all challenged, giving rise to anger on both sides of the generational divide.

He echoed ideas we had heard from the speaker of the Knesset yesterday: once Israel and Palestine accepted the principles of equality and symmetry, the zero-sum game (a Palestinian state in all of Palestine vs. a Jewish state in all the Land of Israel) ended, and the two nations could work constructively to design a life of side-by-side sovereignty, sharing the land.

Regarding the historical baggage of claims and counter-claims, of displacement, rejectionism, occupation, terrorism, colonialism, and so on, he argued that all of these were significantly defused by the very fact of mutual acceptance and recognition—but that neutralizing such deep feelings is a long and challenging process. He mentioned an ongoing truth and reconciliation project of which I had been unaware. Reuven later promised that we would encounter it directly in the days ahead.

We were on our own for lunch. I had—and loved—my first *sabich* sandwich: eggplant, hardboiled egg, salad, and tachina (tahini). Turns out *sabich* originated with Iraqi Jews in Israel and has become a new street food fad in Palestine.

Afternoon

After lunch we toured the Samaria region; visited and learned about the ancient Samaritan community in Nablus; and drove (slowly) past permaculture farms laid out on terraces, small communities old and new, and a stunning, newly discovered mosaic in the excavation of an ancient synagogue.

We stopped at a village founded by Jewish settlers shortly after the Six-Day War, where Reuven had arranged a meeting with some young members, some doing their national service, others already in college. After a short panel presentation, we divided into small groups for informal conversations over *bourekas* (ubiquitous Middle Eastern cheese pastries) and cold drinks. This community had been founded as part of the movement of Orthodox Zionists to settle the newly conquered territories, both for the religious experience of living in the sacred heartland and for the messianic political purpose of securing Jewish sovereignty over the land. Over the years of head-to-head national conflict, the Palestinians saw communities like this one as colonialist outposts: physical obstacles and symbolic mockeries of the dream of Palestinian self-determination. While the founders of this particular community had tried to foster good neighborly relations with the Palestinians around them, the underlying tension could not be defused.

However, our Orthodox hosts, who have grown up since the new order was established, have not carried forward the founders' messianic conceptions. As full and equal citizens of the secular state of Palestine (the father of one of our hosts is currently serving his third term in the Palestinian parliament), they feel uninhibited in their ability to live according to their interpretation of *halakhah*, on land they see as holy, with free and open access to the Jewish national home next door, with all its cultural resources. Working together with their Palestinian neighbors and partners, the community has discovered and harnessed the tremendous economic potential in sophisticated permaculture and xericulture; the region now feeds itself and the entire Jerusalem metropolitan area. And in this generation's focus on building a holy life on holy land in the here and now, it seems that they have largely stuffed the messianic genie back into the bottle.

On the way back to the bus, some of our hosts showed us their preparations for the upcoming sabbatical year. Having decided to observe it as faithfully to the Torah's description as they can, they have been processing and preserving a portion of every harvest by canning, freeze-drying, and dehydrating, thereby accumulating reserves for their own use and for sale to Jews who want to avoid eating sabbatical produce. In addition, of course, they have synchronized their personal sabbatical savings plans. Next year they will all take their sabbaticals simultaneously, and receive a salary to supplement their reduced income from produce sales.

Evening

Back in Jerusalem, after dinner, Reuven led us on a night tour along the parapet of the Old City walls. It was a clear, starry night. Old walled cities everywhere have a certain magic for me; Jerusalem combines that with a tradition of holiness and centuries of historical memories. No words.

Day 7, Wednesday: The Dead Sea

Morning

We left early for the Dead Sea. It's fascinating to see how Jerusalem really sits on the edge of civilization—we had barely crossed the city limits when we were surrounded by desert. And we barely noticed the border signs as we passed into—and then out of—Palestine on our way down.

After visits to a couple of interesting archaeological sites around Jericho (actually, what I most remember is the heat), we drove to a dock at the northern tip of the Dead Sea and boarded a tour boat. Just to the east of our departure point we saw a large mass of towers and pipes—a geothermal power station, using deep wells to extract volcanic heat to generate electricity. We then cruised along the west coast while Reuven reviewed highlights of history and pointed out important sites. In particular, he spoke of Masada, the famous fortress where the Jewish rebels made their last stand against the Romans in 73 CE. The contemporary historian Josephus described a mass suicide by the last holdouts, a story that captured the imagination of Zionists looking for heroic role models; however, admiration for such extremism has waned over the years, and some scholars question whether Josephus's account even reflects real events. When we protested skipping Masada, Reuven agreed that it is a beautiful site with interesting excavations, but given our limited time, it is not a high priority. We have already gotten used to his refrain, "On your next visit. . . ."

Near the southern tip of the sea, we disembarked to visit the outflow of the Red-Dead Canal, a complex of pools, channels, and dams that regulate the flow and chemical composition of seawater from the Red Sea (near Eilat) into the Dead Sea. This joint Israeli-Jordanian project aimed at replenishing the Dead Sea and generating hydroelectric power was repeatedly held up or stopped over the years over concern for all the environmental unknowns it entailed. But finally, after years of experiments, virtual and real simulations, and pilots to try to account for all possible negative consequences, the project went forward. And indeed, after ten years of full operation, the concerns seem to have been put to rest. The sea has expanded almost to its original dimensions, undoing decades of ecological and economic damage caused by falling water levels. The canal produces significant electric power for Jordan, Israel, and Palestine. The mineral industry continues, but tourism has significantly expanded: on the bus trip back north we passed several ecotourist villages along the shore.

Afternoon

We stopped at one of those villages for lunch, and then went in the water and took the traditional weird pictures of ourselves floating. Later in the afternoon we drove to Ein Gedi and hiked up the stream of this wonderful oasis. Reuven, of course, filled us in on the drama that had occurred there between David and Saul. By the time we pulled into our hotel, everyone was sound asleep.

Evening

Free evening; went out to dinner in the restaurant district of the western city, met Israelis and Palestinians, drank, danced, talked about life and stuff. I can't believe what a great time I am having.

Day 8, Thursday: Judean Foothills

Morning

We drove west to a large new archaeological park in the Judean Foothills (intermediary between the coastal plain and the mountains of Jerusalem). This rich site, excavated over the past twenty years, contains a wealth of material from the centuries associated with the biblical monarchy. In excavations of this age, the findings are sometimes hard for laypeople to understand, even if one can keep up with the guide's explanations. Here, the National Parks Authority has created a living history experience that we all found quite successful. Families can apply to live in the park for one-week stints, rent free. However, they have to live as close an approximation as possible to a biblical life style: no electricity or plastic or running water; authentic foods, clothes, utensils, and furniture. Ten biblical houses are occupied in this way. While of course the occupants have their private areas, much of the day is spent struggling with their daily tasks before the eyes of tourists passing through. Reality TV without TV. It was great fun, though not all the occupants' children seemed convinced of that.

We were served a "biblical" lunch—flat bread, coarse hummus, a salad of pungent greens, pickles, and olives.

Afternoon

After lunch we met in an air conditioned (!) conference room in the site's visitors' center for a seminar on the uses of archaeology. Conducted by three young archaeology graduate students, using examples from this site and slides and maps illustrating other sites around Israel and the world, they got us thinking and talking about Israel's obsession with archaeology—and our own assumptions about it.

For example, after decades of research and ever ongoing excavations, the controversy over the historical truth of the biblical account is still going strong. Religious, nationalistic, and scientific considerations get all tangled up. On one level, one can say: but does it really matter? Does it really matter whether the walls of Jericho actually collapsed? Or where the boundaries of Solomon's empire lay—or even if there was a Solomon who ruled an empire? But then, can one really just walk away from these questions? That is—does it really *not* matter? And to whom does it matter: to religious believers, to Jewish and Palestinian nationalists, to historians? And if it does matter, why does it matter? Do sites have messages—or do we impose our messages on the sites?

Evening

We went to a play generating a lot of buzz. It dramatized original and modern versions of several stories that appear both in the Bible and in the Quran. Some characters spoke Hebrew and others spoke Arabic, and projected subtitles assisted Jerusalem theater-goers who were not fluent in both languages. Exploring the possible reasons for the slight differences between the versions—and the differing interpretations that have developed over the years—the play highlighted cultural affinities and differences. For example, both Judaism and Islam have found theological meaning in different traditions regarding which son—Isaac or Ishmael—was almost sacrificed by their shared patriarch Abraham. The play also asked universal moral questions, such as how to respond when supreme obligations—love of God, love of one's child—appear to collide.

Day 9, Friday: Jordan Valley

Morning

We started the day descending again toward Jericho, but then turned north and drove up the Jordan Valley. We passed a number of small villages and towns, Jewish and Palestinian (and mixed), surrounded by a patchwork of green fields and orchards. Very pastoral.

Reuven explained that years ago, this area was largely desolate, but the "permaculture revolution" has changed the landscape, leading to a burgeoning of sustainable family and small communal farms. The main innovation—a dense integration of fruit trees, vegetable beds, and pasture tailored to the particular terrain and microclimate on small farms—has facilitated high productivity with minimal water and mechanization. As a result, small farming has largely been revived as a livelihood. The combination of a trend towards living in smaller, more intimate communities, and the realization that large-scale industrial farming was damaging the soil and the climate has led to a decline in large farms. Many kibbutz fields, for example, have been subdivided into family farms, while the communal structures have been retained for supply and marketing—a revival of the twentieth-century model of smallholder communities known as the *moshav ovdim* (workers' settlement).

Thus the population in this periphery has been growing. Some formerly suburban-style "community settlements" have been reorganized into agricultural villages. Some of these have experimented—with some success—with food autarky; that is, becoming totally self-sufficient in food production.

Afternoon

We stopped at a popular baptismal site, an archaeological dig, and a reconstructed village from early pioneering days. After a relaxed swim in the Sea of Galilee, we ate a picnic lunch on a pebbly beach, where Reuven told us about the years of constant worry about the falling water level in the lake. Nowadays, on account of the permaculture revolution and cheap seawater desalination, the region has plenty of water, and the Sea of Galilee has been restored to its original size.

Later we stopped at the excavation at Korazin (an ancient village mentioned in the New Testament) overlooking the Sea of Galilee, and

Reuven led us in a study session on Christian traditions relating to the Galilee, based on the biblical accounts of Jesus' life. We arrived at our hotel in Safed a couple of hours before the Sabbath.

Evening

Because of its storied history as a center of activist Kabbalah in the sixteenth century, its airy location, and the artists' colony that developed in the mid-twentieth century, Safed continues to be a magnet for spiritual searchers. It seems to be an amalgam of ultra-Orthodox, New-Age seekers, purveyors of tourist kitsch, serious artists, and just ordinary people trying to live normal lives in a peripheral town. The municipality struggles to keep all that in balance, not always successfully. In any case, some of our group went synagogue-hopping before dinner (I rested); and after dinner at our hotel we sat and sang. Reuven had prepared a booklet of Sabbath songs, many from Psalms, some by the sixteenth-century kabbalists of Safed.

Day 10, Saturday: Safed

Morning

We got up early for a hike along the Amud stream nearby. Lush vegetation, rushing cool water, time to just sit and think or meditate.

Afternoon

An artist came to our hotel to speak about her life mission: expressing Jewish mystical ideas through visual imagery. She seemed authentic, and certainly talented, but kabbalistic concepts like the ten *sefirot* ("emanations" of God in the world) — even illustrated in color — went over my head.

After she left, we continued the discussion with Reuven. It developed into a lively debate. Some of our group, like me, feel alienated by the whole world of Jewish mysticism; others feel attracted and connected to it. Reuven pointed out that there has always been ambivalence toward mysticism in Judaism and probably always will be.

Evening

Went to a bar with live music — a Korean klezmer band. Go figure.

Day 11, Sunday: Haifa

Morning

Driving southwest across the Galilee, we passed through a now-familiar lush patchwork of small farms surrounding villages and towns. Eco-tourism and WWOOFing (World Wide Opportunities on Organic Farms, a global network for volunteers) are important features of the economies in many of these communities.

Suddenly it dawned upon us that we had not seen billboards anywhere in our travels. Reuven confirmed that Israel has draconian—and strictly enforced—anti-billboard laws.

In Haifa, we went first to the Haifa University campus atop Mount Carmel. There, on the southern edge of the campus, we visited a some-what odd-looking compound. A complex of small buildings, trans-ported or reconstructed from various historical locations—Jewish pioneering settlements, Palestinian villages—encircled a central auditorium/classroom building and a large hostel. This complex is the Center for Truth and Reconciliation, a joint project of Israel and Palestine. For over two decades, Israeli and Palestinian staff members have been collecting archival materials and personal testimonies of violence perpetrated against the "other" in the course of the preceding century. Changing exhibits document painful events during the period, with texts and recordings telling both the backstories and motivations of perpetrators and the backstories and suffering of victims. The center aims to help both sides modify their collective memory to include empathy for those on the other side who suffered—and national responsibility for causing that suffering. Forgiveness is not the objective. The point is to listen, really listen, to the other side of the story.

As at Yad Vashem, some exhibits were hard to look at and some stories were hard to listen to. And I understood why this center is still somewhat controversial in both Israel and Palestine. Many Israelis and Palestinians avow that it fosters false equivalencies, or lumps justified and unjustified violence together. Sitting down with us later, the center's codirectors acknowledged that these concerns are basically unavoidable—but they do demand a response. Thus, the center runs courses, conferences, seminars, and a publications program on the abstract issues underpinning its work—on collective and historical responsibility, justice and mercy, bystander responsibility, the uses and misuses of violence, romantic and liberal nationalism. The Israeli and Palestinian education ministries sponsor a program whereby every high school student in both countries attends a four-day seminar at the center in the course of eleventh or twelfth grade; generally at least two schools, one Palestinian and one Israeli, participate together. The center also has a curriculum-development and teacher-training wing. I found the concept movingly impressive—and the challenge daunting.

Afternoon

We needed to air out, so Reuven led us on a walk from the business district on the Mount Carmel ridge down a chain of stairways from level to level, from neighborhood to neighborhood, crossing the whole city from top to bottom, and ending up at a noisy, funky, working-class restaurant in the port. Nearby was a huge construction site. Reuven explained that this was to be the terminal for the high-speed rail line to Istanbul scheduled to open in two years: a six-hour ride, with connections to all of Europe. Meanwhile, a line to the east is in its final planning stages.

Evening

We stayed the night in a kibbutz guest house on the beach, a short drive south of Haifa. After dinner we went for a walk on the beach, and Reuven helped us organize a campfire. He taught us a selection of Israeli folk and popular songs relating to the sea. After all the attention devoted over the past week to the "heartland," and to Israel's place in the Middle East, I was struck by the cultural importance of Israel's location on the Mediterranean coast, symbolizing the open horizon—and the link to European culture.

Day 12, Monday: The Negev

Morning

Early on Monday we boarded a high-speed express train to Beersheba. After the hour ride, we traveled by bus for another hour through the desert to the campus of Sde Boker. There we toured the country's major desert research center. We saw researchers working on pilot devices in solar energy labs; fields and hothouses for plant breeding; a control room full of screens monitoring every aspect of the Red-Dead canal operation; and a demonstration permaculture farm complete with goats, chickens, a fish pond, fruit trees, vegetable beds, and a monitor displaying annual yields of various products as well as water and fuel consumption.

The idea of "making the desert bloom" has often been associated with David Ben-Gurion, who lived here at Kibbutz Sde Boker in his later years. We toured his home and visited his grave. There's something sad about the fact that visionaries usually don't live to see their visions become reality. Moses, or Herzl, for example.

Afternoon

Our itinerary billed the next stop as a "Bedouin experience." We were expecting something romantic and kitschy—like every "authentic folklore experience" in every tour itinerary in the world. And, indeed, we did start out with a visit to a large goat-hair tent in the middle of nowhere, where we were served bread baked in the coals, goat *labaneh* (yogurt cheese), and bitter coffee. And an older man in traditional dress did regale us with stories and proverbs about the "old way" of Bedouin life, along with the challenges it has faced in the past century.

But then we got back on our bus and discovered that this little tent camp with its goat pen was actually on the outskirts of a large village that was surprisingly green and felt prosperous and modern. In another goat-hair tent, this one in the courtyard of a spacious community center, we met the village's youth director, a vivacious woman wearing a hijab who had clearly honed her "stand-up" style. She vividly depicted for us the transition the Bedouin population has undergone in the course of her lifetime. Sixty years ago, when her parents were born, Bedouin communities were characterized by a patriarchal social structure (including polygyny and inmarriage), and loyalty to their old way of life. Most Bedouins continued to reside in clan-based villages, but since these were off the planning grid, they could not receive building permits, and thus Bedouins continued to live in shanties and tents not linked to water, sewer, and electric networks. Others moved to towns established for them by the state, but found the urban lifestyle too foreign to their traditional family customs and the economic opportunities too limiting. Soon the towns had high rates of unemployment, crime, and drug use. The early Zionist settlers had romanticized the Bedouins and even sought to imitate some of their customs (e.g., dress, food, slang); but by the end of the twentieth century the Bedouins' image in Israeli popular culture had shifted from quaint to frightening, from a model of Middle Eastern authenticity to a vexing social and economic challenge to the state.

Then, some years ago, a few young Bedouin university graduates working at the Sde Boker center mapped out a strategy and managed, by dint of brains, commitment, charisma, and luck, to parlay their ideas into a movement that ultimately came to dominate the social and political life of most Bedouin communities. Their plan had two major components:

1. A massive investment in quality education, from early childhood through college, with a conscious and sophisticated effort to harmonize knowledge of and respect for traditional mores with knowledge and skills needed to function in the modern world. This was not a simple challenge, given the inherent conflicts between tradition and modernity, especially in the status of women and the power of the clan. Community organizers worked with the older generations to create local community centers that preserved and transmitted traditional culture, while at the same time educating for incremental change. Meanwhile, Beersheba University established a teacher-training program and structured its curriculum to interweave modern and traditional culture. The program's graduates then led a makeover of the schools serving the Bedouin communities.

2. Development of a new model for Bedouin economic development rooted in the melding of traditional and modern agricultural practices. By the time this process started, the Bedouins' livelihood already came mainly from work as day laborers outside the village; they herded goats not out of necessity but as a cultural marker (indeed, the women and children tended the goats). The revolution consisted in restoring village-based agriculture as a livelihood. Modern xericulture methods could make the desert productive, and permaculture principles could allow the development of mixed farming (livestock, fruit, vegetables, grasses) in the desert. Thus shantytowns became villages supported by local family farms. Today, the markets of Beersheba are stocked with produce from Bedouin farms.

Over the years, as the movement spread—and with it education and prosperity—the standard of living improved, and stability and hope came to characterize the Bedouin population.

Of course, she added, let's not get carried away with the old Zionist idea of return to the soil. Nowadays, thousands of Bedouins work in construction, education, medicine, technology, transportation, and other professions. Many with no patience for village life have moved to the city.

Evening

Late afternoon, as the heat subsided, we took a short hike in the Ramon Crater, thrilling to the beauty and the vastness of the lunar-like landscape. We stayed overnight in the youth hostel in Mitzpeh Ramon, the funky town perched on the rim of the crater. Some of us went out walking along the rim path at night. Stars!

Day 13, Tuesday: Tel Aviv

Morning

Back to Beersheba, short train ride to Tel Aviv, rest of the morning free — shopping, beach. . . .

Afternoon

After lunch we gathered for a wrap-up conversation at the same spot on the beach promenade where Reuven had given his introduction — seems like a year ago! He presented the various visions that have driven the creation of current Israeli reality as a series of conflicting but overlapping utopias, all based on the fundamental Jewish aspiration to create an ideal society in the Promised Land. Over the years, realities on the ground have shaped — but also been shaped by — that aspiration. The history of Israel reflects a complex dynamic between real-life circumstances and a set of sometimes congruent and sometimes conflicting utopian visions: social justice, cultural self-determination, state power, secure borders, commitment to Jewish law, universal values of freedom and equality. The balance among these (and others) has always been uneasy, a constant work in progress. But, he contended, progress there has been.

So, he concluded, too good to be true?

Yes, I thought. *Well . . . no.*

And then we were off to the airport.

Notes

Introduction

1. Nevo, *Neuland*, 531.

1. The Eternal Quest for Utopia

1. McClintock, "Big Rock Candy Mountains."
2. Seeger, "Oleanna."
3. Pleij, *Dreaming of Cockaigne*, 3–6, 26–27, 283, 294, 426.
4. More, *Utopia*, 76.
5. Tihany, "Utopia in Modern Western Thought," 37.
6. Jennings, *Paradise Now*, 79–148.
7. Jennings, *Paradise Now*, 149–241.
8. Jennings, *Paradise Now*, 243–92.
9. Bach, "Seeking Emptiness."
10. Katscher, "Owen's Topolobampo Colony."
11. Wilkinson, "'New Norway.'"
12. Levitas, *Concept of Utopia*, 41–67.
13. And beyond; see, for example, Fokkema, *Perfect Worlds*.
14. Levitas, *Concept of Utopia*, 221.
15. Polak, *Image of the Future*, vol. 2, 447.
16. Berlin, *Two Concepts of Liberty*, 52.
17. For example, see Sagi, *Jewish Religion after Theology*, 211–20.
18. Plato, *Republic*, 192.

2. Paradise Lost, Remembered, and Promised

1. Delumeau, *History of Paradise*, 55.
2. Kramer and Albright, "Enki and Ninhursag," 11.
3. Hesiod, *Works and Days*, 67–75 (lines 109–201).
4. Homer, *Odyssey*, 56 (lines 135–36); Plato, *Critias*, 111–21 (113–121).
5. Brody, *Other Side of Eden*, 73–97.

281

6. Manuel and Manuel, *Utopian Thought*, 43.

7. Gordis, "Significance of the Paradise Myth," 90–92.

8. Babylonian Talmud *Sanhedrin* 38b.

9. Amit, "Biblical Utopianism," 11–17.

10. Midrash *Yalkut Shimoni*, Breisheet 20.

11. Eisenstein, *Otzar Midrashim*, Rabbi Akiba, 430.

12. Babylonian Talmud *Ketubot* 62b.

13. Ahad Ha'am, *Kol Kitvei Ahad Ha'am*, 286.

14. Galnoor, *Partition of Palestine*, 111.

15. Uffenheimer, "Utopia Umetziut Bamachshavah Hamikra'it," 10–16.

16. Babylonian Talmud *Arachin* 32b–33a.

17. Greenberg, "Biblical Conception of Asylum," 132–133.

18. Babylonian Talmud *Makkot* 10a.

19. Kugel, *How to Read the Bible*, 1–47, 296–316.

20. Mishnah *Sanhedrin* 2:1–2.

21. Babylonian Talmud *Sanhedrin* 19a–b.

22. Rashi, *Teshuvot Rashi*, 251–52 (no. 224).

23. Soloveitchik, *Halakhic Man*, 28.

24. Kochan, "A Model for Jewish Historiography," 265.

3. Utopia, Apocalypse, Messiah

1. Hertzberg, *Zionist Idea*, 430.

2. Kugel, *How to Read the Bible*, 652.

3. Collins, *Apocalyptic Imagination*, 4–41.

4. Sandmel, *Genius of Paul*, 17–21.

5. Urbach, *Sages and Their Beliefs*, 651.

6. Babylonian Talmud *Sanhedrin* 97a–b.

7. *Midrash Shmuel* 13:4.

8. Babylonian Talmud *Baba Batra* 75a–b.

9. *Pesikta Rabbati* 1b.

10. Babylonian Talmud *Berachot* 34b.

11. Babylonian Talmud *Sanhedrin* 99a.

12. Urbach, *Sages and Their Beliefs*, 649.

13. Manuel and Manuel, *Utopian Thought*, 35–55.

4. A Torah Society

1. Yedidya, "Chadash Mi-lo Yashan."

2. According to rabbinic tradition, after the Roman destruction of Jerusalem in 70 CE, the coastal town of Yavneh became the center of Torah learning and jurisprudence for about fifty years.

3. Babylonian Talmud *Berachot* 49b.

4. Yedidya, "Chadash Mi-lo Yashan," 90–105.

5. See the discussion of Hartman in Troy, *Zionist Ideas*, 257–58; and Buber, "Debate on Zionism and Messianism."

6. Maimon, "Chiddush Hasanhedrin," 64.

7. Fishman, *Judaism and Collective Life*, 61–67.

8. The first of the daily morning blessings in the traditional liturgy praises God for "giving the rooster the understanding to distinguish between night and day."

9. Or, "Boker Chag Bakfar."

10. Likhovski, "Invention of 'Hebrew Law.'"

11. Babylonian Talmud *Avodah Zarah* 64b.

12. Herzog, "T'chokah Le-yisrael," 18.

13. State of Israel, Ministry of Justice, "Hamishpat Ha'ivri Bapsikah," accessed May 2020 https://www.justice.gov.il/Units/MishpatIvri/MishpatIvriBapsika/Pages/MishpatIvriBapsika.aspx.

14. Babylonian Talmud *Ketubot* 111a.

15. Abramov, *Perpetual Dilemma*, 74.

16. *Yishuv* means "settlement," but before 1948, the term referred to the Jewish population of Palestine. The Old Yishuv comprised the pre-Zionist Orthodox communities; the New Yishuv referred to the Zionist communities.

17. Blau, "Yesodot Lechukah."

18. Abramov, *Perpetual Dilemma*, 127.

19. Babylonian Talmud *Sanhedrin* 32b.

20. Navon, *Kol Haderech*, 113–17.

21. For a succinct summary of the development of responses to *shemitah* see Golinkin, *Teshuvot*, 1:37–45.

22. Abramov, *Perpetual Dilemma*, 47–50.

23. Aviner, *Torat Eretz Yisrael*, 339.

24. Aviner, *Torat Eretz Yisrael*, 358.

5. Holy Community

1. Birthright Israel, accessed November 2019, https://www.birthrightisrael.com/about_us.

2. Almog, *Sabra*, 233.

3. For example, Nisbet, *Community and Power*, 1–11, 33–53.

4. Bauman, *Community*, 1–20.

5. For the story of how *Life Is with People* came to be written, see Zipperstein, "Underground Man."

6. Zborowski and Herzog, *Life Is with People*, 216–32.

7. Goren, *New York Jews*, 25.

8. Kaplan, *Judaism as a Civilization*, 288.

9. Kaplan, *Judaism as a Civilization*, 428.

10. Kaplan, *Judaism as a Civilization*, 425–27.

11. Siegel et al., *Jewish Catalog*, 278.

12. Krippner-Martinez, "Invoking 'Tato Vasco,'" 1–13.

13. Sarna, *Jacksonian Jew*, 62.

14. Pease and Pease, *Black Utopia*, 18–20.

15. Herscher, *Jewish Agricultural Utopias*, 29–107.

16. Buber, *Paths in Utopia*, 141–42.

17. Buber, *Paths in Utopia*, 141–42.

18. Kropotkin, *Memoirs of a Revolutionist*, 398–99.

19. Mandel Leadership Institute, "*Vayachof Kol Yisrael*," 5–24.

6. A National Home

1. State of Israel, Knesset, Sefer Hachukim [Book of laws] 2743 (July 26, 2018), accessed May 2020, https://fs.knesset.gov.il/20/law/20_lsr_504220.pdf.

2. State of Israel, Knesset, accessed May 2020, https://www.knesset.gov.il/docs/eng/megilat_eng.htm.

3. Plaut, *Growth of Reform Judaism*, 34.

4. Herzl, *Jewish State*, 4–5.

5. Hobsbawm and Ketzer, "Ethnicity and Nationalism," 7.

6. Troy, *Zionist Ideas*, 106–12.

7. Lewinsky, *Masa L'eretz Yisrael*, 37.

8. Mishnah *Ta'anit* 4:8; this cryptic reference to a national matchmaking day has morphed, as Lewinsky prophesied, into a sort of Jewish Valentine's Day in twenty-first century Israel.

9. Lewinsky, *Masa L'eretz Yisrael*, 41.

10. Lewinsky, *Masa L'eretz Yisrael*, 48–54.

11. Lewinsky, *Masa L'eretz Yisrael*, 54–56.

12. Lewinsky, *Masa L'eretz Yisrael*, 57–58.

13. Although there were a few "new women" in this literature, the vast majority of references are masculine, whether by convention or by intent.

14. Crevecoeur, *Letters from an American Farmer*, 54–55.

15. Commager, *Empire of Reason*, xi.

16. Paul, *Myths That Made America*, 369–79.

17. Chernyshevsky, *What Is to Be Done?*, 199.

18. Wohl, *Generation of 1914*, 5–18, 27, 57, 82, 169, 204–15.

19. A chilling artistic depiction of this process is the Fred Ebb song "Tomorrow Belongs to Me," in the 1966 musical *Cabaret*.

20. Rosenstein, "*Hayehudi Hechadash*," 26–58, 269–79.

21. Lehman, *Ra'ayon Vehagshamah*, 113–15.

7. Statehood and Power

1. Fackenheim, "Jewish Return into History," 226.

2. Rosenstein, *Galilee Diary*, 153.

3. Buber, *Writings*, 304.

4. Jabotinsky, "Tristan da Runha," 162.

5. Jabotinsky, "Tristan da Runha," 165–68.

6. Jabotinsky, "Tristan da Runha," 193–96.

7. Jabotinsky, "Tristan da Runha," 199–202.

8. Troy, *Zionist Ideas*, 63–74.

9. Halkin, *Jabotinsky*, 156.

10. Buber, *Kingship of God*, 70–80.

11. Lorberbaum, *Disempowered King*, 2–34.

12. Lorberbaum, *Disempowered King*, 2–34.

13. See, for example, Aviezer Ravitzky's analysis of selected thinkers, *Religion and State in Jewish Philosophy*.

14. Tosefta *Sanhedrin* 4:5.

15. *Sifrei Deuteronomy* 156.

16. *Deuteronomy Rabbah Shoftim* 8:8.

17. Herzl, *Old New Land*, 79.

18. Gorny, *From Binational Society to Jewish State*, 17–108; and Shumsky, *Beyond the Nation-State*, 222–32.

19. Buber, draft resolution at Twelfth Zionist Congress, 1921, quoted in Hattis, *Binational Idea*, 30–31.

20. Ahad Ha'am, *Kol Kitvei Ahad Ha'am*, 10.

21. Weizman, Actions Committee, 1930, quoted in Hattis, *The Binational Idea*, 89.

22. Ben Gurion, Mapai council 1934, quoted in Hattis, *The Binational Idea*, 98.

23. Jabotinsky, Peel testimony, 1937, quoted in Gorny, *From Binational Society to Jewish State*, 103.

24. ESCO Foundation, *Palestine*, 1085.

25. Tamir, *Why Nationalism*, 31.

8. Enlightenment and Normalization

1. Herzl, *Jewish State*, xvi–xvii.

2. Lowenthal, *The Diaries of Theodore Herzl*, 373–74.

3. Herzl, *Old New Land*, 105–6.

4. Herzl, *Old New Land*, 177–78.

5. Herzl, *Old New Land*, 79.

6. Herzl, *Old New Land*, 139.

7. Herzl, *Old New Land*, 122–24.

8. Herzl, *Old New Land*, 95.

9. Herzl, *Old New Land*, 248–51.

10. Funkenstein, *Perceptions of Jewish History*, 347–48.

11. Hyland et. al., *Enlightenment*, 29.

12. Mendelssohn, *Jerusalem*, 129.

13. Mendelssohn, *Jerusalem*, 133–38.

14. Satanow, *Divrei Rivot*, 4a.

15. Satanow, *Divrei Rivot*, 38a–b.

16. Satanow, *Divrei Rivot*, 47a–b.

17. Satanow, *Divrei Rivot*, 47a–b.

9. Promised Borders

1. Tuan, *Space and Place*, 154.

2. Buber, *Israel and the World*, 111.

3. Wazana, *All the Boundaries of the Land*, 125.

4. Brodsky, "Interpretation of Maps," 438.

5. Wazana, *All the Boundaries of the Land*, 131–32.

6. Wazana, *All the Boundaries of the Land*, 234.

7. Wazana, *All the Boundaries of the Land*, 166.

8. Blakeley, "Reconciling Two Maps," 49, and see references cited therein.

9. Wazana, *All the Boundaries of the Land*, 295.

10. Zusman, "Baraita D'tchumei Eretz Yisrael," 246.

11. Herodotus, *Histories* 3.91, p. 252.

12. Feldman, "Some Observations on the Name Palestine," 16–17.

13. Biger, "Boundaries of Israel," 73.

14. Biger, "Boundaries of Israel," 77–78; Tuchman, *Bible and Sword*, 310–48.

15. Galnoor, *Partition of Palestine*, 111–12.

16. Neuman, *Havikuach al Gvulot Hamedinah*, 32–38.

10. A Model of Social Justice

1. For an informative case study illustrating the tensions within socialism, see Berlin, *Life and Opinions of Moses Hess*, 5–45.

2. Frankel, *Prophecy and Politics*, 171–257.

3. Levin, *While Messiah Tarried*, 319.

4. Berlin, *Life and Opinions of Moses Hess*, 16–25.

5. Hess, *Rome and Jerusalem*, 220.

6. Hess, *Rome and Jerusalem*, 120–21.

7. Hess, *Rome and Jerusalem*, 36.

8. Hess, *Rome and Jerusalem*, 159.

9. Shapira, "Labour Zionism and the October Revolution," 631.

10. Borochov, *Nationalism and the Class Struggle*, 205.

11. Sternhell, *Founding Myths of Israel*, 72–73.

12. N. Syrkin, *Die Judenfrage und der Socialistische Judenstaat*, 61.

13. N. Syrkin, *Die Judenfrage und der Socialistische Judenstaat*, 62.

14. N. Syrkin, *Die Judenfrage und der Socialistische Judenstaat*, 63.

15. N. Syrkin, *Die Judenfrage und der Socialistische Judenstaat*, 65.

16. N. Syrkin, *Die Judenfrage und der Socialistische Judenstaat*, 64–65.

17. N. Syrkin, *Die Judenfrage und der Socialistische Judenstaat*, 57.

18. Hertzberg, *Zionist Idea*, 333–34.

19. N. Syrkin, *Die Judenfrage und der Socialistische Judenstaat*, 67.

20. Hess, *Rome and Jerusalem*, 159.

21. Mossinson, "Hatanach B'vet Hasefer," 26, 111.

22. Hertzberg, *Zionist Idea*, 611; and Troy, *Zionist Ideas*, 151.

23. Scholars suggest that "He shall strike down a land" in 11:4 should be emended to "He shall strike down a wicked ruler," based on a scribal substitution of *eretz* (land) for *'aritz* (wicked ruler). See Zakovitz, *Mashmia Shalom Mevaseir Tov*, 86–87.

24. The author's interpretation of this passage is based on an analysis by Zako-vitz, *Mashmia Shalom Mevaseir Tov*, 71–101.

25. The word for "shoot" in 11:1, *choter*, can also mean "staff," "rod," or "scepter."

26. Plato, *Republic*, 192–93.

27. Sternhell, *Founding Myths of Israel*, 72–73.

11. Visions in Collision

1. Rivlin, address at Herzliya Conference.

2. DellaPergola, "World Jewish Population, 2018," 5.

3. Buzaglo, *Safah Lene'emanim*, 47–58.

4. Yizhar Smilansky, "Sod Hakiyum Hayehudi."

5. Sternhell, *Founding Myths of Israel*, 5.

6. Alterman, "Shir Boker."

7. Shalev, *B'ikar Al Ahava*, 34.

8. Maimonides, Mishneh Torah, Laws of Kings 5:9–12.

9. Midrash *Vayikrah Rabbah* (Vilna) 4:6.

Bibliography

Abramov, S. Zalman. *Perpetual Dilemma: Jewish Religion in the Jewish State*. Rutherford NJ: Fairleigh Dickinson University Press, 1976.

Ahad Ha'am [Asher Ginsberg]. *Kol Kitvei Ahad Ha'am* [Collected works of Ahad Ha'am]. Jerusalem: Jewish Publishing House, 1965.

Almog, Oz. *The Sabra: The Creation of the New Jew*. Translated by Haim Watzman. Berkeley: University of California Press, 2000.

Alterman, Nathan. "Shir Boker." In *Pizmonim Veshirei Zemer* [Ditties and popular songs], vol. 2, 302–3. Tel Aviv: Hakibutz Hameuchad, 1977–79.

Amit, Yaira. "Biblical Utopianism: A Mapmaker's Guide to Eden." *Union Seminary Quarterly Review* 44 (1990): 11–17.

Anderson, Benedict. *Imagined Communities*. New York: Verso, 2006.

Appiah, Kwame Anthony. *The Lies That Bind: Rethinking Identity*. London: Profile, 2018.

Aviner, Shlomo, ed. *Torat Eretz Yisrael: The Teachings of Harav Tzvi Yehuda Hacohen Kook*. Jerusalem: Torat Eretz Yisrael Publications, 1991.

Avineri, Shlomo. *Theodor Herzl and the Foundation of the Jewish State*. Translated by Haim Watzman. London: Phoenix, 2014.

Bach, Ulrich. "Seeking Emptiness: Theodor Hertzka's Colonial Utopia *Freiland* (1890)." *Utopian Studies* 22, no. 1 (2011): 74–90.

Bauman, Zygmunt. *Community: Seeking Safety in an Insecure World*. Malden MA: Polity Press, 2001.

Ben Porat, Guy. *Between State and Synagogue: The Secularization of Contemporary Israel*. Cambridge: Cambridge University Press, 2012.

Ben-Rafael, Eliezer. *Crisis and Transformation: The Kibbutz at Century's End*. Albany NY: SUNY Press, 1997.

Berlin, Isaiah. *The Life and Opinions of Moses Hess*. Cambridge: Jewish Historical Society of England, W. Heffer and Sons, 1957.

———. *Two Concepts of Liberty*. London: Oxford University Press, 1958.

Biger, Gideon. "The Boundaries of Israel—Palestine Past, Present, and Future: A Critical Geographical View." *Israel Studies* 13, no. 1 (Spring 2008): 68–93.

Blakely, Jeffry A. "Reconciling Two Maps: Archaeological Evidence for the Kingdoms of David and Solomon." *Bulletin of the American Schools of Oriental Research* 327 (August 2002): 49–54.

Blau, Moshe. "Yesodot Lechukah Lemedinah Hayehudit" [Foundations for a constitution for the Jewish state]. *Yavneh—A Religious Academic Journal* 3 (Nisan 1949): 37–41.

Borochov, Ber. *Nationalism and the Class Struggle: A Marxian Approach to the Jewish Problem*. Westport CT: Greenwood Press, 1972. First published by Poale Zion-Zeire Zion of America (New York), 1937.

Brenner, Michael. *In Search of Israel: The History of an Idea*. Princeton NJ: Princeton University Press, 2018.

Brodsky, Harold. "Interpretation of Maps Based on the Bible." *Geographical Review* 82, no. 4 (October 1992): 430–40.

Brody, Hugh. *The Other Side of Eden: Hunters, Farmers, and the Shaping of the World*. New York: North Point Press, 2000.

Buber, Martin. "A Debate on Zionism and Messianism." In *The Jew in the Modern World—A Documentary History*, edited by Paul Mendes-Flohr and Jehuda Reinharz, 651–55. Oxford: Oxford University Press, 2011.

———. *Israel and the World*. New York: Schocken, 1948.

———. *Kingship of God*. New York: Harper and Row, 1967.

———. *Paths in Utopia*. Translated by R. F. C. Hull. London: Routledge and Kegan Paul, 1949.

———. *The Writings of Martin Buber*. Edited by Will Herberg. New York: World Publishing, 1956.

Buzaglo, Meir. *Safah Lene'emanim* [A language for the faithful]. Jerusalem: Mandel Foundation, 2008.

Chernyshevsky, Nikolai. *A Vital Question; or What Is to Be Done?* Translated by Nathan Dole and S. Skidelsky. New York: Thomas Crowell, 1886.

Collins, John J. *The Apocalyptic Imagination*. Grand Rapids MI: William B. Eerdmans, 1998.

Commager, Henry Steele. *Empire of Reason: How Europe Imagined and America Realized the Enlightenment*. Garden City NY: Anchor/Doubleday, 1977.

Cook, Stephen L. *Prophecy and Apocalypticism: The Postexilic Social Setting*. Minneapolis: Fortress Press, 1995.

Crevecoeur, J. Hector St. John. *Letters from an American Farmer*. New York: Fox, Duffield, 1904.

Dan, Yosef. *Apokalipsa Az Ve'achshav* [Apocalypse then and now]. Tel Aviv: Yediot Acharonot, 2000.

Delanty, Gerard. *Community*. New York and London: Routledge, 2003.

DellaPergola, Sergio. "World Jewish Population, 2018." In *The American Jewish Year Book*, edited by Arnold Dashefsky and Ira M. Sheskin, vol. 118, 361–452. Dordrecht: Springer, 2018. Behrman Jewish DataBank 23 (2018). Accessed May 2020. https://www.jewishdatabank.org/content/upload/bjdb/2018 -World_Jewish_Population_(AJYB,_DellaPergola)_DB_Final.pdf.

Delumeau, Jean. *History of Paradise: The Garden of Eden in Myth and Tradition*. Translated by Matthew O'Connoll. New York: Continuum, 1995.

Eisenstein, J. D. *Otzar Midrashim*. New York: J. D. Eisenstein, 1915.

Elboim-Dror, Rachel. *Hamachar shel Etmol: Ha-utopiot Hatzioniot* [Yesterday's tomorrow: The Zionist utopias]. Jerusalem: Yad Ben-Zvi, 1993.

Eliav-Feldon, Miriam. "'If you will it, it is no fairy tale': The First Jewish Utopias." *Jewish Journal of Sociology* 25, no. 2 (December 1983): 85–104.

———. *Realistic Utopias: The Ideal Imaginary Societies of the Renaissance 1516-1630*. Oxford: Clarendon Press, 1982.

Elon, Menachem. *Jewish Law: History, Sources, Principles*. Philadelphia: The Jewish Publication Society, 1994.

ESCO Foundation for Palestine. *Palestine: A Study of Jewish, Arab, and British Policies*. New Haven CT: Yale University Press, 1949.

Fackenheim, Emil. "The Jewish Return into History: Philosophical Fragments on the State of Israel." In *Jewish Philosophy and the Academy*, edited by Emil Fackenheim and Raphael Jospe, 223–40. Teaneck NJ: Fairleigh Dickinson University Press, 1996.

Feiner, Shmuel. *The Jewish Enlightenment*. Translated by Chaya Naor. Philadel-phia: University of Pennsylvania Press, 2004.

Feldman, Louis H. "Some Observations on the Name Palestine." *Hebrew Union College Annual* 61 (1990): 1–23.

Fishman, Aryei. *Judaism and Collective Life: Self and Community in the Religious Kibbutz*. London: Routledge, 2002.

Fokkema, Douwe. *Perfect Worlds: Utopian Fiction in China and the West*. Amster-dam: Amsterdam University Press, 2011.

Frankel, Jonathan. *Prophecy and Politics: Socialism, Nationalism, and the Russian Jews, 1862-1917*. Cambridge: Cambridge University Press, 1981.

Funkenstein, Amos. *Perceptions of Jewish History*. Berkeley: University of California Press, 1993.

Galnoor, Itzhak. *The Partition of Palestine: Decision Crossroads in the Zionist Movement*. Albany NY: SUNY Press, 1995.

Gans, Chaim. *A Just Zionism*. New York: Oxford University Press, 2008.

Gilbert, Martin. *Jewish Historical Atlas*. London: Weidenfeld and Nicolson, 1976.

Gillman, Neil. *The Death of Death: Resurrection and Immortality in Jewish Thought*. Woodstock VT: Jewish Lights, 1997.

Gitelman, Zvi. *The Quest for Utopia: Jewish Political Ideas and Institutions through the Ages*. Armonk NY: M. E. Sharpe, 1992.

Golinkin, David, ed. *Teshuvot Va'ad Hahalacha shel Knesset Harabanim Beyisrael* [Responsa of the Halakhah Committee of the Rabbinical Assembly in Israel]. Vol. 1. Jerusalem: Masorti Movement in Israel, 1986.

Gordis, Robert. "The Significance of the Paradise Myth." *American Journal of Semitic Languages and Literatures* 52, no. 2 (January 1936): 86–94.

Goren, Arthur. *New York Jews and the Quest for Community: The Kehillah Experiment, 1908–1922*. New York: Columbia University Press, 1970.

Gorny, Yosef. *From Binational Society to Jewish State: Federal Concepts in Zionist Political Thought, 1920–1990, and the Jewish People*. Leiden: Brill, 2006.

———. "Thoughts on Zionism as a Utopian Ideology." *Modern Judaism* 18, no. 3 (October 1998): 241–51.

Goswell, Greg. "Messianic Expectation in Isaiah 11." *Westminster Theological Journal* 79 (2017): 123–35.

Greenberg, Moshe. "Biblical Conception of Asylum." *Journal of Biblical Literature* 78, no. 2 (June 1959): 125–33.

Halkin, Hillel. *Jabotinsky: A Life*. New Haven CT: Yale University Press, 2014.

Hattis, Susan Lee. *The Bi-National Idea in Palestine during Mandatory Times*. Haifa: Shikmona, 1970.

Havrelock, Rachel. "The Two Maps of Israel's Land." *Journal of Biblical Literature* 126, no. 4 (Winter 2007): 649–67.

Herodotus. *The Landmark Herodotus: The Histories*. Translated by Andrea L. Purvis. New York: Pantheon, 2007.

Herscher, Uri. *Jewish Agricultural Utopias in America, 1880–1910*. Detroit: Wayne State University Press, 1981.

Hertzberg, Arthur. *The Zionist Idea*. Philadelphia: The Jewish Publication Society, 1959.

Hertzka, Theodor. *Freeland: A Social Anticipation*. Translated by Arthur Ransom. St. Loyes, Bedford UK, 1891.

Herzl, Theodor. *The Diaries of Theodore Herzl*. Translated by Marvin Lowenthal. New York: Grosset and Dunlap, 1962.

———. *A Jewish State: An Attempt at a Modern Solution of the Jewish Question*. Translated by Sylvie D'Avigdor. New York: Maccabaean Publishing, 1904.

———. *Old New Land*. Translated by Lotta Levensohn. Princeton NJ: Wiener, 1997.

Herzog, Isaac Halevi. *T'choka Le-yisrael al pi Hatorah* [Legislation for Israel according to the Torah]. Jerusalem: Mossad Harav Kook, 1989.

Hesiod. *Hesiod's Works and Days*. Translated by David Tandy and Walter Neale. Berkeley: University of California Press, 1996.

Hess, Moses. *Rome and Jerusalem: A Study in Jewish Nationalism*. Translated by Meyer Waxman. New York: Bloch Publishing, 1918.

Higger, Michael. *The Jewish Utopia*. Baltimore: Lord Baltimore Press, 1932.

Hobsbawm, E. J., and David J. Kertzer. "Ethnicity and Nationalism in Europe Today." *Anthropology Today* 8, no. 1 (February 1992): 3–8.

Homer. *The Odyssey*. Translated by Walter Shewring. Oxford: Oxford University Press, 1980.

Hyland, Paul, Olga Gomez, and Francesca Greensides, eds. *The Enlightenment: A Sourcebook and Reader*. London: Routledge, 2003.

Inbari, Motti. *Messianic Religious Zionism Confronts Israeli Territorial Compromises*. Cambridge: Cambridge University Press, 2012.

Jabotinsky, Vladimir. "Tristan da Runha." In *A Pocket Edition of Several Stories Mostly Reactionary*, 141–202. Paris, 1925.

Jennings, Chris. *Paradise Now: The Story of American Utopianism*. New York: Random House, 2016.

Kaplan, Mordecai. *Judaism as a Civilization: Toward a Reconstruction of American Jewish Life*. Philadelphia: The Jewish Publication Society, 1980.

Katscher, Leopold. "Owen's Topolobampo Colony, Mexico." *American Journal of Sociology* 12, no. 2 (September 1906): 145–75.

Katz, Jacob. *Tradition and Crisis: Jewish Society at the End of the Middle Ages*. New York: Schocken, 1971.

Klieman, Aaron S. "The Controversy over Partition for Palestine." *Jewish Social Studies* 42, no. 2 (Spring 1980): 147–64.

Kochan, Lionel. "A Model for Jewish Historiography." *Modern Judaism* 1, no. 3 (December 1981): 263–78.

Kramer, Samuel N., and W. F. Albright. "Enki and Ninhursag: A Sumerian 'Paradise' Myth." *Bulletin of the American Schools of Oriental Research, Supplementary Studies* 1 (1945): 1–40.

Krippner-Martinez, James. "Invoking 'Tato Vasco': Vasco de Quiroga, Eighteenth–Twentieth Centuries." *The Americas* 56, no. 3 (January 2000): 1–28.

Kropotkin, Peter. *Memoirs of a Revolutionist.* Boston: Houghton and Mifflin, 1899.

Kugel, James. *How to Read the Bible: A Guide to the Scripture, Then and Now.* New York: Free Press, 2007.

Kymlicka, Will. *Multicultural Citizenship.* Oxford: Oxford University Press, 1995.

Lehman, Siegfried. *Ra'ayon Vehagshamah* [Idea and realization]. Edited by Abraham Yakel. Tel Aviv: Tarbut Vechinuch, 1962.

Levin, Nora. *While Messiah Tarried: Jewish Socialist Movements 1871–1917.* New York: Schocken, 1977.

Levitas, Ruth. *The Concept of Utopia.* Oxford: Peter Lang, 2011.

Lewinsky, Elchanan Leib. *Masa L'eretz Yisrael Beshnat 5800* [A trip to the land of Israel in 2040]. Berlin: Klal, 1922.

Likhovski, Assaf. "The Invention of 'Hebrew Law' in Mandatory Palestine." *American Journal of Comparative Law* 46 (Spring 1998): 339–73.

Litvak, Olga. *Haskalah: The Romantic Movement in Judaism.* New Brunswick NJ: Rutgers University Press, 2012.

Lorberbaum, Yair. *Disempowered King: Monarchy in Classical Jewish Literature.* London: Continuum, 2011.

Luz, Ehud. "Utopia and Return: On the Structure of Utopian Thinking and Its Relation to Jewish-Christian Tradition." *Journal of Religion* 73, no. 3 (July 1993): 357–77.

Maimon, Judah L. "*Chiddush Hasanhedrin*" [Renewal of the Sanhedrin]. In *Dat Yisrael Umedinat Yisrael* [The religion of Israel and the State of Israel], 38–51. New York: World Zionist Organization Department of Education and Culture, 1950.

Mandel Leadership Institute. "*Veyachof Kol Yisrael Leilech Bah*": *Al Achifa Datit Lehalachah Ulema'aseh* ["He forces all Israel to walk in the way": On religious coercion in theory and practice]. Jerusalem: Mandel Leadership Institute, 2012.

Manuel, Frank E., and Fritzie P. Manuel. *Utopian Thought in the Western World.* Cambridge MA: Belknap Press, 1979.

McClintock, Harry. "Big Rock Candy Mountains." Accessed May 2020. https://www.stlyrics.com/lyrics/obrotherwhereartthou/inthebigrockcandymountains.htm.

Mendelssohn, Moses. *Jerusalem: Or on Religious Power and Judaism*. Translated by Allan Arkush. Hanover NH: University Press of New England, 1983.

Meyer, Michael. *The Origins of the Modern Jew: Jewish Identity and European Culture in Germany, 1749–1824*. Detroit: Wayne State University Press, 1967.

More, Thomas. *Utopia*. Translated by Clarence Miller. New Haven CT: Yale University Press, 2001.

Mossinson, Ben Zion. "Hatanach B'vet Hasefer" [The Bible in the school]. *Hachinuch* 1 (1911).

Murphy, Frederick J. *Apocalypticism in the Bible and Its World*. Grand Rapids MI: Baker Academic, 2012.

Navon, Isaac. *Kol Haderech* [All the way]. Edited by Eyal Meron. Jerusalem: Keter, 2005.

Neuman, Kalman. *Havikuach al Gvulot Hamedinah, Sugiah shel Dat Umedinah?* [The debate over the borders of the state: A question of religion and state?]. Jerusalem: Israel Democracy Institute, 2013.

Nevo, Eshkol. *Neuland* [New land]. In Hebrew. Or Yehuda: Kinneret-Zmora Bitan-Dvir, 2011.

Nisbet, Robert. *Community and Power*. New York: Oxford University Press, 1962.

Or, Meir. "Boker Chag Bakfar" [Festival morning in the village]. *Batirah* 2 (October 20 1950): 13.

Paul, Heike. *The Myths That Made America: An Introduction to American Studies*. Bielefeld, Germany: Transcript Verlag, 2014.

Pease, William H., and Jane Pease. *Black Utopia: Negro Communal Experiments in America*. Madison WI: State Historical Society of Wisconsin, 1963.

Plato. *The Republic*. Translated by Robin Waterfield. Oxford: Oxford University Press, 1993.

———. *Timaeus and Critias*. Translated by Robin Waterfield. Oxford: Oxford University Press, 2008.

Plaut, W. Gunther. *The Growth of Reform Judaism: American and European Sources until 1948*. New York: World Union for Progressive Judaism, 1965.

Pleij, Herman. *Dreaming of Cockaigne: Medieval Fantasies of the Perfect Life*. Translated by Diane Webb. New York: Columbia University Press, 2001.

Polak, Fred. *The Image of the Future*. 2 vols. New York: Oceana Publications, 1961.

Rainey, Anson R., and R. Steven Notley. *The Sacred Bridge: Carta's Atlas of the Biblical World*. Jerusalem: Carta, 2006.

Rashi [Rabbi Shlomo Yitzhaki]. *Teshuvot Rashi* [Rashi's responsa]. Edited by Israel Elfenbein. New York, 1953.

Ravitzky, Aviezer. "Is a Halakhic State Possible?: The Paradox of Jewish Theocracy." *Israel Affairs* 11, no. 1 (2005): 137–64.

———. *Religion and State in Jewish Philosophy: Models of Unity, Division, Collision, and Subordination*. Translated by Rachel Yarden. Jerusalem: Israel Democracy Institute, 2002.

Rivlin, Reuven. Address at Herzliya Conference, June 7, 2015. Herzliya Interdisciplinary College. Accessed May 2020. https://www.idc.ac.il/en/research/ips/Documents/4-Tribes/PresidentSPEECH2015.pdf.

Rosenstein, Marc. *Galilee Diary*. New York: URJ Press, 2010.

———. *"Hayehudi Hechadash": Hazika Lemesoret Hayehudit Bechinuch Hatichoni Hatzioni Haklali Be'eretz Yisrael Mereishito Ve'ad Kom Hamedina* [The "New Jew": The place of the Jewish tradition in general Zionist secondary education in Palestine, from its beginnings until the establishment of the state]. PhD dissertation, Hebrew University of Jerusalem, 1985.

———. "Toward a Vision of a Democratic Jewish State." *CCAR Journal: The Reform Jewish Quarterly*, Spring 2016: 5–29.

Rubenstein, Sondra Miller. *The Communist Movement in Palestine and Israel, 1919–1984*. Boulder CO: Westview Press, 1985.

Sagi, Avi. *Jewish Religion after Theology*. Brighton MA: Academic Studies Press, 2009.

Sandmel, Samuel. *The Genius of Paul*. New York: Farrar, Straus and Cudahy, 1958.

Sapir, Gideon, and Daniel Statman. *State and Religion in Israel: A Philosophical-Legal Inquiry*. Cambridge: Cambridge University Press, 2019.

Sarna, Jonathan D. *Jacksonian Jew: The Two Worlds of Mordecai Noah*. New York: Holmes and Meier, 1981.

Satanow, Isaac. *Divrei Rivot* [Matters of dispute]. Constantina, Romania, 1793.

Scholem, Gershom. "Toward an Understanding of the Messianic Idea." In *The Messianic Idea in Judaism and Other Essays on Jewish Spirituality*, 1–36. New York: Schocken, 1971.

Seeger, Pete. "Oleanna." Accessed May 2020. https://www.lyricsondemand.com/p/peteseegerlyrics/oleannalyrics.html.

Shalev, Meir. *B'ikar Al Ahava* [Mainly about love]. Tel Aviv: Am Oved, 1995.

Shapira, Anita. *Israel: A History*. Translated by Anthony Berris. Waltham MA: Brandeis University Press, 2012.

———. "Labour Zionism and the October Revolution." *Journal of Contemporary History* 24, no. 4 (October 1989): 623–56.

Shumsky, Dmitry. *Beyond the Nation-State: The Zionist Political Imagination from Pinsker to Ben-Gurion*. New Haven CT: Yale University Press, 2018.

Siegel, Michael, Michael Strassfeld, and Sharon Strassfeld. *The Jewish Catalog: A Do-It-Yourself Kit*. Philadelphia: The Jewish Publication Society, 1973.

Smilansky, Yizhar. "*Sod Hakiyum Hayehudi*" [The secret of Jewish existence]. *Davar*, January 29, 1988.

Soloveitchik, Joseph. *Halakhic Man*. Philadelphia: The Jewish Publication Society, 1983.

Sternhell, Zeev. *The Founding Myths of Israel: Nationalism, Socialism, and the Making of the Jewish State*. Translated by David Maisel. Princeton NJ: Princeton University Press, 1998.

Syrkin, Marie. *Nachman Syrkin: Socialist Zionist: A Biographical Memoir*. New York: Herzl Press and Sharon Books, 1961.

Syrkin, Nachman. *Die Judenfrage und der Socialistische Judenstaat* [The Jewish question and the socialist Jewish state]. Bern: Steiger, 1898.

Tal, Alon. *The Land Is Full: Addressing Overpopulation in Israel*. New Haven CT: Yale University Press, 2016.

Tamir, Yael. *Why Nationalism*. Princeton NJ: Princeton University Press, 2019.

Tihany, Leslie. "Utopia in Modern Western Thought: The Metamorphosis of an Idea." In *Ideas in History*, edited by Richard Herr and Harold T. Parker, 20–38. Durham NC: Duke University Press, 1965.

Troy, Gil, ed. *The Zionist Ideas: Visions for the Jewish Homeland, Then, Now, Tomorrow*. Philadelphia: The Jewish Publication Society, 2019.

Tuan, Yi-Fu. *Space and Place*. Minneapolis: University of Minnesota Press, 1977.

Tuchman, Barbara. *Bible and Sword: England and Palestine from the Bronze Age to Balfour*. New York: Funk and Wagnalls, 1956.

Uffenheimer, Benjamin. "Utopia Umetziut Bamachshavah Hamikra'it" [Utopia and reality in biblical thought]. *Shnaton: An Annual for Biblical and Ancient Near Eastern Studies* (1980): 10–26.

Urbach, Ephraim. *The Sages and Their Beliefs*. Translated by Israel Abrahams. Jerusalem: Magnes Press, 1975.

Wazana, Nili. *All the Boundaries of the Land: The Promised Land in Biblical Thought in Light of the Ancient Near East*. Winona Lake IN: Eisenbrauns, 2013.

Wilkinson, Norman B. "'New Norway'—A Contemporary Account." *Pennsylvania History: A Journal of Mid-Atlantic Studies* 15, no. 2 (April 1948): 120–32.

Wohl, Robert. *The Generation of 1914*. London: Weidenfeld and Nicolson, 1980.

Yakobson, Alexander, and Amnon Rubinstein. *Israel and the Family of Nations: The Jewish Nation-State and Human Rights*. Translated by Ruth Morris and Ruchie Avital. London: Routledge, 2009.

Yedidya, Asaf. "Chadash Mi-lo Yashan: Ha-utopia Hagenuza shel Zeev Yaavetz" [New from the not old: Zev Yavetz's unpublished utopia]. *Cathedra* 148 (June 2013): 71–108.

Zakovitz, Yair. *Mashmia Shalom Mevaseir Tov* [Announcing happiness, heralding good fortune]. Haifa: Haifa University Press, 2004.

Zborowski, Mark, and Elizabeth Herzog. *Life Is with People*. New York: Schocken, 1969.

Zerubavel, Yael. *Recovered Roots: Collective Memory and the Making of Israeli National Tradition*. Chicago: University of Chicago Press, 1995.

Zipperstein, Steven. "Underground Man: The Curious Case of Mark Zborowski and the Writing of a Modern Jewish Classic." *Jewish Review of Books* (Summer 2010). Accessed May 2020. https://jewishreviewofbooks.com/articles/275 /underground-man-the-curious-case-of-mark-zborowski-and-the-writing -of-a-modern-jewish-classic/.

Zusman, Y. "Baraita D'tchumei Eretz Yisrael" [The Baraita on the borders of the Land of Israel]. *Tarbiz* 45 (1976): 213–57.

Index

222, 226–27; open, 259, 260; utopian, 169. *See also* boundaries

Borochov, Ber, 185

Bosnia, 225

boundaries, 21, 96, 122, 166, 167, 171, 173; halakhic, 169; state, 134. *See also* border

bourgeois, 186

Brave New World, 12

Britain, 88

British Mandate for Palestine, 88, 89, 129, 131, 171, 235

British Raj, 134

Brit Shalom, 130

Brueghel, Pieter, 4

Buber, Martin, 85–87, 116, 130, 157–58, 222

Bull, Ole, 9

Bund, 182

bureaucracy, 125

burial, 249

Cabet, Etienne, 8, 13, 87

cabinet, 250

cactus, 109

calendar, 110, 256; Jewish, 211

Calypso, 17

Camelot, 10

Camelot (Alan Jay Lerner and Frederick Loewe), 258–59

camels, parable of the two, 66, 208

Campanella, Tomas, 6–7

camps, Jewish summer, 82

Canaan, 22–24, 25, 26, 122, 162, 164, 167, 169

Canaanites, 60; driving out, 70

Canaanites (movement), 211

Canal, Red-Dead, 268

Candide (Voltaire), 7

canon, 38, 40

cantons, 131

capacity: absorptive, 177; carrying, 229

capitalism, 99, 226

capitalists, 186

car, private, 232

card, identity, 93

Carmel (mountain). *See* Mount Carmel

Carmina Burana, 4

carts, parable of the two, 66

center: cultural, 97, 100, 129, 233, 259, 262; religious, 262

centers: community, 243; Jewish community, 82

Central Conference of American Rabbis, 94

character: Israeli, 205; Jewish, 138

charedi, 204, 207–9, 211. *See also* ultra-Orthodox

charter, 129

Chazon Ish. *See* Karelitz, Rabbi Abraham

Chernyshevsky, Nikolai, 7, 9, 102–3

chief rabbi, 35, 60, 89, 207, 249

chief rabbinate, 51, 64, 66, 67, 88

chieftains, tribal, 123

child-rearing, 85

children's houses, 85

Chovevei Tzion, 97, 98, 101, 139, 140, 141, 182, 187

Christianity, 40

Christians, 61, 142, 219

Church Fathers, 19
circumcision, 64
cities, 230; holy, 63; mixed, 261
citizens, 89, 134–35, 138, 153, 154,
    248; Arab, 206; Palestinian, 223;
    senior, 223
citizenship, 225, 244; shared, 226
City of the Sun (Tomas Campanella), 6
clan, 276–77
class, 102, 145, 154; economic, 207;
    social, 181, 189; socioeconomic, 221
coalition, 66, 199, 208, 209, 216, 222
Cockaigne. *See* Land of Cockaigne
coercion, religious, 65
collective, 55
colonialism, 226
colonies, 121
Columbus, Christopher, 17
commandment, 66, 127, 128, 212,
    218, 234
committees, admissions, 256
commonwealth, Jewish, 133. *See also*
    state: Jewish
commune, 54, 180
communist, 183
Communist Manifesto (Karl Marx), 183
communitarians, 181
community, 55, 76, 135, 181, 215, 243,
    256, 249, 265; agricultural, 186;
    all-encompassing, 81; anti-Zionist
    Orthodox, 65; autonomous, 64, 75,
    146; Bedouin, 223, 276; diaspora,
    88, 236; egalitarian, 222; halakhic,
    89, 146, 207, 208, 209, 220; holy,
    79, 87, 89; homogeneous, 261,
    296; ideal, 236; imagined, 96, 110;
    insulated, 84; intentional, 83–84;

intimate, 57, 271; Jewish, 63, 74,
76, 80, 88, 89, 97, 175, 215, 218–19,
237, 238; Jewish agricultural, 84;
local, 96; lost, 75, 77, 82; medieval,
75; multidimensional, 81; native
American, 82; non-Jewish, 88;
non-utopian, 84; old-time, 76;
Orthodox, 63, 104; peasant village,
87; preindustrial, 96; premodern,
86, 90; reconstructed, 80, religious, 88–89, 94, 253; sectarian,
80; self-governing, 80; semiautonomous, 74, 79, 217; smallholder, 271; socialist, 223; super-,
74; Torah, 64, 110; traditional, 63,
65, 75, 217, 221; traditional Jewish,
76, 89; utopian, 11, 13, 25, 59, 76,
79, 82, 83; utopian Jewish, 74
concubine of Gibeah, 124–25
Condorcet, Nicolas de, 13, 145
conflict: Israel-Palestine, 259, 261;
national, 266
congestion, 247
conquest, 164, 167, 168, 175, 177;
Asyyrian, 125; Babylonian, 125
constitution, 59, 62–64, 66, 247–48,
259, 260
constitutionalists, 117
continuity, Jewish, 235
contractors, labor, 225
conversion, 52, 95, 212, 220, 249, 256
converts, Reform, 93
cooperatives, 180
cooperative society, 188
cosmopolitanism, 146, 180–82, 184,
186–87
cottage cheese, 221

court, 27, 31, 33, 64, 88; British government, 60; rabbinical, 60, 64; supreme, 53, 250

covenant, 23, 24–25, 27, 29, 38, 42, 45, 78, 94–95, 108, 115, 135, 165, 184, 192, 197; grant, 42

cowardice, 133

Crevecoeur, St. John, 102

crime, 199

criminals, 117

Crusades, 170

cuisine, 110

cult, sacrificial, 27

cultural renewal, 100

culture, 95, 97, 130, 256; bilingual, 260; European, 275; global, 211; Hebrew, 211; Israeli, 101, 108; Jewish, 133, 182, 213, 217; Jewish national, 132; Jewish secular, 108; literary, 119; mainstream, 110; national, 97, 211; secular, 261

curriculum, 108, 119, 253; Bible, 191; core, 253; general studies, 208

customs, 60, 96, 260; ancient, 98

Daedalus, 13–14

Damascus, 170

Daniel (biblical book), 35–38, 39

David, 42, 125, 167–68, 194–95

day care, 223

Dead Sea, 230, 267–68

Deborah, 122–23

debts, remission of, 68

Declaration of Independence, 92, 134, 138, 226, 248

defense, 65, 132, 190

defensibility, 177

Degania, 85

democracy, 210, 238; cosmopolitan, 262; popular, 147

demonstrations, 223

denominations, Christian, 88

desalination, 230, 271

desert, 24–26, 42–43, 125, 128, 145, 148, 170, 176, 195, 228, 229, 275, 277. See also wilderness

determinism, apocalyptic, 190

deterrence, mutual, 117, 121, 233

development, 228; economic, 206

diaspora, 33, 60, 63, 100, 104, 135, 215, 234

dignity, 133

dilemma, utopian, xx, 13, 27, 34, 52, 62, 83, 135, 177

diplomacy, 167

discrimination, 61, 145, 154, 206, 212, 249

disobedience, civil, 210

divorce, 64, 208, 220, 249, 256

dogma, 86

donors, 236

Don Quixote, 10

draft, 52

dream: American, 265; messianic, 45

dynasty, 126; Davidic, 125, 127, 195

dystopia, 12, 110, 116

Eber-hanahar, 168

eco-tourism, 273

Eden, 3, 4, 10, 17–20, 24, 32, 167, 195; expulsion from, 24. See also Paradise

Edom, 167

education, 57, 75, 104, 141, 144, 151–
52, 153, 182, 189, 236, 252; basic,
209; bilingual, 253; boards of Jewish, 80; Bureau of, 79; general, 65;
higher, 209; Israeli, 108; Ministry
of, 68, 108, 258; sectarian, 208;
yeshiva, 208; Zionist, 191
educators: Jewish, 245–46; Zionist,
105–6
egalitarianism, 188, 198
Egypt, 22–24, 26, 28, 170, 173, 175
Ein Gedi, 268
elders, 124; seventy, 195
election, 142, 249; primary, 249
Eliezer, Rabbi, 40–42, 45
emancipation, 74–75, 80, 104, 140,
145, 146, 148, 150, 153
emigration, 181, 186
emirate, autonomous, 171
empathy, 273
emperors, 161
empire, 122, 125, 168; Israelite, 167;
multicultural, 168; Solomon's, 46,
145, 167
employees, 258
employers, 258
empowerment, 128
end of days, 44
energy: geothermal, 247; hydroelectric, 247; solar, 247, 275
enforcement, 57, 64, 68, 77, 219;
religious, 66
Engels, Friedrich, 9
English (language), 109, 211, 254
Enlighteners, 144

Enlightenment, 7, 46, 76, 84, 101, 102,
104, 121, 141, 144–49, 150, 153, 154,
181, 262. See *Haskalah*
Entebbe, 113
environment, 228
epic, national historical, 108
equality, 92, 99, 144, 146, 152, 265;
gender, 220; social, 142
Eretz Israel, 21, 130, 173. *See also* Land
of Israel
Eritrea, 225
Eruv, 55–56
Ethiopia, 225–26
Ethiopian (ethnic group), 223
ethnicity, 138, 154, 249
Europe, 96, 99, 101, 103–4, 138–39,
146, 149, 183, 225; old, 103–4
eutopia, 6, 27
Eve, 18–19
exile, 55, 56, 63, 122, 128, 194, 226, 229,
235; Babylonian, 169; end of, 235
exiles, ingathering of, 46
Exodus (Leon Uris), 109
Exodus, 95
expression: free, 211; freedom of, 249
extortion, 66
Extraordinary Zionist Conference, 133
extremism, 268
Ezekiel (book), 100, 165–67
Ezra (book), 169

Fackenheim, Emil, 114, 133
fairy-tale, xx, 11
faith, 25, 43, 95, 145, 147; religious, 176
falafel, 110
Falastin, 170

farmers, 68, 153, 223, 229, 257–58; Jewish, 64

farming, industrial, 271

farmland, 27

farms, 243, 271; family, 271

federation, 131

federation, labor. See *Histadrut*

federations, Jewish, 80

femicide, 199

fiction, legal, 68

fiction, utopian, xix, 5, 11

Fiddler on the Roof, 77

Fifteenth of Av. *See* Tu B'av

Finland, 96

First Aliyah, 52

First World War. *See* World War I

Fishman. *See* Maimon, Rabbi Yehudah

Flood, 196

folkdances, 96

folklore, 3

folk-personality, 140

folksongs, 96

folkways, 97, 110

food: growth, 258; kosher, 64, 256; non-kosher, 52, 256; preparation, 258

forcing the end, 63, 209

forgiveness, 132, 274

Former Soviet Union, 225–26

founding fathers, 130

Fourier, Charles, 8, 87, 181

France, 131

freedom, 61, 65, 92–93, 98, 138, 144, 150, 152, 153, 188, 248–49; economic, 85; human, 144; national, 130

Freeland, 8

free-market, 181, 197

free will, 38, 39, 44

frontiers, 161

fund, sabbatical, 258

Funkenstein, Amos, 144

Galilee, 170, 224

garbage, 246

gardens, roof, 247

Garibaldi, Giuseppe, 132

Gaza strip, 175

gender, 154, 249. *See also* sex

general assembly, 87

genocides, 262

gentile, 56, 60, 67–68, 141–42, 210, 224

geography, historical, 159

Gerar, 22

Germany, 57, 96, 104, 182

ger toshav, 60–61, 207

ghetto, 74, 80

Gibeah, 124–25

Gideon, 122–23, 126

Gini Index, 257

Glaucon, 14

gleaning, 99

God, 18–19, 20, 21–23, 24–25, 26, 27, 29, 38, 39, 41, 44, 63, 70, 78, 89, 94–95, 97, 108, 123, 125, 126–27, 128, 143, 145, 164, 165, 181, 192, 195, 218, 262

Golan Heights, 170, 175

gold, 120

golden age, 10, 17, 42, 96, 103

governance, 26, 33, 56, 65, 126, 132, 146; rational, 232

homogeneity, 96, 219; ethnic, 134

hope, messianic, 190

house (of parliament): lower, 249–50; upper, 249

housing: affordable, 221; discrimination in, 93

Hula swamp, 228

humaneness, 213

humanism, 39, 144, 152

humanitarianism, 145

humanities, 253

hummus, 110

Hungary, 96

hunter-gatherer, 18

Hythloday, Raphael, 44

Icaria, 8, 13

Icarus, 13–14

identity, 115, 260, 261; ethnic, 207; ethno-cultural, 110; human, 146; individual, 147; Israeli, 74; Israelite, 25; Jewish, 33, 74, 114, 181, 187, 197, 211, 214, 236, 246, 265; Jewish national, 97, 170, 183; national, 96, 110, 129, 146, 147, 176; particular, 147; shared, 226

idolatry, 192, 194

idol worship, 128

Imagined Communities (Benedict Anderson), 96

immersion, Hebrew, 246

immigrants, 236, 243–44, 246; absorption of, 171; European, 109; Jewish, 234, 261; Vietnamese, 225; Zionist, 104

immigration, 130, 133, 154, 215, 224–28, 229, 234, 235; Jewish, 91–92, 132, 141, 153, 225, 226, 231; mass, 97, 225–26, 230, 235; quotas, 225

immorality, 18–19, 56

immunity, judicial, 31

impact, environmental, 258

income, minimum, 223

independence, 88, 131, 226; Jewish, 186; judicial, 211. *See also* Declaration of Independence

Independence Hall, 248

India, land bridge to, 171

individual, 39–40; rights of, 75

industrial revolution, 7, 12

industry, 189

inequality, 28, 257; income, 221, 222

inflation, 222

ingathering, 46, 91–92, 100, 128, 146, 215, 226, 233, 235

injustice, 56, 192, 197

in-marriage, 276

integration, 80, 84, 140, 146, 148, 209

interest: great power, 177; Jewish, 154; public, 232

Interior: Minister of, 93; Ministry of, 51, 212

internet, 226

Iraq, 173

iron, 6, 120, 121

iron wall, 121

Isaac, 22

Isaiah, 193–97

Israel, kingdom of. *See* kingdom of Israel

Israel, Land of. *See* Land of Israel

Israel, State of. *See* State of Israel

Israel Defense Forces, 205

Lenin, Vladimir, 9, 182, 186

Letters from an American Farmer (St. John Crevecoeur), 102

Levitas, Ruth, 11, 15

Levites, 166

Lewinsky, Elchanan Leib, 55, 97–101, 107, 109, 141, 144, 153, 181, 211, 213, 215, 217, 218, 226, 229, 230, 231, 232, 233, 236

Lewis, Sinclair, 76

lexicographer, 108

liberation, national, 191

Life Is with People (Zborowski and Herzog), 77–79

literature: apocalyptic, 35, 37, 40; halakhic, 127; Jewish, 261; popular, 77; rabbinic, 19, 40, 108; talmudic, 46; utopian, 5

liturgy, traditional, 128

longing, 75, 103, 158, 159, 190, 229; nostalgic, 122

Looking Backward (Edward Bellamy), 7

Lovers of Zion. See *Chovevei Tzion*

loyalty, dual, 260

Lucian of Samosata, 4

Luilekkerland (Pieter Brueghel), 4

Magnes, Rabbi Judah, 79, 130

Maimon, Rabbi Yehudah, 57–58

Maimonides. *See* Rambam

Main Street (Sinclair Lewis), 76

majority, Jewish, 231

manna, 24

map, 159; biblical, 162; Ezekiel's, 165–67; halakhic, 170

marital relations, 20

marriage, 51, 64, 208, 212, 220, 249, 256; civil, 51, 249

Marx, Karl, 9, 180–81, 183, 187, 189

Marxism, 46, 186

Masada, 267–68

maskil, 147, 149, 152, 153

masorti, 212

masses, 186

mass transit, 232. *See also* transportation electric

materialism, 29, 185, 217, 220

Matters of Dispute (Isaac Satanow), 149–53

meat, nonkosher, 64

mechanization, 271

medical care, 179. *See also* health care

Mediterranean coast, 275

mellah, 77

memory: collective, 115, 158, 273; historical, 96, 97, 110

Mendelssohn, Moses, 104, 147–49

mercy, 215

Messiah, 30, 38, 43, 44, 60, 69, 110, 140; days of the, 44; false, 140

messianism, 44, 45, 184, 192

metal, 117, 120

Mexico, 9, 82

Michoacan, 82

Middle Ages, 45, 132, 169

Middle East, 226, 261

Middle Eastern (ethnic group), 223

midrash, apocalyptic, 40

Midrash *Sifrei Devarim*. See *Sifrei Devarim*

milieu, cultural, 219

military, 205

militia, 173, 190, 224

Minister of Religious Affairs, 57

ministers, government, 250

minority, 61, 65, 154; Arab, 92, 121; Jewish, 250; Muslim, 137; national, 207, 260; observant, 208; Palestinian Arab, 250; religious, 64

Minsk, 187

Mishnah, 29–30, 31, 127, 234

Mitzpeh Ramon, 278

Mizrachi, 21, 53, 57

Moab, 167

modernization, 75, 84, 104, 134, 218

monarch, 125, 128, 152; Davidic, 145

monarchists, 124, 196

monarchy, 7, 27, 33, 42, 123, 124, 127, 152, 164, 192, 196, 218; absolutist, 147; centralized, 125; David's, 128, 129, 170; divine-right, 126; hereditary, 125; limited, 126; Near Eastern, 125; sacred, 126

morality, 147, 213

More, Thomas, xix, 5–6, 10, 44, 82, 139, 144

"Morning Song" (Nathan Alterman), 228

Morris, William, 7–8

Moses, 23–24, 25, 99, 195

moshav ovdim, 271

Moslems, 142

mosques, 254

Mossinson, Ben-Zion, 191

Mount Carmel, 173–74

Mount Herzl, 262

Mount Sinai, 24–26, 42, 78, 94–95

movement: Conservative, 146, 212; democratic, 145; Jewish national, 235; kibbutz, 222; liberal, 212; messianic, 46; mystical, 46; nationalist, 52, 104; neo-Orthodox, 146; Orthodox, 146; Palestinian national, 129; Reconstructionist, 146, 212; Reform, 146, 212; Romantic, 147; youth, 57, 104

movement, freedom of, 249

municipality, 118

Muslims, 61, 88, 170, 219

mysticism, 272–73

myth, origin, 19, 21

mythology: Greek, 17; Sumerian, 17

Nablus, 265

Narodniks, 181

nasi, 101

Nathan, 125–26

nation, 25, 50, 94, 121, 135, 159; Jewish, 95, 106, 133, 140, 191, 236, 238

national home, 88, 90, 100, 106, 107, 109, 129, 133, 134, 171, 177, 207, 209, 210, 213, 215, 217, 219, 220, 221, 231, 237, 238, 259, 262, 266; Palestinian, 260

National Insurance Institute, 198, 223

nationalism, 76, 96, 132, 180, 221, 262, 274; hyper-, 262; Jewish, 187; liberal, 132, 176; Palestinian, 175; romantic, 59–60, 176, 184, 210

nationalists, 142; Jewish, 109

nationality, 93, 94–95, 102, 181, 184; Jewish, 93

National Library, 261

religion, 63, 77, 94, 95, 135, 138, 146, 148, 150, 154, 159, 181, 182, 184, 212, 249; established, 248–49; freedom from, 217; freedom of, 217; Jewish, 52

Religious Communities Organization Ordinance, 88

Renaissance, 5–6, 7, 8, 12, 144

renewal, cultural. *See* cultural renewal

Renewal, Jewish. *See* Jewish Renewal

rent-return-reuse, 247

repentance, 40–41, 132

Rephaim, 161

representation, proportional, 249

Republic (Plato), 4–5, 14, 196–97

Reschid Bey, 141–42

residency, freedom of, 249, 256

resident alien. See *ger toshav*

resources: allocation of, 236; natural, 232

responsa, 76

responsibility, collective, 78

restoration, 10, 43, 46, 56, 63, 69, 94, 127, 128, 146, 170, 182, 186, 210; messianic, 70

resurrection, 44

return, 128, 186, 226, 231; mass, 130

returnees, 169

reuse, 247

revelation, 29, 95

review, judicial, 250

Revisionists, 116

Revisionist Zionist Alliance, 116

revolt, Bar Kokhba, 170. *See also* rebellion: Bar Kokhba

revolution, 153, 180, 181, 182, 183, 186; democratic, 145, 147; Russian, 185, 186

right (political), 176

rights, 61, 65, 92, 130, 145; citizenship, 140; equal, 65, 121; equality of, 138; group, 154; human, 93; individual, 75, 154; minority, 211; natural, 134; water, 175; women's, 213

ritual, 87, 88

Rivlin, Reuven, 204–5, 209, 211

Rockwell, Norman, 76

roles, gender, 265

Romans, 170

romanticism, 182

Rome and Jerusalem (Moses Hess), 183–85

roofs, 243; green, 247

rootedness, 59, 79, 104, 107–8, 215, 229

rootlessness, 96, 234

Rosh Hashanah, 58

Rousseau, Jean-Jacques, 10, 147

Russia, 57, 97, 102, 181, 182

Sabbath, 20–21, 27, 29, 32, 33, 52, 55–56, 64, 143, 183–84, 208, 212, 214, 216–21, 251; *oneg*, 220; public observance of, 65; rest, 220

sabbatical year, 27–28, 55, 64, 67–69, 169, 234, 257–58, 266–67. See also *shemitah*

sabra, 105, 109

The Sabra (Oz Almog), 74

sacrifices, 128, 144, 146; Temple, 168

Safed, 63, 272

safety-net, 181

turbines, wind, 247

2001 Space Odyssey (Stanley Kubrick), 12

tycoons, 199, 221, 229, 236

tzedakah, 236

Uganda, 158

ultra-Orthodox, 207–9. See also *charedi*

Una, Moshe, 61

union, labor, 181

Union of Israel. *See* Agudat Israel

United Nations, 60, 65, 69, 173–75, 216

United States, 97

universalism, 142

university, 252

upcycling, 246

uprising, Arab, 173

Urbach, Ephraim, 43–44

Uris, Leon, 109

Utopia (Thomas More), xix, 5–6, 10, 44, 82, 144

utopia: American, 79; biblical, 183; national, 25, 138; nostalgic, 96; socialist, 182, 221–22, 224, 231; Torah, 208; Torah state, 62, 66, 95, 217; Zionist, 132

utopianism, xix, 20, 39, 44, 45, 84

utopians: Enlightenment, 144; realistic, 144; socialist, 8

Utopus, 44

values, Jewish, 141, 154, 214, 245

vassals, 167

vengeance, 28

Versailles, 171; peace conference, 171

Vespucci, Amerigo, 5

viability, economic, 171

victimhood, 223, 260

victories, 70

Vienna, 144

village: Palestinian, 206; youth, 153

violence, 96

visa, 225, 259

Voltaire, 7

wages, 61

wanderers, 107

wandervogel, 104

warlords, 122

warming, global, 226

Washington DC, 154

waste management, 260

water, 230, 260, 271

Wazana, Nili, 162, 164–65, 168

weakness, 133

weapons, 98

Weizmann, Chaim, 130–31

welfare, 26, 65, 75; Jewish, 182; social, 27, 222

West Bank, 175–76; conquest of, 69

Western Wall, 100, 237–38, 255

What Is to Be Done? (Nikolai Chernyshevsky), 7, 102–3

What Is to Be Done? (Vladimir Lenin), 9

wilderness, 25. *See also* desert

withdrawal, 176

women, 237–38; status of Bedouin, 277

work, 188

worker, 61; foreign, 227; Jewish, 182; temporary, 225

world to come, 19, 20, 40, 44

World War I, 12, 104, 116, 134, 171

World War II, 12

World Zionist Organization, 116
worship, freedom of, 249

xericulture, 266, 277

Yad Vashem, 261–62
Yannai, Alexander, 30–31, 168
Yavetz, Zev, 52–56, 59, 101, 141, 153,
    208, 211, 215, 217, 218, 226, 229,
    232, 233
Yavneh, 53–54
yeshivah, 87, 109, 207
Yiddish, 182
Yishuv, 85, 107, 179, 198
yordim, 234
Yugoslavia, 134

Zborowski, Mark, 77
Zechariah, 115

Zerubbabel, 115
Zevi, Sabbetai, 46, 69
Zionism, 10, 35, 52, 57, 62–63, 69, 88,
    89, 104, 130, 153, 179, 182, 185, 187,
    190; apocalyptic, 70; cultural, 95,
    101, 116; mainstream, 132; Ortho-
    dox, 46, 69, 209–11; socialist, 185
Zionist Conference, Extraordinary.
    See Extraordinary Zionist Con-
    ference
Zionist Congress, 21, 133; first, xix,
    139; twentieth, 173
Zionist Organization, 53, 139–40
Zionist proposal, 171
Zionists, 59, 101, 104, 121, 129, 130,
    131, 171; armchair, 263; cultural,
    100, 129, 144; Orthodox, 65, 209–
    11, 266; romantic, 159; secular, 65,
    95, 235; socialist, 191, 197